From Health Behaviours to Health Practices

D0761359

Sociology of Health and Illness Monograph Series

Edited by Professor Ian Rees Jones
Cardiff School of Social Sciences
WISERD
46 Park Place
Cardiff
CF10 3BB
Wales, UK

Current titles

From Health Behaviours to Health Practices
Critical Perspectives

Edited by

Simon Cohn

WILEY Blackwell

This edition first published 2014
Originally published as Volume 36, Issue 2 of *The Sociology of Health & Illness*
Chapters © 2014 The Authors.
Book Compilation © 2014 Foundation for the Sociology of Health & Illness/Blackwell Publishing Ltd.

Blackwell Publishing was acquired by John Wiley & Sons in February 2007. Blackwell's publishing program has been merged with Wiley's global Scientific, Technical, and Medical business to form Wiley-Blackwell.

Registered Office
John Wiley & Sons Ltd, The Atrium, Southern Gate, Chichester, West Sussex, PO19 8SQ, United Kingdom

Editorial Offices
350 Main Street, Malden, MA 02148-5020, USA
9600 Garsington Road, Oxford, OX4 2DQ, UK
The Atrium, Southern Gate, Chichester, West Sussex, PO19 8SQ, UK

For details of our global editorial offices, for customer services, and for information about how to apply for permission to reuse the copyright material in this book please see our website at www.wiley.com/wiley-blackwell.

The rights of Simon Cohn to be identified as the author of the editorial material in this work has been asserted in accordance with the UK Copyright, Designs and Patents Act 1988.

All rights reserved. No part of this publication may be reproduced, stored in a retrieval system, or transmitted, in any form or by any means, electronic, mechanical, photocopying, recording or otherwise, except as permitted by the UK Copyright, Designs and Patents Act 1988, without the prior permission of the publisher.

Wiley also publishes its books in a variety of electronic formats. Some content that appears in print may not be available in electronic books.

Designations used by companies to distinguish their products are often claimed as trademarks. All brand names and product names used in this book are trade names, service marks, trademarks or registered trademarks of their respective owners. The publisher is not associated with any product or vendor mentioned in this book. This publication is designed to provide accurate and authoritative information in regard to the subject matter covered. It is sold on the understanding that the publisher is not engaged in rendering professional services. If professional advice or other expert assistance is required, the services of a competent professional should be sought.

Library of Congress Cataloging-in-Publication Data

From health behaviours to health practices : critical perspectives / edited by Simon Cohn.
    p. ; cm.
"Originally published as Sociology of health & illness ; v. 36, issue 2."
Includes bibliographical references and index.
    ISBN 978-1-118-89839-0 (paperback)
  I. Cohn, Simon, editor. II. Sociology of health & illness.
[DNLM: 1. Health Behavior–Collected Works. 2. Sociology, Medical–Collected Works. W 85]
RA418
362.1–dc23
2014018415

A catalogue record for this book is available from the British Library.

Set in 9.5/11.5 pt TimesNewRomanMTStd by Toppan Best-set Premedia Limited
Printed and bound in Malaysia by Vivar Printing Sdn Bhd

1 2014

Karen MacKinnon

Contents

Notes on contributors

Thomas Abel Department of Social and Preventive Medicine, University of Bern, Switzerland

John Anderson Centre for Addictions Research of British Columbia, University of Victoria, Canada

David Armstrong Department of Primary Care and Public Health Sciences, King's College London, UK

Fran Baum Southgate Institute for Health, Society & Equity, Flinders University, South Australia

Cecilia Benoit Centre for Addictions Research of British Columbia and Department of Sociology, University of Victoria, Canada

Peter Bower Health Sciences, Manchester University, UK

Patrick John Burnett Department of Sociology, University of British Columbia, Canada

Sinead Charbonneau Centre for Addictions Research of British Columbia, University of Victoria, Canada

Simon Cohn London School of Hygiene & Tropical Medicine, London, UK

Carol Emslie Institute for Applied Health Research, School of Health & Life Sciences, Glasgow Caledonian University, Scotland

Matthew Fisher Southgate Institute for Health, Society & Equity, Flinders University, South Australia

Katherine L. Frohlich Department of Social and Preventive Medicine, School of Public Health and IRSPUM, Université de Montréal, Canada

Judith Green Department of Health Services Research and Policy, London School of Hygiene & Tropical Medicine, London, UK

Helga Hallgrimsdottir Department of Sociology, University of Victoria, Canada

UK

Christine Horrocks Department of Psychology, Manchester Metropolitan University, UK

Kate Hunt   Medical Research Council/Chief Scientist Office, Social and Public Health Sciences Unit, Glasgow University, Scotland

Sally Johnson   Division of Psychology, University of Bradford, UK

Anne Kennedy   Health Sciences, Manchester University, UK

Antonia C. Lyons   School of Psychology, Massey University, New Zealand

Karen MacKinnon   School of Nursing, University of Victoria, Canada

Lenora Marcellus   School of Nursing, University of Victoria, Canada

Annemarie Mol   Amsterdam Institute for Social Science Research, University of Amsterdam, The Netherlands

Andrew Morden   Arthritis Research UK Primary Care Centre, Keele University, UK

Sarah Nettleton   Department of Sociology, University of York, York, UK

Bie Nio Ong   Arthritis Research UK Primary Care Centre, Keele University, UK

Rachel Phillips   Centre for Addictions Research of British Columbia, University of Victoria, Canada

Jane C. Richardson   Arthritis Research UK Primary Care Centre, Keele University, UK

Anne Rogers   Health Sciences, Manchester University, UK

Tom Sanders   Arthritis Research UK Primary Care Centre, Keele University, UK

Erica van der Sijpt   Amsterdam Institute for Social Science Research, University of Amsterdam, The Netherlands

Sudeh Cheraghi-Sohi   Arthritis Research UK Primary Care Centre, Keele University, UK

Camille Stengel   School of Social Policy, Sociology and Social Research, University of Kent, UK

Fiona Stevenson   Primary Care and Population Sciences, Royal Free and University College London Medical School, UK

Gerry Veenstra   Department of Sociology, University of British Columbia, Canada

Else Vogel   Amsterdam Institute of Social Science Research, University of Amsterdam, The Netherlands

Kate Weiner   Department of Sociological Studies, University of Sheffield, UK

Catherine M. Will   Department of Sociology, University of Sussex, UK

Pilar Zazueta   Division of Medicine, University of Victoria, Canada

1

From health behaviours to health practices: an introduction

Simon Cohn

Changes in demographics and the widespread decline of communicable disease in both Western and non-Western populations has resulted in the rise of so-called chronic illnesses, and in particular, 'lifestyle conditions'. This has led health professionals to turn their gaze from eradicating external agents of disease to altering a wide range of interacting factors identified as causing, or having the potential to cause, ill health. As a result, the idea that smoking, diet, alcohol consumption and physical activity should now be a central focus for intervention has become an established and uncontested position not only in health research but among policymakers, the media and the public more generally.

Derived from health psychology, the concept of health behaviour underpins many of these developments and has led to the generation of new typologies and fields of academic expertise. The assumption that there are easily identifiable and observable forms of health behaviour has almost universally been adopted by those involved in (and funded to do) healthcare research. Yet a great wave of research over the last two decades attempting to develop techniques and evidence of behavioural change has proved to have surprisingly limited success. Usually, explanations of negative findings focus on the nature of the intervention, its theoretical underpinnings, problems with its delivery or the outcome measures used. Very rarely, if ever, is the validity or usefulness of the pivotal concept of health behaviour itself ever questioned. In addition, critics have suggested that the concept insidiously supports variations of neoliberal ideology and responsibilisation, for example through such creative terms as liberal paternalism.

The collection of chapters in this book responds to the fact that surprisingly little critical attention has been paid to how health behaviour is actually conceptualised, whether this might explain why attempts to change what people do for any extended period seem to be so difficult, and what the limitations of the term might be. Collectively, these contributions show that across this burgeoning corpus of work there is remarkably little discussion of power or conceptualisation of sociality beyond a largely epidemiological idea of population. They explore whether there are alternative ways to both theorise and conduct research into what people do and don't do in relation to their health. And, given that very little in this field of research has attempted to capture the specific and detailed qualities of people's activities in particular situations, they demonstrate how investigating local minutiae might actually be crucial to provide general insight. Thus, by drawing on a range of theoretical approaches and empirical studies, the chapters highlight the potential of sociology, and the

From Health Behaviours to Health Practices: Critical Perspectives, First Edition. Edited by Simon Cohn. Chapters © 2014 The Authors. Book Compilation © 2014 Foundation for the Sociology of Health & Illness / Blackwell Publishing Ltd.

social sciences more generally, to provide complementary or alternative ways of considering human activities that relate to health.

As a way of introducing the chapters, and pre-empting the ways in which they critically engage with the concept of health behaviour, I want to spend just a little time describing something of the underlying logic that determines not simply how health behaviour is conceived in the abstract, but perhaps more significantly how it is constructed through research activities designed to address contemporary health problems. Implicitly I draw on my experiences working in a multidisciplinary team consisting of health psychologists and behavioural scientists, primary and secondary care medics, epidemiologists, statisticians and the like. While this is in part a caricature, my intention is to be provocative. It is not simply to pave the way for the more substantive contributions, but to help catalyse a further debate that needs to be had: that, as social scientists often working alongside other disciplines in health research environments, we have, ourselves, in many instances accepted the concept of health behaviour far too readily.

Originally healthy behaviour (Kasl and Cobb 1966), or health-protective behaviour (Harris and Guten 1979) referred to the strategies people might adopt to prevent disease. In a much cited piece of research, Belloc and Breslow (1972) argued that personal lifestyle (sleep, diet, physical activity and smoking) impacted on health in diffuse ways and that there was a direct correlation between them and the risks of ill-health. Interestingly, Matarazzo (1983) later drew directly on a biomedical paradigm to describe this kind of behaviour as a behavioural pathogen and contrasted this with health-protective behaviour, which he labelled a behavioural immunogen. What was significant was that, by adopting the clear distinction informed by biomedicine that some behaviour is unequivocally good whilst other kinds are detrimental, the behaviour itself became abstract and removed from any comprehensive, detailed description of what people were actually doing. And, although the original emphasis of health behaviour was on its positive role in illness prevention, because the primary focus came to be on behavioural change most research has come to focus on negative health behaviour. Even physical activity has, in recent years, been recast to fit this schema, as research has shifted from its promotion to addressing the 'problem' of sedentarism.

Initial attempts to encourage certain kinds of health behaviour, while discouraging others, were aimed at modifying people's health beliefs through education initiatives. By assuming that what people did was the result of deliberation and reasoning, addressing motives and intentions became central. As a result, Levanthal's self-regulatory model (Leventhal et al. 2003) was highly influential, since it proposed the ways in which individuals reflect on what they do prior to action. Drawing on both individual attitudes and socially determined norms, this psychological approach created the space into which researchers felt confident they could intervene. However, as studies began to report that there is often a gap between intentions and behaviour, Bandura's notion of self-efficacy (1977) was increasingly adopted. Further adapted by Ajzen, this general orientation proposed that as well as attitudes and subjective norms influencing intentions, certain beliefs affect levels of perceived control and that this might explain why intentions are not always translated into actions (Ajzen 1991). More recently, some psychologists have drawn from behavioural economics to explore alternative ways in which non-deliberate or automatic processes might explain why people behave the way that they do, rather than the more reason-based models that initially shaped behavioural science (Thaler and Sustein 2008).

A key point in all this, however, is that despite the evolution of the concept of health behaviour in the psychological literature, what has remained central is the linear order that conceives of various psychological determinants, potentially modified by social norms and triggered by environment cues, which then determine someone's behaviour. In other words, health behaviour is seen as the an outcome of an individual who is presented as the obvious focus of both the processes preceding behaviour and the agent of the behaviour itself. Thus, although contemporary behavioural science might not equate directly with classic behaviourism, because of its focus on mediating cognitive processes, behaviour is nevertheless conceived of as a definitive and observable entity that should not require abstract concepts or assumptions to identify or interpret it (Baumeister *et al.* 2007), just as Watson argued a century ago (Watson 1930).

In contemporary research, specific forms of health behaviour tend to be combined with other disease-related elements so that useful, multifactorial accounts can be established (Abraham *et al.* 2000). They have to be drawn out from the inherently chaotic variation of human activity and sufficiently standardised to resemble other items, such as demographic and physiological factors. Often a range of graphic representations during the research process and in final publications further confirm the epistemological parity between health behaviour and other variables; flow charts, tree diagrams, drawings of multiple boxes and arrows all map out the mix and the hypothesised relationships between them. Two key assumptions underlie this process: that kinds of behaviour can be considered to be distinct from each other and that they can potentially be controlled or altered once an accurate causal explanation is established.

The imperative to consider specific forms of behaviour as unique variables that can be studied and assembled alongside others means that they must be conceived of as discrete, stable, homogeneous, observable and, crucially, measurable. Often a distinction is made between subjective and objective measures. The former consist of various methods of participant selfreporting – usually by questionnaires or diaries – and tend to be regarded as unreliable. In contrast, the term objective measures increasingly refers to various forms of electronic technologies that can record data relatively unobtrusively and independently of the participant. Thus, embedded in the very objects of study is a preconceived notion not only of what they are, but also how they function.

But because research is only conducted on kinds of behaviour that already fulfil these criteria, other health-related activities or variations of what people do in different situations that escape the parameters of measurement are excluded. The social, affective, material and interrelational features of human activity are effectively eliminated, as behaviour becomes viewed as an outcome of the individual and determined only by such things as motives, intentions and the subjective reception of norms and cues. In response, there has been a growing acknowledgement that the specifics of context are significant and somehow need to be taken in to account. However, citing context to situate individuals in their physical and social environment indirectly serves to reinforce what is of primary importance and fore grounded. Health behaviour remains contrasted against a backdrop of interrelated factors that fall outside the specifics of research because they have not, or often cannot, be rendered into variables. As a consequence, although discussion of context may ostensibly resemble adoption of a more sociological perspective, by preserving the delineated characteristics of health behaviour and pre-empting a focus for causal explanation, its inclusion frequently serves simply to maintain, rather than revise, conceptualisations of health behaviour.

So why is problematising the category of health behaviour important? After all, it would be reasonable to argue that not only are these weaknesses inevitable, but they are actually highly productive and necessary in order to construct a particular kind of object of enquiry. But a danger of this is that the notion of behaviour becomes so reified that it fails to provide any critical insight into what people actually do and why. In this, then, lies the inherent conservatism of adopting categories of behaviour a priori. The issue is not simply that they continuously get reproduced from one research project to another but that they increasingly become naturalised the more they are 'understood'. It is also clear that the focus on health behaviour unavoidably presents a particular moral explanation, as issues of responsibility and agency are distributed in specific ways along causal pathways that inevitably converge on the individual. Although not necessarily intentional, this individualising characteristic can all too easily align itself, and further legitimate, public health and policy strategies that ignore the complex structural issues that underpin the political economy of health.

This collection of chapters contends, in different ways, that many of the limitations and consequences of the concept of health behaviour can be potentially addressed by drawing on a broader notion of *health practices*. In contrast to the idea of specific behaviour, everyday practices are always locally situated and composite. They are not a direct result or outcome of mental processes but emerge out of the actions and interactions of individuals in a specific context. Thus, the word practice has the potential to resist both the psychologising and the individualising features that ultimately have come to define the term health behaviour. However, adopting such a conception means it is perhaps impossible and even undesirable to try and identify when exactly an action starts and when it ends, or the extent to which one action is distinct from another. It also potentially resists the search for causal explanations, in the form of identifying determinants, and instead embraces the idea that practices are contingent on a whole variety of social and material factors. This is not, however, an argument designed to champion the impossibility of the social sciences genuinely engaging with contemporary health problems. But by being aligned with a language of systems, complexity, interactions and irreducibilities, such an approach must inevitably be modest, since it can only ever offer a partial interpretation. Nevertheless, it also means that issues of power and politics cannot be bracketed off but must be recognised as central features of any proposed method to influence or change people.

Identifying a variety of problems associated with the concept of health behaviour, and considering what possibilities a more practice-orientated approach might offer, the contributions in this monograph address many of the issues raised above in a variety of ways. As a result, grouping chapters together represents just one way in which the overlapping and cross-cutting themes in the collection might be navigated. A first set explores some of the theoretical approaches from sociology that have the potential to provide a counter to the individualised notion of health behaviour. To begin with, Armstrong argues that the whole shift towards encouraging patients to take control of their behaviour and, as a consequence accept responsibility, is remarkably recent. Importantly, he also suggests that ultimately agency itself has, in the process, come to be equated with health. Horrocks and Johnson extend this theme by critically examining the ideological assumptions associated with such things as self-management and choice. They describe the ways in which health psychology has served to support and reproduce a range of values that inevitably engage more favourably with some groups of people more than others. Veenstra and Burnett also tackle the concept of agency through the influential work of Bourdieu and in particular through his rendering of structure–agency as coconstituting rather than in opposition. They argue, however, that the relational characteristics of many of Bourdieu's terms tend to be underemphasised and that, if accounts of health practice are to be of value for applied work, it is crucial to embrace this ontological imperative. Finally, Frohlich and Abel return to the unequal distribution of health and health-resources with the observation that those who are most deprived are the least likely to alter their health-related practices. By integrating Sen's capability theory with the theories of Bourdieu, the authors make a shift from framing the issue in terms of who possesses what capital to thinking about where there might be social and cultural opportunities for change.

A second group of chapters draw on accounts of particular health initiatives to explore the limitations of behaviour-based interventions and the potential for social science approaches in current health research. In different ways they extend the general theoretical perspectives introduced by the initial chapters to illustrate the extent to which people's actions arise from their interactions both with other people and the material environment. Implicitly drawing on arguments of scale, the chapters present a variety of cases in which apparently individual actions are influenced by forces that can only be conceived of at a social level. This implicitly alters not merely the focus of causal explanations but highlights the ways in which practices emerge from, and are always contingent upon, a wide range of factors that operate alongside, rather than 'prior to'. As some of the authors explicitly propose, this offers new ways to think about health interventions that need to take into account factors that defy reductionism. Firstly, Baum and Fisher continue with the theme of health inequalities and discuss how, despite the weight of evidence for the existence of social determinants of health, governments nevertheless are attracted to behavioural explanations for ideological reasons. Given this trend, they conclude that health policies are unlikely to ever address the broader social foundations of health. Ong *et al.* take up the same issue through a discussion of context and, using two studies as illustrative examples, argue that what is commonly framed as the background features of living with a chronic condition should be refigured to be integrated in existing research designs. Nettleton and Green then draw on case studies to discuss a number of practices relating to transport and physical activity and suggest that a Bourdieusian-informed approach can demonstrate the extent to which existing tacit knowledge and habitus shape the conditions of possibility for change, and therefore that public health must attend to their significance.

The next three chapters extend these arguments by providing detailed qualitative accounts of specific health practices. Addressing the health issue of substance misuse by women who are pregnant, Benoit *et al.* point out that the key to the effectiveness of any intervention is the way that people see substance abuse as problematic. The authors show that views on such things as health risks should not be regarded as individually held beliefs that go on to directly influence behaviour. Instead, they are inherently social discourses that are only meaningful through the ways in which participants talk, compare and situate themselves in relation to others. Complementing this position, Lyons *et al.* focus on the alcohol consumption of people in their mid-life. Similarly rejecting any approach that assumes that drinking is the result of rational decision-making, they describe how many of the factors that shape alcohol consumption are inherently cultural and embodied. In particular, they include aspects relating to gender and, although this is frequently omitted in health behaviour research, the desire to be moderately intoxicated. Finally, adopting a more overtly anthropological orientation, van der Sijpt explores issues relating to reproduction and contraception in Cameroon. Like many of the other chapters, the author explicitly rejects behavioural models that rely on any version of rational choice theory. But she adds to this critique by arguing the same values underlie the notion of individual rights and that these do necessarily translate easily to other cultural contexts. Instead, van der Sijpt suggests that the idea of navigation better captures the practices by which women engage with the different options on contraception and reproduction that they encounter in their daily lives.

The final pair of chapters could be said to critique the concept of health behaviour not by drawing on established perspectives of the social but by conceiving of practice as a means to resist seeking direct causal antecedents – whether they be individual psychological processes or, indeed, more diffuse social influences. Will and Weiner examine people's talk about cholesterol reduction and note the ways that people often accommodate contradictory and inconsistent accounts. Beyond an analysis of discourse, their argument suggests that the processes of talking and making sense of everyday practices never need to be fixed or singular because ultimately these are accounts of activities that are not coherent; they are practices, not behaviour. Finally Vogel and Mol explore how the drive for healthy eating, and the various forms of knowledge that support this, have become the antithesis of eating practices associated with pleasure. They argue that linking eating practices with enjoyment is not natural but a relationship that is acquired. By attending to the variety of social and material elements that enable such practices to be pleasurable, an alternative strategy to traditional interventions intended to correct unhealthy behaviour could potentially be developed.

No overview of the chapters, especially as brief as this, could claim they all share common approaches or conclusions. Nevertheless, it is clear all the authors are uneasy about the dominance of the concept of health behaviour, based on theoretical, methodological or political grounds. The chapters suggest that the concept is too contained, too delineated and too far removed from everyday social life. So perhaps this, then, is the final value of reading the chapters together – that the term health practices ultimately is useful not because it claims to be a direct alternative, or substitute, for psychological and behavioural approaches but precisely because it allows for sufficient degrees of freedom such that no single theory can ever fully stabilise how it can or should be applied.

References

Abraham, C., Norman, P. and Conner, M. (eds) (2000) *Understanding and Changing Health Behaviour: From Health Beliefs to Self-regulation*. Amsterdam: Harwood Academic Press.

Ajzen, I. (1991) The theory of planned behaviour, *Organizational Behavior and Human Decision Processes*, 50, 2, 179–211.

Bandura, A. (1977) Self-efficacy: toward a unifying theory of behavior change, *Psychological Review*, 84, 2, 191–215.

Baumeister, R., Vohs, K. and Funder, D. (2007) Psychology as the science of self-reports and finger movements: whatever happened to actual behaviour? *Perspectives on Psychological Science*, 2, 4, 396–403.

Belloc, N. and Breslow, L. (1972) The relationship of physical health status and health practices, *Preventative Medicine*, 1, 3, 409–21.

Harris, D. and Guten, S. (1979) Health-protective behavior: an exploratory study, *Journal of Health and Social Behavior*, 20, 1, 17–29.

Kasl, S. and Cobb, S. (1966) Health behavior, illness behavior and sick role behavior, *Archives of Environmental Health*, 12, 2, 246–66.

Leventhal, H., Brisette, I. and Leventhal, E. (2003) The common-sense model of self-regulation of health and illness. In Cameron, L.D. and Leventhal, H. (eds) *The Self-regulation of Health and Illness Behavior*. London: Routledge.

Matarazzo, J.D. (1983) Behavioral immunogens and pathogens: psychology's newest challenge, *Professional Psychology: Research and Practice*, 14, 3, 414–16.

Thaler, R. and Sustein, C. (2008) *Nudge: Improving Decisions About Health, Wealth and Happiness*. New Haven: Yale University Press.

Watson, J. (1930) *Behaviorism*. Chicago: University of Chicago Press.

2

Actors, patients and agency: a recent history
David Armstrong

Introduction

When was it first possible to say that patients had agency? The term was certainly used in the 19th century but only in the context of differentiating human action from non-human or 'natural' forces. An outbreak of pestilence and famine in India, for example, identified 'human agency as the instrument of dissemination and contaminated water as the vehicle of infection' (Bombay Sanitary Report for 1897 1898: 1265). More broadly, events were construed as 'through the agency of Man' as against, say, 'the agency of insects'. Although this use continued during the first half of the 20th century, agency came more commonly to refer to an organisation that provided a service, as in a voluntary agency or a health agency. In more recent years however, agency, as applied to patients and their behaviour, has taken on a more powerful sense of individual autonomous action. This chapter attempts to describe the emergence of this latter use of agency through contemporary medical, socio-logical, psychological and ethical writing and argues that the new application of the term reflects more than a change of semantic fashion but rather a fundamental reconstruction of patients' identity that began in the second half of the 20th century.

The new patient project

In 1951, when Parsons described the significance of the sick role in medical encounters he identified three salient features of the situation of patients; namely, helplessness, technical incompetence and emotional involvement. The sick person was not regarded as being responsible for his (sic) condition and therefore could not avoid it or mitigate it by willpower. Further, for Parsons, the very nature of patienthood was such that the sick were not com-petent to help themselves; they therefore required professional help that, in its turn, imposed a further disadvantage because patients were not in a position to know what needed to be done or how to do it. Finally, Parsons argued that the situation of illness presented patients and those close to them with complex problems of emotional adjustment that he described as a situation of strain.

Clearly within Parsons' analytic framework there was little space for independent action by the patient. Patients were vulnerable and irrational, dependent on a benevolent medical

From Health Behaviours to Health Practices: Critical Perspectives, First Edition. Edited by Simon Cohn. Chapters © 2014 The Authors. Book Compilation © 2014 Foundation for the Sociology of Health & Illness / Blackwell Publishing Ltd.

profession to address their healthcare needs and assuage the emotional strain of illness. The formal sick role, as conferred by medicine, established expectations and obligations about motivations but little about subsequent behaviour except in generalities such as 'to comply with medical advice'. Patients were docile figures with no responsibility for their predicament and minimal involvement in their own care.

Seven years later, in 1958, Hochbaum published a report of a 'socio-psychological study' entitled *Public Participation in Medical Screening Programs* that investigated the problem of patients who failed to respond to invitations to attend newly developed screening programmes, especially for tuberculosis. His report was one of a number in the immediate post-war years that explored patients' behaviour, most of which were concerned less with behaviour and more with non-behaviour, particularly in the form of non-attendance for health care (Glasser 1958, Koos 1954, Rosenstock *et al.* 1959). Yet, while the failure of patients to attend as expected formed the common theme across these reports, Hochbaum's analysis can be seen, in retrospect, as providing a particularly clear programmatic statement of a post-war project to transform the nature of patienthood.

The main challenge of screening was that it focused on pre-symptomatic disease. In the absence of symptoms patients had no means of knowing whether or not they had the disease in question. Feeling healthy therefore did not equate with actually being healthy: 'In the absence of noticeable symptoms, accepting the possibility of having contracted tuberculosis depends on an additional belief that the absence of such symptoms does not necessarily assure a state of health', observed Hochbaum (1958: 5). The challenge for public health was to raise the patient to a higher level of alertness, to the possibility of diseases that remained hidden from personal experience. As Hochbaum explained:

> In the case of a person who is not aware of symptoms, psychological readiness …
> requires a full acceptance of the possibility that he could have a serious disease such as
> tuberculosis without noticeable warning symptoms. (Hochaum 1958: 6–7)

The task ahead therefore was to promote a constant state of self-appraisal in all patients, a sort of ongoing reflexivity about illnesses both actual and potential. Being alert to the possibility of disease could not, however, be reduced simply to having appropriate knowledge:

> [The] difference in participation in case-finding programs between well-informed and
> poorly informed respondents is not an impressive one … does it mean that we have to
> consider more complex relationships between what people know and what people do?
> (Hochbaum 1958: 15)

In many cases, Hochbaum observed, some patients might know about the dangers of tuberculosis but not really believe them, while others did believe them but thought the danger applied to other people and not themselves. Indeed:

> Information is depersonalised, isolated from the springs of behavior. Information
> alone is not a motivating force, although it is basic to most behavior. Without knowing
> what to do and how to do it, one cannot act. But only when this knowledge is related
> in some way to one's needs will it actually be translated into action. (Hochbaum 1958:
> 16–17)

Patients were not to be instructed, for how could this approach be expected to achieve that desired permanent state of readiness? Instead, patients had to cultivate their subjective awareness and place their behaviour under constant observation. This would require a change in the dialogue and relationship between doctor and patient: it required medicine to use the patient's words in a more subtle way. Instead of listening to the patient's symptoms, filtering out the unreliable ones and focusing on those that might have pathological significance, the symptoms needed to be reframed as mechanisms for accessing an inner patient identity. Symptoms were to be treated as part of a patient's experience irrespective of their clinical significance:

> Symptoms in this report referred to the respondent's interpretation of what constitutes tuberculosis symptoms and not necessarily to medically valid interpretations of the disease. In short we shall be concerned with what people believe not with the correctness of these beliefs. (Hochbaum 1958: 5)

Hochbaum's analysis pointed in three new directions. The first was the refining and fine-tuning of those psychological mechanisms that underpinned the state of readiness; the second, the application of that psychological state to symptom appraisal; and the third, the promotion of autonomous action based on these appraisals and interpretive processes. Each of these strategies, in their turn, was to be articulated on the patients' behaviour, initially their healthcare attendance or help-seeking, later, risk and illness management. Were his project to be implemented, Hochbaum claimed, it would not only assist the screening programme for tuberculosis but 'similar principles are likely to be operative with the behavior of the public in other health areas' (Hochbaum 1958: 23).

Hochbaum's design was a radical one: a staged reconstruction of the self and its sense of agency. Patients had to believe themselves vulnerable to unspecified illnesses while at the same time mistrusting their own subjective interpretations of symptoms as indicators of disease. This new scepticism, when combined with the attention to the self implied by the new psychological preparedness, placed every patient in an ambiguous state with regard their health. Over subsequent decades this reconstruction of personal experience engendered that state of reflexivity where knowledge and beliefs were not held as a resource pointing to the world outside the individual but as an analytic frame governing awareness of self.

Hochbaum's ambitious programme could not be established overnight; the project would take many decades to realise and would require the invention of new constructs and new technologies to further its aims. Even so, Hochbaum's statement of the problem and the way forward can be seen as a blueprint for future analysis and discourse – the instillation of a new attribute of agency in the minds and bodies of every patient and the construction of a malleable and willing patient who would be a voluntary participant in health programmes, as the potential for control of the patient was transferred from medicine to the patients themselves.

The appraisal process

Although the problem of non-attendance had been identified in the late 19th and early 20th centuries in terms of defaulting from treatment it was only applied to those health-related activities, such as attendance for compulsory vaccination or treatment for venereal disease, that carried legal or quasi-legal sanctions. But around mid-century the problem was extended to non-participation in public health programmes such as screening using mass miniature radiography (Dick 1945, Hochbaum 1958) and polio vaccination (Rosenstock, Derryberry, and Carriger 1959). And whereas character flaws such as indolence and apathy had formed the main explanatory framework for defaulting, the study of non-participation demanded the investigation of more complex cognitive-behavioural processes that preceded the decision not to attend. Further, such analyses of the ways patients made decisions could also be applied equally to those who chose to attend public health programmes and clinical consultations.

During the immediate post-war years patients presented themselves in the consulting room face-to-face with the doctor, as they had done in previous years, but it seemed increasingly unclear how that manoeuvre was accomplished. In 1961, using Parson's formulation of the 'tendency to adopt the sick role' (measured using responses to hypothetical symptoms) and levels of stress, Mechanic and Volkart (1961) tried to predict the illness behaviour, as they described it, of a group of college students. Like Hochbaum a few years earlier, Mechanic drew attention to the interpretive space that surrounded symptoms:

> [A] symptom viewed by a layman as not serious, may be of great medical
> consequence ... Persons, of course, also sometimes visit the physician unnecessarily,
> thus, wasting valuable medical time. (Mechanic 1962: 193–4)

The patient therefore had to be both attentive and active so as to steer a difficult course between 'early detection [that] might greatly reduce the future consequences of the illness, while, at the same time, discouraging tendencies toward hypochondriasis' (Mechanic 1962: 193–4).

In subsequent studies of the transition of patients between their homes and the consulting room of the medical practitioner, the journey across physical space was used to explore the movement across the interpretive space in which symptoms were located. When social scientists and concerned doctors enquired about symptoms it was increasingly their lay, rather than medical, interpretation that informed the purpose of the interaction together with the promotion of a process of subjective reflection. Researchers such as Leventhal et al. (1980), Kleinman (1980), Locker (1981) and Tuckett et al. (1985) asked patients about how they made sense of symptoms, not to better diagnose disease but to understand the processes by which self-conscious decisions were taken to consider themselves as ill and/or ready to consult the doctor. The advice that doctors should consider eliciting their patients' explanatory models, illness representations and lay theories marked the spread of a generalised approach to the consultation that would bring to life patients' inner interpretive maps (Pendleton et al. 1984, McWhinney 1984).

Hochbaum, together with others in the Behavioural Science Section of the US Public Health Service, continued investigating the decision to make use of health care and in 1966 a colleague, Rosenstock, published a formalised version of the analytic framework called the health belief model to explain why people both used and failed to use health services (Rosenstock 1966). The model had four core elements centred round patients' perceptions of illness and its context: these were the perceived seriousness of the problem, the perceived benefits of action, perceived barriers and perceived susceptibility. The first three components had their origins in existing psychological theories (Rosenstock 1974) that captured the trade-off between costs and benefits of behaviour, but it was the fourth construct that best engaged with Hochbaum's vision of how threats might be personalised. It was not only necessary to recognise the dangers posed by unsuspected disease but also relate these concerns to the self.

In Hochbaum's analysis of 1958 the immediate threat lay in the dangers of asymptomatic disease, but other unseen hazards were also beginning to appear in the social world outside the body of the patients and their unknown pathologies. New concerns about environmental pollution (Carson 1962) multiplied in subsequent decades as the Green movement identified the existence of threats to health and life everywhere. For medicine in this period the form of a persistent, ubiquitous and hidden threat came from the newly discovered risk factor (Kannel *et al.* 1961). Risk factors were initially identified as existing within the human body (such as high blood pressure or raised blood cholesterol) but over the course of the 1960s they were extended to embrace external risks including behaviour (as in, for example, the dangers of smoking). By the mid-1970s many of these risks could be captured by the notion of lifestyle, at once a descriptor of a way of living and a sum of everyday activities, but also a catalogue of hazardous factors. Everyone was at risk, constantly.

A risk factor perspective, like screening and early diagnosis, was a pre-symptomatic technology. Being at risk required a constant state of vigilance towards the patient's internal and external environment as well as towards the person's own behaviour. According to Hochbaum's analysis it was a question of convincing patients of the threats posed by these proliferating risks and persuading them that the very absence of symptoms did not preclude disease. Being at risk therefore established the perfect machinery for placing the population in a constant state of readiness and awareness in regard their health. Recognition of risks everywhere was but another device for both engendering and reinforcing beliefs in individual susceptibility.

The sense of personal susceptibility embedded in the health belief model might have been a prerequisite for a patient's readiness for action, but there was always the danger that the threat of disease discovery that hovered constantly over an individual's future might lead to a form of psychological paralysis or even denial (Goldstein 1960). How could the capacity of patients to overcome these challenges be identified and promoted? In 1966 Rotter advanced the concept of a locus of control to describe the ability to respond to threat: some people had a strong external locus of control, believing that life was controlled by luck, charms or all-powerful others, while those with an internal locus of control believed that responsibility for action belonged to themselves and their own efforts. A focus on this psychological capacity for action was further enhanced in 1977 when Bandura proposed the construct of self-efficacy, the belief an individual had in their ability to carry out certain behaviour in a specific situation rather than the idea of a generalised reactive style embedded in locus of control. Self-efficacy reflected an important aspect of Hochbaum's notion of psychological readiness: if patients had self-efficacy then they also had the power to act. In 1988 the concept of self-efficacy was incorporated into a revised version of the health belief model (Rosenstock *et al.* 1988).

For most of the latter part of the 20th century the health belief model, adapted and developed, provided the core psychological mechanism for studying and explaining patients' behaviour. The model, reported Rosenstock, Strecher, and Becker (1988), generated more research into explaining, predicting and influencing health-related behaviour than any other theoretical framework. Yet, while the model was widely utilised, its explanatory and predictive power was never large (Harrison *et al.* 1992). Its success, however, should not be assessed in terms of its empirical claims but in its incitement of the very phenomenon it measured. The health belief model was less a theoretical framework and more a technology that promoted the idea of actions based on psychological readiness, a machine for bringing to life Hochbaum's vision in which all patients would show a psychological awareness of the hidden threats contained in everyday life. By the closing decades of the 20th century a framework for describing, explaining and furthering the psychological readiness that Hochbaum had prescribed for a future world were firmly in place; an analytic space had been opened up far removed from the passivity of the patient's role in the consulting room as described by Parsons. The patient was now primed for action.

The path to action

In 1974 Stimson summarised the results of 19 studies published between 1957 and 1969 that were concerned with whether or not patients took their medicine as advised by the doctor. The assumption underlying all of these studies, he noted, was that 'the patient should obey or comply with what the doctor says. It is an ideal of the patient as a passive and obedient recipient of medical instructions' (Stimson 1974: 99). Yet, as Stimson pointed out, people had their own ideas and attitudes about the use of medicines and they were not taking them in a thoughtless vacuum. Their actions in not following medical advice could therefore be construed as rational and deliberate.

In the 1970s the term non-compliance began to replace that of default in sociological writing on medicine-taking (Hayes-Bautista 1976) and a few years later medical writers also began self-consciously to use the expression 'defaulters or non-compliers'. In the 1990s an even more non-judgemental expression, non-adherence, became the preferred descriptor and during the first decade of the 21st century it was joined by another term, concordance, that reflected the idea that if doctor and patient shared treatment decisions the problem of non-adherence should disappear, as no medicine would be prescribed without the patient's endorsement (Royal Pharmaceutical Society of Great Britain 1997).

Concordance implied a greater agreement between doctor and patient on the nature of the problem, the need for treatment and the most appropriate medication. Default and non-compliance had indicated a failure of the patient; lack of concordance reflected a failure of the consultation, mostly through the physician not having elicited the true nature of the patient's problem (Britten et al. 2000) or the patient's real concerns (Barry et al. 2000). Concordance therefore promoted a form of open consultation that encouraged the patient to express their true selves by verbalising their inner life-worlds (Mishler 1985).

The task of generating concordance had been facilitated by a new patient-centredness in the consultation. First identified by Byrne and Long in 1976, the emergence of the idea of a patient-centred consultation exactly paralleled the construction of an independent appraisal of the need for treatment as revealed in the spread of investigations into non-compliance and concordance. Patient-centredness and concordance were therefore two sides of the same coin: research studies demonstrated again and again that patients could be incited to adopt the state of psychological readiness described by Hochbaum in deliberating on medical decisions. It was then for clinicians to introduce these tactics into routine clinical practice (Kahn et al. 1979, Levenstein et al. 1986).

Post-war concerns about whether or not patients were taking prescribed medication as instructed were also mirrored in anxieties about self-medication. Patients choosing self-medication without the guidance of medical expertise risked using inappropriate or useless treatments or, worse, masking a serious illness. The medical view that self-medication was a potentially dangerous activity began to change during the late 1960s as successive reports showed it was not only extremely common but could be viewed as a reasonable alternative to using hard-pressed medical services (Dunnell and Cartwright 1972, Wadsworth et al. 1971). Indeed, in many instances the doctor might endorse the patient's decision and encourage patients to continue with some form of self-medication that the patient had initiated (Scott et al. 1960). By the mid-1970s responsible self-medication was increasingly seen as another part of a comprehensive healthcare package (BMJ 1975) and the term over-the-counter medicine entered common usage.

When in 1981 Dean reported a selected review of the literature on self-care, she found that earlier studies had focused mainly on the utilisation of physician and hospital services, delay in seeking care and patient compliance with medical regimes:

> The implicit, sometimes explicit, assumption of the studies was the patients were only recipients of professional care ... the individual as an active participant on healthcare process was ignored ... Decision-making by the patient, if discussed at all, was considered in terms of complying with medical directives ... The studies approached self-care as behaviour to be avoided or changed ... at the most negative extreme, lay involvement in health care has been denigrated as misinformed and dangerous. (Dean 1981: 674)

More recent research, she pointed out, had shown that self-care occurred independently of professional care. Dean noted, moreover, a recent shift in research focus from a predominant concern with the utilisation of professional services towards a study of self-medication, the role of the family in health maintenance and the self-care of individuals.

In the 1980s self-medication became a legitimate complement to medical action. Indeed, self-medication could be actively promoted as an adjunct to patient care (Morrell *et al.* 1980, Segall and Goldstein 1989). The new vision was of self-caring, self-medicating patients who took increasing responsibility for their own treatment. It was but a small step to self-management, a term Lorig and Holman (2003) claimed had been first used in 1976 (Creer *et al.* 1976). During the 1980s it began to be applied to many chronic diseases such as diabetes, asthma and arthritis. In 2001 Lorig *et al.* developed a chronic disease self-management programme that was adopted by Kaiser Permanente in the USA and the UK's National Health Service's expert patient programme.

There had been earlier lay attempts to promote the self-management agenda, such as the Boston Women's Health Collective (1971) but self-management was not a strategy driven by patients but rather one incited by medicine and complicit social sciences. The patient was an expert who:

> [F]eels confident and in control of their life, aims to manage their condition and its treatment in partnership with healthcare professionals, communicates effectively with professionals and is willing to share responsibility for treatment, is realistic about how their condition affects them and their family and uses their skills and knowledge to lead a full life. (Department of Health 2001)

Accompanying these exhortations to act autonomously, albeit within the constraints of healthcare policies and professional guidance, there was a new emphasis on choice – though always with an expectation that patients would choose health (Department of Health 2004).

Although patients had little option but to take the road of choice this was not a conspiracy by the medical profession to subjugate patients by even more subtle chains. In fact, the medical profession itself was caught within the same machinery of power that elicited and instilled agency in everyone, lay and professional. Just as patients' psychological forces were beginning to be assembled in the 1950s, Balint (1957) was proposing the same self-critical examination of a doctor's own behaviour. By 1987 Neighbour could describe the consultation with patients co-occurring with the doctors' own inner dialogue with themselves (Neighbour 1987). In other words, the new medicine demanded reflexivity from doctor and patient, both of whom were made increasingly responsible for their actions.

The conceptual space of agency

Through practical strategies as diverse as risk factor awareness campaigns, population and patient surveillance, concordance and self-management, clinical medicine demanded of the patient both reflexivity and responsibility. But how could clinical medicine shed its own professional responsibilities for patient welfare to a (hypothetically) autonomous patient? Such a transfer needed a political framework so that agency could be legitimately and safely nurtured: that underpinning was provided by the new discourse of medical ethics.

Emerging in the early 1970s, medical ethics (often described as bioethics), provided the key construct of patient autonomy for a medicine that was just beginning to grapple with the problem of patients' behaviour. The term patient autonomy was almost unknown before the mid-1960s (as shown by Google Ngrams) but became one of the commonest themes in the new *Hastings Centre Reports* (since 1971) and the *Journal of Medical Ethics* (since 1975) and formed a cornerstone of the principlist approach to medical ethics popularised by Beauchamp and Childress (1979). Patient autonomy – particularly as an ethical principle – created a space in which agency could crystallise. This was not a practice, as was so much of medical involvement with promoting a sense of agency in patients, but a set of political and ideological beliefs that defined the contours of a new conceptual and moral space. The corollary was that medicine at once became paternalistic (Weiss 1985): what had once formed the bedrock of collegiate professional practice became an overbearing intrusion into the patient's life-world. After the rejection of paternalism the child/patient (and many metaphors were used in contemporary analyses comparing family life with the relationship between doctor and patient) could be allowed to grow up and find their own voice and their own sense of responsibility as medicine started to engage in a new dialogue with an emancipated patient. In effect, this new form of communication between doctor and patient involved a transfer of that very autonomy that had so recently been identified as a defining characteristic of professional status (Freidson 1970, Johnson 1972) to the patient, as clinical decision-making became increasingly circumscribed by external constraints (Haug 1973).

The idea of patient autonomy was at first a free-floating ethical principle derived, it was claimed, from moral philosophy, but it soon began to mark out the operational field of self-conscious, self-reflexive action by engaging with conditions such as mental illness and dementia that appeared to constrain its spread and proliferation. Debates in the 1960s that informed the anti-psychiatry movement were fundamentally about whether or not those with mental health problems were in a position to show discretion in their behaviour and exercise real choice in their actions. Latterly these limits to autonomy have been explored through dementia (Gubrium 1986, Kitwood and Bredin 1992, Sabat and Harre 1992), asking the key questions that delineate agency: what is mental capacity and does the patient have it?

The increasing belief in the importance of patient autonomy during the closing decades of the 20th century created problems for psychologists and sociologists who were struggling to identify the causes of behaviour. Shifts in explanatory focus from the fixed structures of the mind to more contingent attributes helped to develop a space in which patients' agency could materialise, yet there remained a tension between causal explanations and autonomy: if a patient's actions could be explained by prior factors how could the patient really have exercised choice?

The explanatory constraints of causal models were addressed by a growing turn to qualitative methods that identified patient's reasons for actions rather than their causes. Whereas causes undermined the very notion of autonomy, reasons provided a new explanatory framework in which the patient's own sense of agency was paramount. In 1983, for example, Blaxter explored respondents' own ideas of causes (which, she noted, could be 'factually incorrect') which she ascribed to their need to give meaning to their illness experiences. Or, as Williams observed, patients with chronic illness engaged with a process of narrative reconstruction that subsumed their own version of causality (Williams 1984). Chronic illness was, in fact, less a disease and more an ongoing struggle to define and maintain identity in a cognitive world (Charmaz 1987, 1995).

Debate about the exact relationship between a reason and a cause had in fact (re-)appeared in philosophy in the post-war years (Davidson 1963). Initially, the problem that reasons posed for scientific explanation in the behavioural sciences was managed by subordinating reasons to attributions: reasons offered less a means of explaining action and more a post hoc justi-fication. During the late 1970s and early 1980s, however, just as patients' autonomy and reflexivity were being recognised, reasons began to be liberated from the constraints of attri-bution theory (Buss 1978, Locke and Pennington 1982). This marked the beginning of a new explanatory system that prioritised the autonomous patient unencumbered by the structural social and psychological constraints that were believed to determine or limit action.

In 2006 when Thoits examined the role of conventional causal explanation in stress research she was initially perplexed as to why the relationship between stressful experiences and psychological difficulties was so modest in size. Then, in what she described as a moment of epiphany, she realised that those respondents who seemed protected from the effects of stress were more likely to be exercising personal agency; such individuals through problem-solving efforts and purposeful acts were able to transform or compensate for stressors that they could not avoid or eliminate. In this sense, agency was not some sort of confounder to be eliminated but rather an important factor by which people made deliberate efforts to solve the demands in their lives. There was a component of human behaviour, she suggested, that could not be captured by causes, simply because it had no preceding cause in the con-ventional sense. In effect, the autonomous patient was beginning to exist beyond the reduc-tive science of explanation.

The imputation of agency

Medicine was not alone in promoting agency as the construct appeared in a new and more forceful way across a number of disciplines in the second half of the 20th century. In phi-losophy Taylor described a new theory of agency in 1958 that supposed that 'an act for which an agent is responsible is performed by him, but … he, in turn, is not causally neces-sitated to do it' (Taylor 1958: 227–8). A theory of agency emerged in economics (Ross 1973) when it was realised that, despite extensive work on the theory of the firm and of markets, there was 'no theory which explains how the conflicting objectives of the individual partici-pants are brought into equilibrium so as to yield this result' (Jensen and Meckling 1976: 309). At the same time, sociologists grappled with the problem of how the actions of the autonomous agent could be explored in a world hitherto dominated by structure (Giddens 1979). As Lash and Urry (1984) noted, over the previous half decade or so, forms of agency had increasingly come to take the place of purely structural determinations in explanations of collective action.

With the promotion of agency across medicine the old Parsonian model of patient pas-sivity was rejected. Not only was Parson's insistence that patients should comply with medical advice undercut but the epicentre of the sick role, that the patient was not respon-sible for illness, was inverted. Patients as autonomous actors were, in the final analysis, responsible – responsible for managing the risk factors that threatened illness, responsible for maintaining and monitoring psychological vigilance and responsible for self-manage-ment. The shifting locus of responsibility, captured in the changing debates around medi-calisation (Conrad 1992, Crawford 1980, Illich 1974, Zola 1972), took place as the active patient emerged phoenix-like from the ashes of professional autonomy.

When Hochbaum outlined his grand design for ways in which patients of the future would perceive their bodies and experiences in different ways and act accordingly, he can hardly have imagined the success of his project. His master plan for a new patient identity, one that was psychologically prepared, vigilant for illness threats and making autonomous choices in the name of health, has gradually materialised. Agency is now promoted through a research agenda that has identified important constructs such as the risk factor, self-efficacy and self-management. Clinical practice has then incorporated these research inventions into the routine care of patients such that it becomes increasingly difficult for patients to resist the demands that they be both reflexive and empowered to act. To engage with this new world of hazard requires patients to take increasing responsibility for health-related decisions; in short, to exercise agency: that is the attribute which separates the passive patient of 1958 from the active one today.

References

Balint, M. (1957) *The Doctor, His Patient and the Illness*. Edinburgh: Churchill Livingstone.

Bandura, A. (1977) Self-efficacy: towards a unifying theory of behaviour change, *Psychological Review*, 84, 191–215.

Barry, C.A., Bradley, C.P., Britten, N. and Stevenson, F.A. *et al.* (2000) Patients' unvoiced agendas in general practice consultations: qualitative study, *British Medical Journal*, 320,1246–50. doi: http://dx. doi.org/10.1136/bmj.320.7244.1246

Beauchamp, T.L. and Childress, J.F. (1979) *Principles of Biomedical Ethics*. New York: Oxford University Press.

Blaxter, M. (1983) The causes of disease: women talking, *Social Science & Medicine*, 17, 2, 59–69.

BMJ (1975) Editorial. Ask your friendly pharmacist, *British Medical Journal*, 1, 594, 1.

Bombay Sanitary Report for 1897 (1898) Pestilence and famine in India, *British Medical Journal*, 2, 1265.

Boston Women's Health Collective (1971) *Our Bodies, Ourselves*. Boston: New England Free Press.

Britten, N., Stevenson, F.A., Barry, C.A. and Barber, N. *et al.* (2000) Misunderstandings in prescribing decisions in general practice: qualitative study, *British Medical Journal*, 320, 484–8. doi: http://dx.doi .org/10.1136/bmj.320.7233.484.

Buss, A.R. (1978) Causes and reasons in attribution theory: a conceptual critique, *Journal of Personality and Social Psychology*, 36, 11, 1311–21.

Byrne, P.S. and Long, B.E.L. (1976) *Doctors Talking to Patients*. London: HMSO.

Carson, R. (1962) *Silent Spring*. Harcourt: Houghton Mifflin.

Charmaz, K. (1987) Struggling for a self: identity levels of the chronically ill. In Roth, J.A. and Conrad, P. (eds) *The Experience and Management of Chronic Illness*. Greenwich: JAI Press.

Charmaz, K. (1995) The body, identity, and self: adapting to impairment, *Sociological Quarterly*, 36, 4, 357–380.

Conrad, P. (1992) Medicalization and social control, *Annual Review of Sociology*, 18, 209–32.

Crawford, R. (1980) Healthism and the medicalization of everyday life, *International Journal of Health Services*, 10, 3, 365–88.

Creer, T., Renne, C. and Christian, W. (1976) Behavioral contributions to rehabilitation and childhood asthma, *Rehabilitation Literature*, 37, 8, 226–32.

Davidson, D. (1963) Actions, reasons and causes, *Journal of Philosophy*, 60, 23, 685–700.

Dean, K. (1981) Self-care responses to illness: a selected review, *Social Science & Medicine*, 15, 5, 673–87.

Department of Health (2001) *The Expert Patient: a New Approach to Chronic Disease Management for the 21st Century*. London: HMSO.

Department of Health (2004) *Choosing Health: Making Health Choices Easier*. London: HMSO.

Dick, P.W. (1945) Mass miniature radiography of factory groups, *British Medical Journal*, 2, 4425, 568–9.

Dunnell, K. and Cartwright, A. (1972) *Medicine Takers, Prescribers and Hoarders*. London: Routledge.

Freidson, E. (1970) *Profession of Medicine*. New York: Dodd Mead.

Giddens, A. (1979) *Central Problems in Social Theory: Action, Structure and Contradiction in Social Analysis*. London: Macmillan.

Glasser, M.A. (1958) A study of the public's acceptance of the Salk vaccine program, *American Journal of Public Health*, 48, 141–6.

Goldstein, M.J. (1960) The relationship between coping and avoiding behaviour and response to fear-arousing propaganda, *Journal of Abnormal and Social Psychology*, 60, 1, 37–43.

Gubrium, J. (1986) The social preservation of mind: the Alzheimer's disease experience, *Symbolic Interaction*, 9, 37–51.

Harrison, J.A., Mullen, P.D. and Green, L.W. (1992) A meta-analysis of studies of the health belief model with adults, *Health Education Research*, 7, 1, 107–16.

Haug, M.R. (1973) Deprofessionalization: an alternate hypothesis for the future, *Sociological Review Monograph*, 20, 195–211.

Hayes-Bautista, D.E. (1976) Modifying the treatment: Patient compliance, patient control and medical care, *Social Science & Medicine*, 10, 5, 233–8.

Hochbaum, G.M. (1958) *Public Participation in Medical Screening Programs: a Socio-Psychological Study*. Washington: Public Health Service Publication no, p. 572.

Illich, I. (1974) *Medical Nemesis*. London: Caldar Boyars.

Jensen, M.C. and Meckling, W. (1976) Theory of the firm: managerial behavior, agency costs and owner-ship structure, *Journal of Financial Economics*, 3, 4, 305–60.

Johnson, T.J. (1972) *Professions and Power*. London: Heinemann.

Kahn, G., Cohen, B. and Jason, H. (1979) The teaching of interpersonal skills in the United States medical schools, *Journal of Medical Education*, 54, 1, 29–35.

Kannel, W.B., Dawber, T.R., Kagan, A., Revotskie, N., *et al.* (1961) Factors of risk in the development of coronary heart disease–six year follow-up experience: the Framingham study, *Annals of Internal Medicine*, 55, 1, 33–50.

Kitwood, T. and Bredin, K. (1992) Towards a theory of dementia care: personhood and well-being, *Ageing and Society*, 12, 3, 269–87.

Kleinman, A. (1980) *Patients and Healers in the Context of Culture: an Exploration of the Borderland Between Anthropology, Medicine, and Psychiatry*. Berkeley: University of California Press.

Koos, E. (1954) *The Health of Regionville: What the People Thought and Did About It*. New York: Hafner.

Lash, S. and Urry, J. (1984) The new Marxism of collective action: a critical analysis, *Sociology*, 18, 1, 33–50.

Levenstein, J.H., McCracken, E.C., McWhinney, I.R., Stewart, M.A., *et al.* (1986) The patient-centred clinical method. 1. A model for the doctor-patient interaction in family medicine, *Family Practice*, 3, 1, 24–30.

Leventhal, H., Meyer, D. and Nerenz, D. (1980). The common sense representation of illness danger. In Rachman, S. (ed.), *Contributions to Medical Psychology and Health*, Vol. 2. New York: Pergamon Press.

Locke, D. and Pennington, D. (1982) Reasons and other causes: their role in attribution processes, *Journal of Personality and Social Psychology*, 42, 2, 212–3.

Locker, D. (1981) *Symptoms and Illness: the Cognitive Organization of Disorder*. London: Routledge.

Lorig, K.R. and Holman, H.R. (2003) Self-management education: history, definition, outcomes, and mechanisms, *Annals of Behavioral Medicine*, 26, 1, 1–7.

Lorig, K.R., Ritter, P., Stewart, A.L., Sobel, D.S., *et al.* (2001) Chronic disease self-management program: 2-year health status and health care utilization outcomes, *Medical Care*, 39, 11, 1217–23.

McWhinney, I.R. (1984) Changing models: the impact of Kuhn's theory on medicine, *Family Practice*, 1, 1, 3–8.

Mechanic, D. (1962) The concept of illness behaviour, *Journal of Chronic Diseases*, 15, 2, 189–94.

Mechanic, D. and Volkart, E.H. (1961) Stress, illness behavior, and the sick role, *American Sociological Review*, 26, 1, 51–8.

Mishler, E.G. (1985) *The Discourse of Medicine: Dialectics of Medical Interviews*. Norwood: Ablex.

Morrell, D.C., Avery, A.J. and Watkins, C.J. (1980) Management of minor illness, *British Medical Journal*, 280, 6216, 769–71.

Neighbour, R. (1987) *The Inner Consultation*. Lancaster: MTO Press.

Parsons, T. (1951) *The Social System*. New York: Free Press.

Pendleton, D., Schofield, T., Tate, P. and Havelock, P. (1984) *The Consultation: an Approach to Learning and Teaching*. Oxford: Oxford University Press.

Rosenstock, I.M. (1966) Why people use health services, *Milbank Memorial Fund Quarterly*, 44, 3, 94–127.

Rosenstock, I.M. (1974) Historical origins of the health belief model, *Health Education Monographs*, 2, 4, 328–35.

Rosenstock, I.M., Derryberry, M. and Carriger, B.K. (1959) Why people fail to seek poliomyelitis vaccination, *Public Health Reports*, 74, 2, 98–103.

Rosenstock, I.M., Strecher, V.J. and Becker, M.H. (1988) Social learning theory and the health belief model, *Health Education Quarterly*, 15, 2, 175–83.

Ross, S.A. (1973) The economic theory of agency: the principal's problem, *American Economic Review*, 63, 2, 134–9.

Rotter, J.B. (1966) Generalized expectancies for internal versus external control of reinforcement, *Psychological Monographs*, 80, 1, no. 609.

Royal Pharmaceutical Society of Great Britain (1997) *From Compliance to Concordance: Towards Shared Goals in Medicine Taking*. London: RPS.

Sabat, S.R. and Harre, R. (1992) The construction and deconstruction of self in Alzheimer's disease, *Ageing and Society*, 12, 4, 443–61.

Scott, R., Anderson, J.A.D. and Cartwright, A. (1960) Just what the doctor ordered, *British Medical Journal*, 2, 5194, 293–9.

Segall, A. and Goldstein, J. (1989) Exploring the correlates of self-provided health care behaviour, *Social Science & Medicine*, 29, 2, 153–61.

Stimson, G.V. (1974) Obeying doctor's orders: the view from the other side, *Social Science and Medicine*, 8, 97–104.

Taylor, R. (1958) Determinism and the theory of agency. In Hook, S. (ed.) *Determinism and Freedom In the Age of Modern Science*. New York: Collier.

Thoits, P.A. (2006) Personal agency in the stress process, *Journal of Health and Social Behaviour*, 47, 4, 309–23.

Tuckett, D., Boulton, M., Olson, C. and Williams, A. (1985) *Meetings Between Experts: an Approach to Sharing Ideas in Medical Consultations*. London: Tavistock.

Wadsworth, M.E.J., Butterfield, W.J.H. and Blaney, R. (1971) *Health and Sickness: the Choice of Treatment*. London: Tavistock.

Weiss, G.B. (1985) Paternalism modernised, *Journal of Medical Ethics*, 11, 4, 184–7.

Williams, G. (1984) The genesis of chronic illness: narrative reconstruction, *Sociology of Health & Illness*, 6, 2, 175–200.

Zola, I.K. (1972) Medicine as an institution of social control, *Sociological Review*, 20, 4, 487–504.

3

A socially situated approach to inform ways to improve health and wellbeing

Christine Horrocks and Sally Johnson

The problem with health as a form of behaviour

The dominant neoliberal ideology pervasive in late capitalist societies is based on the expansion of an economic rationality to all domains of social life. This ideology encourages a particular kind of individual entrepreneurial enterprise whereby what were previously deemed to be the state's responsibilities have been devolved to responsible, rational individuals (Lemke 2001). This ideology has become entrenched in health promotion, in which self-management is central to the project. However, Miller and Rose (2008: 39) argue that the achievement of such political ends is exercised indirectly through the notion of action at a distance. They argue that self-regulation is normalised through expertise. This expertise includes psychological understanding which can be used to manage domains such as health. Health psychology is a form of expertise that informs many contemporary approaches to health promotion and policy.

Mainstream health psychology and approaches to health behavioural change assume a particular ontology of personhood that is in concordance with neoliberalism. It centres on the idea that people are driven and cognitively motivated as individuals; and their health beliefs and attitudes are framed as the favoured mechanisms to target in order to bring about behaviour change. This cognitive approach is epitomised by the dominant social cognition models of our time. These models essentially conceptualise health behaviour, or more commonly intentions, within a cost-benefit, decision-making framework.

However, critiques of these cognitive approaches to health behaviour change emerged during the 1970s and 1980s. A more contextualised understanding of health and illness emanating from anthropological, sociological and psychological scholarship began to develop. This scholarship emphasised, for instance, the importance of social representations and culture in understanding health behaviour (see, for example, Blaxter 1983, Herzlich 1973). In conjunction with this literature, the developing critique of psychology as a discipline over the past 20 years (see, for example, Fox *et al.* 2009) provided the conditions for a similar critique of health psychology, to the extent that critical health psychology is now a movement in its own right. Criticisms of mainstream health psychology centre on epistemology, ontology and methodology. Four interrelated key areas of critique include questions about the nature of health behaviour, a problematisation of the view that people are rational

From Health Behaviours to Health Practices: Critical Perspectives, First Edition. Edited by Simon Cohn. Chapters © 2014 The Authors. Book Compilation © 2014 Foundation for the Sociology of Health & Illness / Blackwell Publishing Ltd.

decision-makers, questioning the degree to which the social context is taken into account, and highlighting the problems in the quantification of health-related activities.

Firstly, cognitive approaches are seemingly premised on the idea that health behaviour is easily identified and unitary in character, with meanings that do not change across the diverse range of contexts and settings in which they might be carried out. Mielewczyk and Willig (2007) argue that health behaviour defined in this way does not exist. They reconceptualise behaviour as a set of health-related activities that cannot be divorced from the meaning and importance bestowed upon them by wider social practices. Therefore, they argue, it would be better to focus on the 'wider social practices of which such actions form a part' (Mielewczyk and Willig 2007: 829). Secondly, despite the early promise of cognitive psychology, Stainton Rogers (2012: 46) argues that cognitive approaches in health psychology conceptualise people crudely as naive scientists (simplistically testing hypotheses as in attribution theory) or accountants (calculating the costs and benefits in theories of behaviour change) rather than social actors. Further, the price of a decision-making, neoliberal approach is that a self-determining, good citizen is characterised as one who makes the right choices and takes personal responsibility for their health (Crawford 2006, Davies 2005); therefore being blamed if they make seemingly irresponsible or irrational choices.

Certain cognitive models do take into account social aspects of behaviour. For example, the theory of planned behaviour includes the concept of subjective norms, which consist of beliefs about the attitudes of important others, and their behaviour and motivation to comply with others (see, Ajzen and Madden 1986). However, the third critique points out that these models do not substantially incorporate social and contextual aspects of health and illness. This is because they investigate social cognitions, such as attitudes and control beliefs (Mielewczyk and Willig 2007), which are, inevitably, individual perceptions of social phenomenon. Finally, the value of social cognitive models rests on their ability to predict health behaviour; which they do in a particular way. Variables such as attitudes towards the behaviour, self-efficacy, perceived costs and perceived barriers, which aim to assess the subjective dimensions of behaviour, are measured by means of questionnaires. In what Stainton Rogers (1991: 55) refers to as 'cognitive algebra' models, these variables are subject to increasingly sophisticated methods of statistical analysis. However, Crossley (2008: 23) suggests that critical health psychologists ask important questions about such techniques, specifically: 'Is something essential being lost in the attempt to quantify subjective experiences in this way?' She suggests that the quantification of health-related activities results in simplistic representations of experience which, by their nature, are infused with ambiguity and complexity.

Therefore, critical health psychologists are broadly in agreement that it is more useful to focus on health behaviour as a set of social and situated practices. To this end they adopt different epistemological, ontological and theoretical stances from those of mainstream health psychology (including social constructionism, post-structuralism, feminism and Marxism). In addition, they tend to employ qualitative and participatory methods (for example, discourse analysis, participatory action research and narrative analysis) to develop more socially grounded and relational understandings. This involves investigating health-related practices (rather than behaviour) which can only be understood through their relationship with wider social activities. As Crossley (2008) and Murray and Poland (2006) make clear, health and illness are rooted in more than biomedical explanations; they are enmeshed in broader social, cultural, political and historical contexts. While the initial focus of critical health psychologists was on critiquing mainstream health psychology, recent debates have moved on to consider how a reformulation of health psychology might take place (see the collection of articles in the *Journal of Health Psychology* 11, 3, 2006, and Crossley, 2008 for an extended discussion of these debates). Recent directions include developing action to improve health (see Horrocks and Johnson 2012). In this chapter we therefore draw upon our own research, which has adopted a socially situated and relational position, acknowledging the interactive and structural nature of health practices.

Contemporary healthcare relations: responsible and reflexive consumers

In engaging with some of the more situated and relational positioning of health practices it is important to consider the nature of contemporary health care. In a time of economic austerity, governments are looking for ways to limit and reduce healthcare spending while at the same time engaging in a dialogue that offers assurances on maintaining levels of service. There is growing interest in the delivery of 'lean healthcare' (see Waring and Bishop 2010) with an emphasis on eliminating waste and simultaneously adding value to customer/ patients (de Souza 2009). There are also ongoing debates on proposed reforms and restructuring, with claims that managerialism has replaced professionalism in the social organisation of health care (Kitchener 2000). Alongside what is termed modernisation and different modes of interaction come new forms of governance in health care with ever-changing relationships.

The involvement of the public in the management and provision of public services is now prominent in economically developed countries. This involvement connects with notions of co-production, whereby those in receipt of services are no longer characterised as passive. Instead, there has been a shift towards the notion of exchanging information and shared decision-making (Realpe and Wallace 2010). In the UK the concept of patient and public involvement (PPI) in health is promoted in which 'citizens' are encouraged to participate in the difficult process of managing and commissioning health care, and 'service users', who have experiential knowledge and treatment insight, are consulted in relation to their care. While issues of representation and inclusion are fundamental challenges linked to PPI and the notion of participating citizens, it is the later characterisation of service user involvement that is a priority for this section of the chapter.

As has been noted above, in the health psychology domain the focus is primarily on individuals, and health promotion efforts attempt to change individual behaviour by promoting self-management by rational decision-makers. Embedded in this notion is an implicit narrative of responsibility, in that, if we are unable to self-manage our health and wellbeing, then we are in deficit at a very personal level. Associated with the emphasis on self-management is the notion of the expert patient, which under the aegis of co-production and democratisation, has emerged in the UK health policy (Department of Health 2001, Fox et al. 2005).

Work to transform the healthcare professional/doctor–patient relationship from a professional-led interaction to one that is more of a healthcare professional–patient partnership seems a laudable goal. Here service users are conceived as expert and informed patients who are able to articulate their individual needs (self-manage), thus deploying their expert knowledge and exercising informed decision-making in relation to appropriate treatment and action. Without doubt patients often have expertise in their own illnesses and on how to promote their health, and they have intimate knowledge of the circumstances in which they live. Nevertheless, this may not in itself be sufficient to understand the technical complexities of the causes of disease (Prior 2003).

However, it is claimed that, with the growth of web-based health-related information, interactive forums and consumer websites, people have been transformed into reflexive consumers of health care (Henwood *et al.* 2003). This growth is enhanced by the availability of a range of other media in which the apparent information needs of patients/consumers are being met (see Eysenbach 2000). Arguably, this availability of information has served to usurp the monopolies of health professionals over their knowledge base. Nonetheless, these changes should not blind us to the recognition that, as Fox *et al.* 2005: 1308) suggest that:

> If the 'expert patient' is to be understood as a reflexive project of self-governance, then it is indeed a 'technology of the self', a disciplining of the body in relation to systems of thought.

A cautionary message is embedded in such observations, which demonstrate that people are being positioned as being responsible for the self-management of their health and wellbeing. Notions of empowerment, sharing of power and user-led health care do offer avenues for action and change by resisting the imposition of power, but it is important to also envisage other implications embedded in these concepts.

Significantly, not all patients may wish to or are able to lay claim to the material resources and technical competence necessary to take responsibility for their health. Alternatively, constraints related to the discursive environment, including moral obligations and medical authority, may be so strong that they leave little room for questioning and decision-making in which to operate, as we generally understand it. Nettleton and Burrows (2003) specifically point out that the utility of Internet information relies on the reflexive capacities of users to interpret, discern and marshal this information to achieve positive outcomes. Hence self-management requires more than merely being positioned as a rational decision-maker; the individual is also required to be skilful and able to garner expertise and technical competence in order to secure their health and wellbeing. Here, practising health as an activity is the key. Martin (2008) explains that now that the clinician is no longer conceived as the sole source of expertise; experiential sensibility becomes enmeshed with the technical detail of medical science. Arguably, the delivery of lean health care requires of the self-managing patient lay expertise and compliance. This prompts the question whether the democratisation of knowledge we are seeing is responsible for constructing us all as able to make fully informed health/lifestyle choices that ensure we are aligned with current governmental authority. There are a range of intersecting difficulties and constraints entangled within these conceptualisations of individual action. It fails to take account of the wider social, relational and discursive environments in which people operate and live their lives. Therefore, the two research examples we now move on to serve to demonstrate how these modernising and democratising developments in health care may empower some but can also effectively bypass certain groups and impose choice on others.

Socially situated action for change

Notions of self-management and alignment are critical to understanding existing approaches to health promotion and the impact of aspects of democratisation in health care. Martin-Baro (1994: 22) asks us to consider how individualism reinforces existing structures, reducing all structural problems to personal problems. He goes on to argue that psychologists should adopt a 'preferential option for the poor'. While there has long been a focus on the ways in which people live their lives, it is fair to say that individualised approaches in health psychology are indifferent to the endemic social inequalities that prevail both at a global and a national level. *Fair Society: Healthy Lives* (Marmot Review 2010) corroborates the extensive existing evidence of the widespread nature of health inequalities in the UK (Menville *et al.* 2009, Scarborough *et al.* 2008). Also acknowledged in such work is the stark fact that social and economic inequalities underpin the determinants of health with associated interacting variables shaping health and wellbeing. Graham (2000) describes these interacting variables in terms of material, behavioural and psychosocial factors. Material factors relate to the physical environment of the home, the community and the workplace, and standards of living obtained through forms of income. Behavioural factors include smoking, exercise and diet and psychosocial factors include the perceived personal and emotional costs of living in an unequal society. It is widely accepted that these factors are clustered with people in low socioeconomic groups experiencing an increased risk of being exposed to all three factors. As argued earlier, health and illness are enmeshed in broader social, cultural, political and historical contexts (Crossley 2008, Murray and Poland 2006). Therefore, self-management and alignment with governmental authority may not be possible for some people due to a range of intersecting factors.

Yet much of the health promotion activity is predictable, being exemplified in campaigns underpinned by the social cognitive models outlined earlier that are targeted at changing individual lifestyles. Such campaigns are distanced from the sociocultural milieu of people's lives yet they often conveniently target the behaviour of those experiencing material disadvantage (Nettleton and Bunton 1995). Implicit in these campaigns is the idea that people have a choice in the lifestyles they adopt, and are able to engage in positive health behaviour and to refrain from engaging in negative health behaviour (Lyons and Chamberlain 2006). Often overlooked is the much wider application of health promotion outlined by, for example, Tones and Green (2002), who suggest that health promotion has a dual purpose: to reduce the existing external barriers to empowered choice, developing supportive environments, and to build upon the capacities of individuals so they are better able to control the environment around them. This formulation acknowledges that people live as socially situated selves and are engaged and active, while at the same time experiencing certain restrictions. The need to empower individuals and communities is at the centre of the Marmot Review's vision for reducing health inequalities. However, empowerment is a much used term that can indicate both a process and a goal. For example, Gutierrez (1990: 149) sees empowerment as a 'process of increasing personal, interpersonal or political power so that individuals can take action to improve their life situations'. Rappaport (1987: 121) suggest it means more of an end-point or goal, being 'both a psychological sense of personal control or influence and a concern with actual social influence, political power and legal rights'.

CH has recently been involved in evaluating a public health-promoting intervention that was a joint initiative between a UK National Health Service (NHS) commissioning officer and a social housing provider. The NHS commissioned the social housing provider to pilot a project where health support workers (HSW) were actively working in the community to provide a support and signposting service to people living in local rented accommodation. The aim was to work in the community supporting and enabling individuals and families to take action to make changes that might improve their health status. This work primarily involved listening to people and helping them to find solutions to some of the difficulties they were experiencing in their lives. One of the most revealing aspects of this work was that individuals and families were experiencing multiple mental and physical health difficulties, with 92 per cent of tenants in the pilot project naming health issues as a priority ($n = 327$). Action for change is not easily achieved, many of tenants had lifestyles that were impacting on their health and wellbeing, with alcohol and drug use an issue for some and for many exercise and more general activity, low. Financial worries were prevalent for 38 per cent ($n = 124$) of those working with the health support workers. Poverty and social exclusion are known to limit people's access to health-related knowledge (Campbell and Jovchelovitch 2000); they lack the power to shape their life course and are less likely to believe that they can take control of their health. Indeed, many of the communities targeted for community health interventions experience what Leonard (1984) calls involuntary social marginality due to a range of social, economic and cultural issues. Similarly, Burton and Kagan (2003) refer to psychosocial-ideological threats: certain communities have a marginalised identity that has become internalised, impacting on individuals' self-esteem and motivation.

When interviewed about the services provided by HSWs, it was revealing to hear just how far some of the participants were from the notion of empowered choice and active engagement. Their talk showed that the work of the HSWs was crucial in terms of providing essential support to families who had not become reflexive consumers of health care. Many clients said they did not know about the support they could receive or where to go for services. Maggie described the time her husband came home from hospital and they did not know where to go to get benefits as they had always had paid work:

> When he first had his stroke and he'd come home … it's like we'd just been dumped at home on us own and nobody told us where to go, what form to ask for, nothing. And we were living on I think it were about … what was it? A very, very small amount and I was feeding him and not myself.

Judith described how the HSW was able to get a bath adapted for her disabled nephew:

> And the HSW just went to the right people and just moved it along, moved it along and got things moving. I mean it took me 12 months to get somebody to come out and have a look at it. The HSW spoke to somebody and within 3 month they actually said, 'Yes we can do it'.

Rather than being reflexive consumers those receiving support from the HSW required a navigator, someone to guide their journey through services. The primary focus of the pilot project was to 'support wellbeing and independent living' for families and communities. For tenants and families experiencing multiple disadvantages, supporting action to improve their life situations may be ameliorative, targeted at the personal and relational level, rather than politically transformative, framed more in terms of collective wellbeing and challenging the status quo (Nelson and Prilleltensky 2005). This being accepted, there is a danger that the rush toward democratisation of health care and the continuation of health promotion will leave some people further disempowered, more isolated and marginalised.

This is not to suggest that participation in health care and taking informed action should be discouraged. However, together with the Internet revolution and the growth of technical competence we need to consider their impact, or lack of impact, on the breadth of health practices. At the psychosocial level an emphasis on the importance of participatory democracy in all strata of life incorporates the view that involving people and communities affects their self-esteem and self-confidence and this in turn improves their health and wellbeing (Department of Health 2000). As an aside, it is useful to note that ideology rooted in individual action and participation underpins modern conservativism, which is the position of the UK government at the time of writing with regard to civic society taking the lead in combating disadvantage (Page 2010). However, Bandura (2009: 505), who is an advocate of social cognitive approaches, rightly argues that 'Failure to address the psychosocial determinants of human behaviour is often the weakest link' in policy initiatives'. Research suggests that low levels of social integration and loneliness can significantly increase mortality (see for example Bennett 2002). Also, the most powerful sources of stress have been found to be associated with low status and the lack of social networks, especially for parents with young children (Wilkinson and Pickett 2009). In a world of changing social relationships it is important to consider a range of social locations and participatory modes. Perhaps the role of navigator undertaken by the HSWs is no less important than that of the Google search engine for those in need of information and support.

Mothers' engagement with responsible health practices

Being informed about, and individually responsible for, one's health has since the mid-1970s increasingly become a middle-class, western, moral stance (see Crawford 2006). In the extracts described above, such middle-class ideologies seem far removed the everyday lives of the participants. In this section, the example of mothers taking responsibility for the health of their child in the practice of immunisation is explored. Engagement in this practice is discursively explored in order to elucidate the centrality of the social context. Crawford (2006) points out that, following the turn to language, scholars highlight the value of seeing social practices such as health as discursive events. Thus, being informed about, and taking responsibility for health is an obligation not only to oneself but, in certain circumstance, to others as well. Lee et al. (2010) state that responsibility for another person's health, particularly a child's, has taken on a particular significance. Lee et al. draw on Murphy (2004) to argue that, in our increasingly risk-averse culture, the avoidance of harm has become a moral obligation that is further intensified when it intersects with constructions of motherhood. This intersection of risk and motherhood therefore ensures that mothers are morally accountable to make responsible health choices in relation to their children. Within the ideologies of motherhood, mothers are portrayed as devoted to caring for their children (Bassin et al. 1994) and children are primarily the responsibility of individual mothers (Hays, 1996). To meet these responsibilities mothers are said to engage in a range of 'maternal practices' including nurturing and protecting their children (Arendell 2000: 1194). This meeting of ideologies of motherhood and risk means that mothers' engagement in responsible health practices in relation to their children is seen as a marker of a good mother.

In research conducted by the SJ and a colleague, mothers' negotiation of decisions in relation to their child's health; childhood immunisation, specifically the combined measles, mumps and rubella (MMR) vaccination, was explored. Since the controversy (widely covered in the media) surrounding the MMR vaccination erupted following a report by Wakefield et al. (1998) that linked the MMR vaccination to autism and Crohn's disease there has been a proliferation of research investigating its impact on the uptake of the MMR. In 2010 the journal retracted the original paper (Editors 2010). Much of this research has investigated parents' (predominantly mothers) choices in relation to the MMR. Such studies are generally conceptualised within a decision-making framework, with participants seen as weighing up the costs and benefits of the MMR (for example, Wroe et al. 2005). In a review of these studies, parents were shown to be behaving in line with their attitudes towards the MMR (see Brown et al. 2010). In order to change their attitudes and beliefs, which are seen to emerge from a lack of accurate or trusted information, the provision of appropriate support and information are seen as central to increasing these parents' compliance with the vaccination (for example, Casiday et al. 2006, Hilton et al. 2007, Smailbegovic et al. 2003). One such cognitively informed approach is the development of decision aids that aim to 'empower' parents to make more 'informed choices' in relation to the MMR (Jackson et al. 2010: 75).

Such aids provide both written and graphic information related to healthcare decisions. Aids generally are said to help people to make informed choices through developing more accurate expectations of possible benefits and harms in a given action, and enable people to reach choices that are more consistent with their informed values (see Stacey *et al.* (2011) for a systematic review of decision aids). Decision aids in relation to the MMR have been produced and trialled in booklet (for example, Wroe *et al.* 2005) and web-based forms (for example, Jackson *et al.* 2010, Wallace *et al.* 2005) in the UK and Australia. The web-based aid consisted of an assessment of parents' initial thoughts about the MMR; frequently asked questions; numerical and graphic data comparing risks of the vaccine with risks of measles, mumps and rubella; different views about the vaccination; a decision-making exercise and useful websites for information (see Jackson *et al.* 2010). Such aids therefore buy into neoliberal notions of choice, but choice through self-regulation governed through expertise and action at a distance (Miller and Rose 2008). They also support the goals of lean health care and co-production in that information is expected to be resourcefully exchanged and decisions supposedly shared. However, this model of choice negates broader social and relational aspects of such health choices.

The study undertaken involved an exploratory focus group with UK mothers of children over 13 months of age (when the MMR is usually administered through the NHS) who had had their children vaccinated. In this study agency in relation to the MMR decision was largely constructed as being out of the mothers' control in contrast to the previous literature (Capdevila and Johnson 2012). The mothers questioned the trustworthiness of the advice available through the Internet and were aware of concerns about the MMR, constructing media coverage as alerting them to the potential dangers in comparison to other vaccinations by using the metaphor of a red flag: 'I think it's a red flag, when you see it: a red flag. I remember seeing a news report about that whereas all of the others' [vaccinations] (Anna).

Nonetheless, participants ultimately described conformity to, and compliance with, the system and society as determining MMR decisions; as they put it 'you are driven by the system' (Louise), 'it's one of the things you're just expected to do isn't it?'(Anna), 'that's just what's expected of you ... it's a society thing isn't' (Louise). The process of having vaccinations was predominantly constructed as a mundane, routine procedure and mechanical metaphors were used to convey an unstoppable system-deep process: 'the wheel in motion ... prompted by the whole, the cogs that go round when you have a child' (Louise). Thus, the individualised decision-making framework that dominates the MMR literature did not capture the ways in which these mothers came to have their children vaccinated. We argue that these mothers largely followed the power of governmental authority surrounding medical advice and expertise. In addition, the guilt and worry that is inevitably associated with motherhood was said to be managed by having such decision taken away from you:

You just can feel that you're doing the right thing [having your child vaccinated] and not stressed about it, feel guilty about it and worry about it 'coz, let's face it unfortunately, no one tells you that being a parent is all about guilt. (Louise)

The decision being taken away was also linked to the time mothers have to make such decisions:

Louise: Well, I quite like that, though, that I don't have to make that decision ... I think, you know 'coz you have like you say, got so much on your plate ...

Helen: Hmm: that's taken care of.

Here the ideology of intensive mothering, whereby mothers are portrayed as investing a great deal of time and effort in raising their children (Hays 1996), enabled the responsibility of taking decisions in relation to the MMR to be evaded. The negotiation of MMR decisions did not occur in the context of their attitudes and beliefs but rather in practical, contextual issues (busyness, tiredness, 'too much on their plate'). This example shows how motherhood and risk intersect. This supports the view that health behaviour is not an individual act but is governed by dominant discourses of motherhood and governmental authority in relation to risk, which intensifies the obligation of mothers to do the right thing for their child and for society (Lee *et al.* 2010, Murphy 2004), thereby making them morally accountable for engaging in responsible health practices. Rather than the apparent democratisation of knowledge increasing choice, such knowledge exchange appears to be an imposition, with technological details becoming a burden that provokes compliance rather than the use of experiential sensibility and expertise.

Conclusions

Health psychology as an area of expertise is a relatively new field of research and practice (see Murray 2012 for a review) which, as demonstrated, has a tendency to utilise social cognitive approaches, making no reference to wider social structures and issues of power and authority. While there is a movement that provides a more critical, socially situated and contextual version of health psychology, changes in healthcare delivery, framed as modernisation and democratisation, generally have at their core outmoded and reductionist conceptualisations of human action. This may be due to a political and economic climate that points towards the government's role as enabling rather than providing, but the extent to which these operating practices are effective, feasible, efficient or desirable remains open to question. In a time when there is a drive for lean health care, it might be wise to consider the breadth of implications and whether something is being lost in the apparent process of acting to bring about change. Self-management and individual responsibility for health is at the centre of the mainstream health psychology project as well as contemporary healthcare systems, and while notions such as the 'reflexive consumer' at first are presented as alternatives suggesting empowering practices, the question remains: empowering of whom?

In a world of widening social inequalities health psychology, as an area of practice, should engage more fervently and critically with the debate on giving people responsibility for their own health. The sustained reliance on social cognitive statistical models serves to distance health psychology from the communities that Martin-Baro (1994) suggests should be its 'preferential option' when collaborating to improve health and wellbeing. The democratisation of knowledge and health promotion activities, such as decision aids that rely on a notion of faulty cognition, hardly seems relevant in the health-related contexts we have discussed above. People live their lives as socially situated beings and, as we have seen, all too often an information flow can be either ineffective or overwhelming when set within the whirlwind of people's lives. In addition, the smokescreen of democratisation and choice masks constraints and the imperative to maximise compliance with certain healthcare regimes. Such approaches to health will be only partially successful as they do not substantially tap into the broader social landscape. Employing a critical health psychology approach enables this landscape to become visible and in doing so offers opportunities to work upon dominant ideologies in order to transform and reconstruct them in less oppressive ways of working (Davies *et al.* 2006, Weedon 1997). While working with people in qualitative and participatory research is one avenue to achieve such change, lobbying for change and creating what Campbell *et al.* (2010) refer to as receptive social environments, that is, with those that hold the power, is also necessary. This said, investing in health interventions that provide navigational networks may run counter to the tide of self-management currently underway. Even so, one would want to believe that health psychology could help people and communities navigate their way to better health practices.

References

Ajzen, I. and Madden, T.J. (1986) Prediction of goal-directed behaviour: attitudes, intentions, and perceived behavioral control, *Journal of Experimental Social Psychology*, 22, 5, 453–74.

Arendell, T. (2000) Conceiving and investigating motherhood: the decade's scholarship, *Journal of Marriage and the Family*, 62, 4, 1192–207.

Bandura, A. (2009) Social cognitive theory goes global, *Psychologist*, 22, 6, 504–6.

Bassin, D., Honey, M. and Kaplan, M.M. (1994) Introduction. In Bassin, D., Honey, M. and Kaplan, M.M. (eds) *Representations of Motherhood*. New Haven: Yale University Press.

Bennett, K.M. (2002) Low level social engagement as a precursor of mortality among people in later life, *Age and Ageing*, 31, 3, 165–8.

Blaxter, M. (1983) The causes of disease: women talking, *Social Science & Medicine*, 17, 2, 59–69.

Brown, K.F., Kroll, J.S., Hudson, M.J., Ramsay, M., *et al.* (2010) Factors underlying parental decisions about combination childhood vaccinations including MMR: a systematic review, *Vaccine*, 28, 6, 4235–48.

Burton, M. and Kagan, C. (2003) Community psychology: why this gap in Britain?, *History and Philosophy of Psychology*, 4, 2, 10–23.

Campbell, C. and Jovchelovitch, S. (2000) *Journal of Community and Applied Social Psychology*, 10, 4, 255–70.

Campbell, C., Cornish, F., Gibbs, A. and Scott, K. (2010) Heed the push from below: how do social movements persuade the rich to listen to the poor?, *Journal of Health Psychology*, 15, 7, 962–71.

Capdevila, R. and Johnson, S. (2012) 'Mother knows best?' Exploring mothers' engagement with scientific-based advice on MMR immunization. Paper presented at the British Psychological Society Psychology of Women Section Annual Conference, 11–13 July, Windsor.

Casiday, R., Cresswell, T., Wilson, D. and Panter-Brick, C. (2006) A survey of UK parental attitudes to the MMR vaccine and trust in medical authority, *Vaccine*, 24, 177–184.

Crawford, R. (2006) Health as a meaningful social practice, *Health*, 10, 3, 401–20.

Crossley, M. (2008) Critical health psychology: developing and refining the approach, *Social and Personality Psychology Compass*, 2, 1, 21–33.

Davies, B. (2005) The (im)possibility of intellectual work in neoliberal regimes, *Discourse: Studies in the Cultural Politics of Education*, 26, 1, 1–14.

Davies, B., Browne, J., Gannon, S., Hopkins, L., *et al.* (2006) Constituting the feminist subject in poststructuralist discourse, *Feminism and Psychology*, 16, 1, 87–103.

de Souza, L.B. (2009) Trends and approaches in lean healthcare, *Leadership in Health Services*, 22, 2, 121–39.

Department of Health (2000) *The NHS Plan. A Plan for Investment*. A Plan for Reform. London: Department of Health.

Department of Health (2001) *The Expert Patient: a New Approach to Chronic Disease Management for the 21st Century*. London: Department of Health.

Editors (2010) Retraction – Ileal-lymphoid-nodular hyperplasia, non-specific colitis, and pervasive developmental disorder in children, *Lancet*, 375, 9713, 445.

Eysenbach, G. (2000) Consumer health informatics, *British Medical Journal*, 320, 7251, 1713–6.

Fox, D., Prilleltensky, I. and Austin, S. (eds) (2009) *Critical Psychology: an Introduction*, 2nd edn. London: Sage.

Fox, N.J., Ward, K.J. and O'Rourke, A.J. (2005) The 'expert patient': empowerment or medical dominance? The case of weight loss, pharmaceutical drugs and the Internet, *Social Science & Medicine*, 60, 6, 1299–309.

Graham, H. (2000) *Understanding Health Inequalities*; Buckingham: Open University Press.

Gutierrez, L.M. (1990) Working with women of colour: an empowerment perspective, *Social Work*, 35, 2, 149–53.

Hays, S. (1996) *The Cultural Contradictions of Motherhood*. New Hale: Yale University Press.

Henwood, F., Wyatt, S., Hart, A. and Smith, J. (2003) 'Ignorance in bliss sometimes': constraints on the emergence of the 'informed patient' in the changing landscapes of health information, *Sociology of Health & Illness*, 25, 6, 589–607.

Herzlich, C. (1973) *Health and Illness: a Social Psychological Analysis. (Transl. Graham, D.)* London: Academic Press.

Hilton, S., Petticrew, M. and Hunt, K. (2007) Parents' champions vs. vested interests: who do parents believe about MMR? A qualitative study, *BMC Public Health*, 7, 42, 1–8.

Horrocks, C. and Johnson, S. (eds) (2012) *Advances in Health Psychology: Critical Approaches*. Basingstoke: Palgrave Macmillan.

Jackson, C., Cheater, F.M., Peacock, R., Leask, J., *et al.* (2010) Evaluating a web-based MMR decision aid to support informed decision-making by UK parents: a before-and-after feasibility study, *Health Education Journal*, 69, 1, 74–83.

Kitchener, M. (2000) The bureaucratization of professional roles: the case of clinical directors in UK hospitals, *Organization*, 7, 1, 129–54.

Lee, E.J., Macvarish, J. and Bristow, J. (2010) Risk, health and parenting culture, *Health, Risk & Society*, 12, 4, 293–300.

Lemke, T. (2001) 'The birth of bio-politics': Michel Foucault's lecture at the College de France on neo-liberal governmentality, *Economy & Society*, 30, 2, 190–207.

Leonard, P. (1984) *Personality and Ideology: Towards a Materialist Understanding of the Individual*. London: Macmillan.

Lyons, A.C. and Chamberlain, K. (2006) *Health Psychology: a Critical Introduction*. Cambridge: Cambridge University Press.

Marmot Review (2010) *Fair Society, Healthy Lives*. Available at http://www.marmotreview.org/ (accessed 29 October 2013).

Martin, G.P. (2008) 'Ordinary people only': knowledge, representativeness, and the publics of public participation in healthcare, *Sociology of Health & Illness*, 30, 1, 35–54.

Martin-Baro, I. (1994) Toward a liberation psychology. In Aron, A. and Corne, S. (eds) *Writings for a Liberation Psychology: Igancio Martin-Baro*. Cambridge: Harvard University Press.

Menville, G., Boshuizen, H., Kunst, A.E., Dalton, S.O., *et al.* (2009) The role of smoking and diet in explaining educational inequalities in lung cancer incidence, *Journal of the National Cancer Institute*, 101, 5, 321–30.

Mielewczyk, F. and Willig, C. (2007) Old clothes and an older look: the case for a radical makeover in health behaviour research, *Theory and Psychology*, 17, 6, 811–37.

Miller, P. and Rose, N. (2008) *Governing the Present: Administering Economic, Social and Personal Life*. Cambridge: Polity Press.

Murphy, E. (2004) Risk, maternal ideologies and infant feeding. In Germov, J. and Williams, L. (eds) *A Sociology of Food and Nutrition*. Oxford: Oxford University Press.

Murray, M. (2012) Social history of health psychology: context and textbooks, *Health Psychology Review*, 1, 1, 1–23.

Murray, M. and Poland, B. (2006) Health psychology and social action, *Journal of Health Psychology*, 11, 3, 379–84.

Nelson, G. and Prilleltensky, I. (eds) (2005) *Community Psychology. In Pursuit of Liberation and Wellbeing*. Basingstoke: Palgrave Macmillan.

Nettleton, S. and Bunton, R. (1995) Sociological critiques of health promotion. In Bunton, R., Nettleton, S. and Burrows, R. (eds) *The Sociology of Health Promotion*. London: Routledge.

Nettleton, S. and Burrows, R. (2003) E-scaped medicine? Information, reflexivity and health, *Critical Social Policy*, 2, 22, 165–85.

Page, R.M. (2010) David Cameron's modern conservative approach to poverty and social justice: towards one nation or two?, *Journal of Poverty and Social Justice*, 18, 2, 147–60.

Prior, L. (2003) Belief, knowledge and expertise: the emergence of the lay expert in medical sociology, *Sociology of Health & Illness*, 25, 1, 41–57.

Rappaport, J. (1987) Terms of empowerment/examplars of prevention: toward a theory for community psychology, *American Journal of Community Psychology*, 15, 2, 122–44.

Realpe, A. and Wallace, L.M. (2010) *What Is Co-production?*. London: Health Foundation.

Scarborough, P., Allender, S., Peto, V. and Rayner, M. (2008) *Regional and Social Differences in Coronary Heart Disease 2008*. London: British Heart Foundation.

Smailbegovic, M.S., Laing, G.J. and Bedford, H. (2003) Why do parents decide against immunization? The effect of health beliefs and health professionals, *Child Care Health Development*, 29, 4, 303–11.

Stacey, D., Bennett, C.L, Barry, M.J. and Nananda, F. *et al.* (2011) Decision aids for people facing health treatment or screening decisions. The Cochrane Library. Available at http://onlinelibrary.wiley.com/doi/10.1002/14651858.CD001431.pub3/full (accessed 29 June 2012).

Stainton Rogers, W. (1991) *Explaining Health and Illness: An Exploration of Diversity*. Hemel Hempstead: Harvester Wheatsheaf.

Stainton Rogers, W. (2012) Changing behaviour: can critical psychology influence policy and practice? In Horrocks, C. and Johnson, S. (eds) *Advances in Health Psychology: Critical Approaches*. Basingstoke: Palgrave Macmillan.

Tones, K. and Green, J. (2002) The empowerment imperative in health promotion. In Dooher, J. and Byrt, R. (eds) *Empowerment and Participation: Power, Influence and Control in Contemporary Health Care*, Vol. 1. London: Quay Books.

Wakefield, A.J., Murch, S.H., Anthony, A., Linnell, J., *et al.* (1998) Ileal-lymphoid-nodular hyperplasia, non-specific colitis, and pervasive developmental disorder in children, *Lancet*, 351, 9103, 637–41.

Wallace, C., Leask, J. and Trevena, J. (2005) Effects of a web based decision aid on parental attitudes to the MMR vaccination: a before and after study, *British Medical Journal*, 332, 7534, 146–9.

Waring, J.J. and Bishop, S. (2010) Lean healthcare: rhetoric, ritual and resistance, *Social Science & Medicine*, 71, 7, 1332–40.

Weedon, C. (1997) *Feminist Practice and Poststructuralist Theory*. 2nd edn. Oxford: Blackwell.

Wilkinson, R. and Pickett, K. (2009) *The Spirit Level: Why More Equal Societies Almost Always do Better*. London: Allen Lane.

Wroe, A.L., Turner, N. and Owens, R.G. (2005) Evaluation of a decision-making aid for parents regarding childhood immunizations, *Health Psychology*, 24, 6, 539–47.

4

A relational approach to health practices: towards transcending the agency-structure divide
Gerry Veenstra and Patrick John Burnett

Introduction

The potential of Pierre Bourdieu's theory of practice for situating healthy and unhealthy practices in the interplay between agency and structure has been well established (see Abel 2007, 2008, Abel and Frohlich 2012, Cockerham 2005, 2007, Cockerham *et al.* 1997, Frohlich *et al.* 2001, Korp 2008, Veenstra 2007a, Williams 1995, Williams 2003). Williams (1995) provides one of the earliest and most persuasive justifications of the utility of this theoretical framework for understanding health practices, summarising the major elements of Bourdieu's attempt to construct a theoretical model of social practices that bridges, or better yet, transcends, the agency–structure divide. Briefly, practices of all kinds are located in time and space and, while they are not always performed consciously, they are nevertheless performed with purposeful and practical intent. They are intimately interconnected with habitus, acquired systems of dispositions that generate them; fields, structured systems of social positions with their own internal logics within which practices are situated; and capitals, the resources that are at stake in fields. Practices are, therefore, simultaneously entwined with dispositions of mind and body and supra-individual contexts defined by relations of power.

While he is mostly supportive of the potential of Bourdieu's theory for explicating the logic of healthy and unhealthy practices in particular, Williams (1995) has one major caveat:

> [U]ltimately Bourdieu remains trapped within an objectivist point of view which largely strips agency of its critical reflexive character ... and, as a consequence, 'choice' is largely underplayed. (p. 588)

The criticism of determinism is a familiar theme in scholarly receptions of Bourdieu's work more generally[1] and is one with which other prominent health scholars seemingly concur. For instance, Cockerham, Ruuten, and Abel (1997) find that 'the agent in Bourdieu's approach remains abstract' (p. 337). Frohlich, Corin, and Potvin (2001) conclude that Bourdieu, in attempting to transcend the objectivism–subjectivism dichotomy, 'awards epistemological priority to objective conditions over subjectivist understanding' (p. 789) such

From Health Behaviours to Health Practices: Critical Perspectives, First Edition. Edited by Simon Cohn. Chapters © 2014 The Authors. Book Compilation © 2014 Foundation for the Sociology of Health & Illness / Blackwell Publishing Ltd.

that 'the agent is oddly absent' (p. 790). Abel and Frohlich (2012) find that Bourdieu's conception of habitus does not:

> ... Attempt or mean to explain how structure-based patterns of behaviours are changed, nor does it point to ways in which conditions can be created to alter or increase individual agency for change. (p. 239)

Some of these health scholars see the need to introduce concepts from other theoretical schemas, such as Max Weber's depiction of life choices and life chances (Abel and Frohlich 2012, Cockerham 2005, 2007), Anthony Giddens's structuration theory (Cockerham, Ruuten, and Abel 1997, Frohlich *et al.* 2001) and Amartya Sen's capabilities approach (Abel and Frohlich 2012, Frohlich *et al.* 2001) to address the allegedly deterministic nature of Bourdieu's theory of practice.

Our reading of original writings by Bourdieu (1977, 1984, 1985, 1986, 1988, 1989, 1990, 1998, 2000, 2008) and Bourdieu and Wacquant (1992) and sociological treatises on agency (Emirbayer and Mische 1998), relationality (Emirbayer 1997, Mische 2011, Schinkel 2007) and field theory (Martin 2003) leads us to believe that Bourdieu's theory of practice may be more impervious to the critique of determinism than current evaluations of it in health promotion and public health would suggest. Our case against the charge that Bourdieu's theory of practice is deterministic has two major strands, the first arguing that Bourdieusian fields are imbued with intersubjective agency and the second arguing that, when treated as relationally bound phenomena, Bourdieu's notions of habitus, doxa, capital and field illuminate creative, adaptive and future-looking practices.

We argue that the above-mentioned charges of determinism levelled against Bourdieu's theory of practice are undergirded by substantialism, an ontological perspective invested in the substance of things – of atoms, of trees, of individuals, of social structures – that dominates these research communities. Relationalism, the perspective adopted by Bourdieu, understands the nature and meaning of 'things' in terms of their relatedness to other 'things'. In regards to Bourdieu's theory of practice in particular, we argue that situating agency and action (practices) in the context of relationally constituted fields, where the 'realest real' consists of relations built upon relations, produces a representation of agency that is manifestly intersubjective in nature, thereby undermining the stark distinction between individual agency and social structure. Health scholars with substantialist ontologies have searched for substantialist manifestations of agency in Bourdieu's framework and, unsurprisingly, have come up empty-handed.

Towards further understanding the nature of agency within fields, we consider doxa, a concept used by Bourdieu to describe the 'relationship of immediate adherence that is established in practice between a *habitus* and the field to which it is attuned' (Bourdieu 1990: 68). Doxa is the naturalised, taken-for-granted understanding that people have of their social worlds (of fields), their places within these worlds and their perceptions of the social limits and boundaries that exist for them in the worlds as a result of their life experiences (Bourdieu 1977, 2000). We argue that the consideration of habitus and doxa, linked to one another and to capitals and fields, illuminates creative aspects of individual agency in relation to the strategic actions taken by agents in familiar and unfamiliar fields.

Having made our case that Bourdieu's relational theory of practice encompasses intersubjective agency and creative, adaptive and future-oriented practices, we conclude by commenting on the feasibility of implementing a relational approach to health and health practices in a substantialist health research universe.

Relationality and field theory

In his manifesto for a relational sociology Mustafa Emirbayer (1997) claims that the fundamental distinction in contemporary sociology is not agency versus structure (or individual versus society, or qualitative versus quantitative, or material versus ideal) but rather, substantialism versus relationalism. Substantialism:

> ... Takes as its point of departure the notion that it is *substances* of various kinds (things, beings, essences) that constitute the fundamental units of all inquiry. Systematic analysis is to begin with these self-subsistent entities, which come 'preformed,' and only then to consider the dynamic flows in which they subsequently involve themselves. (Emirbayer 1997: 282–3)

In relationalism, by contrast:

> ... The very terms or units involved in a transaction derive their meaning, significance, and identity from the (changing) functional roles they play within that transaction. The latter ... a dynamic, unfolding process, becomes the primary unit of analysis. (Emirbayer 1997: 287)

Although relationalism has a long history in social thought,[2] substantialist ontologies underpin most contemporary sociological research endeavours and virtually all research on health practices. Bourdieu, heavily influenced by Gaston Bachelard and Ernst Cassirer, opted for relationalism (Bourdieu 1989, 2008).

Bourdieu uses field theory to express the relational logic of social phenomena resulting from the interdependent nature of human actions and complex social relations situated in social environments (Martin 2003). For Bourdieu, the notion of 'society' as a seamless totality is reconstituted in terms of fields wherein the social world is thought to consist of many different fields (such as academic, religious, artistic and healthcare fields) in which people act and are acted upon. Each field represents a socially structured space with its own emergent regulative principles (Bourdieu and Wacquant 1992). Employed as a spatial metaphor, fields can be thought of as social arenas endowed with a specific gravity and force that influence the actions and reactions of social actors who have tacitly agreed to the rules of the game (Bourdieu 1998, 2000, Bourdieu and Wacquant 1992).

Relational field theories of this kind understand social realities to be the emergent result of relational human activities. For instance, classes do not exist as observable entities in society for Bourdieu. Rather, he conceives of classes in terms of the 'social space of differentiation and differences in which "classes" exist in some sense in a state of virtuality, not as something given but as something to be done' (Bourdieu 1998: 12). Indeed, all aspects of Bourdieu's theory of practice, including his conception of power (capital), attain their meanings in relational contexts:

> ... Take the key concept of power, which is typically seen in substantialist terms as an entity or a possession, as something to be 'seized' or 'held.' In the [relational] approach, the concept of power [is] transformed from a concept of substance to a concept of relationship. ... Far from being an attribute or property of actors, then, power is unthinkable outside matrices of force relations; it emerges out of the very way in which figurations of relationships ... are patterned and operate. (Emirbayer 1997: 291–2)

Marx's depiction of capital exemplifies relational logic: 'Capital is not a thing, but a social relation between persons which is mediated through things' (Marx 1990: 932). Like Marx, Bourdieu breaks with common-sense realist representations of capital, that is, as a natural social object with an independent existence, to conceptualising it in terms of relations, that is, as a social phenomenon that emerges within a generative matrix of social factors and forces (within fields).

As one would expect, substantialism and relationalism approach the distinction between agency and structure very differently. The substantialist approach to agency and structure is heir to the Kantian bifurcation of reality into two opposing orders: necessity and freedom. In substantialist thinking, agency (or freedom) 'is commonly identified with the self-actional notion of 'human will,' as a property or vital principle that 'breathes life' into passive, inert substances (individuals or groups) that otherwise would remain perpetually at rest (Emirbayer 1997: 294). Rational choice and game theoretic models, predicated upon the existence of rational and calculating actors, adopt this characterisation of agency. Structure (or necessity) in turn tends to be depicted as an 'autonomous, internally organized, self-sustaining system' (Emirbayer 1997: 294) that exists apart from individual agency, influencing human activity from the outside in or top down.

In contrast with substantialism, 'the relational, field-theoretic point of view sees agency as inseparable from the unfolding dynamics of situations ... much like an on-going conversation' (Emirbayer 1997: 294). In relational terms, agency is not held within the minds, bodies or selves of individuals but instead inheres in relations between individuals in spatial contexts. Agency centres:

> ... Around the engagement (and disengagement) by actors of the different contextual environments that constitute their own structured yet flexible social universes ... Just as consciousness is always consciousness *of* something ... so too is agency always agency *toward* something, by means of which actors enter into relationship with surrounding persons, places, meanings, and events. (Emirbayer and Mische 1998: 973)

Agency is inherently intersubjective and as such is never free of structure (Emirbayer and Mische 1998). In regard to structure, agency's 'counterpart,' Marx argued that 'society does not consist of individuals, but expresses the sum of interrelations, the relations within which these individuals stand' (Marx 1973: 264–5). Somers (1994) prefers the term relational setting to the term structure, defining the former as 'a patterned matrix of institutional relationships among cultural, economic, social, and political practices' (p. 72). Somers' notion of relational settings is remarkably consistent with Bourdieu's depiction of the social world comprising multiple overlapping fields and subfields. Accordingly, with agency manifested in interactions and social structures consisting of relations built upon relations, the stark distinction between agency and structure inherent to substantialist thinking is undermined, even dissolved, in relational field-theoretic thinking. Implementations or adaptations of Bourdieu's relational theory of practice in health promotion and public health research can (and should) spotlight agency, but this is an intersubjective agency, not a Kantian transcendental will.

Substantialism is written into the ontological, epistemological and methodological fibres of the wider health research community, perhaps inevitably so in a field of research that puts individual health at its core. After all, cancer is manifested in the substances of bodies, physical exercise promotes healthy cardiovascular systems in the substances of bodies and mental illness is manifested in the minds of individuals, are they not? And once health is accorded a thing-like status the factors that shape and influence it must be thing-like as well, must they not? Indeed, Norbert Elias noted that substantialism is even written into our grammatical forms:

> There are plentiful examples of the pressure which a socially standardized language puts on the individual speaker to use reifying substantives. Take such sentences as: 'The wind is blowing' or 'The river is flowing' – are not the wind and blowing, the river and flowing, identical? Is there a wind that does not blow, a river that does not flow? (Elias 1992: 43)

Prominent theoretical adaptations of Bourdieu's theory of practice to health practices, such as those of Cockerham (2005, 2007), Frohlich *et al.* (2001) and Abel and Frohlich (2012), display substantialist orientations. Cockerham (2005, 2007) describes a theoretical model of health practices called health lifestyle theory, which is based on the supposition that structural factors such as class circumstances, age, gender, race or ethnicity, and material living conditions inscribe themselves upon people as dispositions to act (habitus) that then inform the patterns of actions and behaviour that characterise healthy or unhealthy lifestyles. Causal directionality runs from structure to practice with a single feedback mechanism from lifestyle practices to habitus.[3] This linear-causal theoretical model sharply distinguishes agency from structure, heavily privileging the latter over the former.

Frohlich *et al.* (2001), inspired by Giddens's structuration theory as well as Bourdieu's theory of practice, call for a recursive and co-dependent dynamic between agency and structure:

> Structure is not possible without action because action reproduces structure. Action is not possible without structure because action begins with a given structure that was the result of prior actions.
>
> … A recursive conception of the relationship between structure and practices moves away from the predominantly deterministic approach taken by researchers in social epidemiology and other sub-fields of public health. (Frohlich *et al.* 2001: 768, 791)

A co-determining dynamic of this kind, both/and in nature, is also incommensurate with a relational world-view (Dépelteau 2008, Martin 2003). Abel and Frohlich (2012) illuminate a variety of ways in which the multiple forms of capital delineated by Bourdieu can interact with one another to influence health practices: for example, the gainful use of economic capital can depend upon having a certain kind of cultural capital and economic capital can facilitate the acquisition of cultural capital. The seemingly universal nature of the capital interactions delineated by Abel and Frohlich is also incompatible with a field-theoretic world-view that is inherently particularistic in nature.[4] Finding insufficient amounts of agency in Bourdieu's theory of practice and/or that the agency that can be identified in it is of the wrong kind are eminently reasonable conclusions from a substantialist perspective. Bourdieu adopted a relational perspective, however, and his theory of practice should be judged on its own terms.

Habitus and doxa in fields

We contribute our understanding of the nature of intersubjective agency manifested within fields by referring to Bourdieu's well-known notion of habitus as well as the underappreciated but important notion of doxa. Our intent here is to provide relational descriptions of habitus, doxa, capital and field as interdependent phenomena that, when taken as an ensemble, give form and coherence to the reflexive, improvisational, innovative and creative practices of actors.

Arguably the most popular concept in Bourdieu's arsenal, habitus is a uniquely subjective concept that reflects the social dispositions and beliefs acquired and stored by social actors over time as they move through social space, encounter different people and fields and reason their way through complex situations. A phenomenon that mediates past experiences and present stimuli, habitus gives 'form and coherence to the various activities of an individual across the separate spheres of life' (Wacquant 1998: 221). It speaks to the ways in which past experiences in social settings and presently available chances and opportunities manifest themselves in relatively durable dispositions that inform the future choices that people make and the actions they may take. Simply put, habitus is the product of history and experience (Bourdieu 1977). People learn and internalise durable dispositions, values and tastes that are formed in relation to the needs and interests that emerge from the social conditions of frequented fields (Bourdieu 1984). Sometimes described as internalised necessity, the arrangement of dispositions that make up the habitus reflect present social conditions and accessible resources (for example, economic, cultural and social capitals) whereby people learn to live with what is available and familiar to them within the context of what they know and understand (Bourdieu 1984, 2000).

Neither habitus nor field has the capacity to explicate social action on its own – each must be understood in relation to the other. The field infuses habitus with its tendencies and rhythms while habitus contributes to constituting the field with value and meaning. Habitus 'is "at home" in the field it inhabits, it perceives it immediately as endowed with meaning and interest' (Bourdieu and Wacquant 1992: 128). In this way, when habitus encounters a social field of which it is the product it is like a fish in water; it possesses a practical sense in the field, a 'feel for the game' that Bourdieu refers to as 'the art of "anticipating" events' (Bourdieu 1990: 66). He notes:

> [P]ractical activity, insofar as it is *makes sense*, as it is *sensée*, reasonable, that is, engendered by a habitus adjusted to the immanent tendencies of the field, is an act of temporalisation through which the agent transcends the immediate present via practical mobilisation of the past and practical anticipation of the future inscribed in the present in a state of objective potentiality. (Bourdieu and Wacquant 1992: 138)

The practical ability to anticipate the forthcoming of events and act in a reasonable way that makes sense is a necessarily creative act intimately tied to a person's relation to the regularities of a field.

Whereas habitus provides form and coherence to a person's relationship with one or many fields, Bourdieu uses the notion of doxa to further illuminate what it means to feel at home in a field, that is, where there is a close fit between the subjective aspects of habitus and the objective structures of a social setting (Bourdieu 1998, Wacquant 1998). Specifically, doxa refers to the preverbal, taken-for-granted understanding of a field that develops when the habitus is closely attuned to its rhythms and regularities (Bourdieu 1990). It is intuitive knowledge shaped by experience, the shared but unquestioned opinions, perceptions and beliefs of the people (groups) whose habitus cohere with the rhythms and regularities of a field (Bourdieu 1998, 1990, 2000). In a sense, the doxa reflects the taken-for-granted order of a field that arises over time from the independent and interdependent experiences, meetings and interactions in familiar fields between people who share a similar habitus (Bourdieu 1984, Eagleton and Bourdieu 1992). When a person feels like a fish in water they do 'not feel the weight of the water, and take the world about itself for granted' (Bourdieu and Wacquant 1992: 127). Over time, as individuals' habitus become accustomed to the patterned social forces of frequented social fields, they develop an embodied sense of their place in the social order. People come to understand which fields do and do not fit neatly with their habitus, what is referred to as a:

> ... Sense of limits ("that's not for the likes of us," etc.) ... which amounts to the same thing, a sense of distances, to be marked and kept, respected or expected. (Bourdieu 1985: 728)

Upon considering habitus, doxa, capital and field as relationally bound concepts we find that agency adopts a necessarily spatial and intersubjective character. Not primarily dependent on external or internal conditions, agency operates at the spatial level of the situation where abilities, potentialities and possibilities for a person to act are linked to the properties and rhythms of a field, the capitals operative in the field, the constitution of habitus and the degree to which the person shares the similar opinions and beliefs of the field (doxa). Having an intimate knowledge and familiarity of the tendencies and patterns of particular fields translates into an ability for improvised and spontaneous strategy. That is to say, in fields to which the habitus is particularly attuned, where a person comprehends the shared set of opinions and beliefs of the field (doxa), we find spaces that are more open to the power of expression and improvised action and where creative actions flow more naturally. It is in 'foreign' fields, where habitus is less adept and a person is less attuned to the shared customs and taken-for-granted regularities of the field (removed from doxa), that the forces of exclusion and difference are more strongly felt and people are comparatively constrained in their potential for free and creative action (Bourdieu 2000).

That said, situations where discontinuities between habitus and field exist do not consign people to be powerless automatons; rather, the discrepancy can trigger innovative actions and reactions intended to strike a manageable balance between one's habitus and the field in question. In this way, a person's sense of their position in a field (that is, the fit between what they know, where they are and who they are around) contextualises agency in a way that considers past experiences in time and across spaces (past experiences with fields) along with sense perceptions of positioning and fit with people and social environments. This point is clearly made by Bourdieu and Wacquant when they state that:

> ... The strategies of agents depend on their position in the field, that is, in the distribution of the specific capital[s], and on the perception that they have of the field depending on the point of view they take *on* the field as a view taken from a point *in* the field. (1992: 101)

As this quote illustrates, strategies for action in a field extend far beyond the possession of relevant capitals and the unconscious direction of a set of preformed dispositions; they emerge at the nexus of field, capitals, doxa and habitus. This means that:

> ... To explain any social event or pattern, one must inseparably dissect both the social constitution of the agent and the makeup of the particular social [field] within which she operates as well as the particular conditions under which they come to encounter and impinge upon each other. (Wacquant 1998: 222)

Embracing the relationality of Bourdieu's concepts allows us to consider the interdependencies of human action (we act and are acted upon) and to understand agency as habitually creative in nature.

A relational approach to health practices would therefore consist of critically examining the complex relations between habitus, doxa, capitals and fields whereby healthy and unhealthy dispositions become naturalised as taken-for-granted realities. Explanations of healthy and unhealthy practices would require identifying the principles and properties of common dispositions within fields and of shared doxa that actors mutually establish. In other words, health researchers seeking to implement a relational field-theoretic approach would benefit from a concerted focus on revealing the complexities of the relations between mental structures (categories of perception and appreciation, systems of preference, perceived limits) and objective structures (fields) that give rise to the 'natural' health-related practices of everyday life.

Conclusion

Although we see great potential in Bourdieu's theory of practice for explicating health practices, implementing field-theoretic ontologies, epistemologies and methodologies in empirical health research endeavours comes with sizeable challenges. For instance, identifying the field or fields within which health practices are made manifest is not a straightforward task. Society comprises many fields. Bourdieu himself referred to the overarching society-wide 'field of power', the field that subsumes all others in a society, as well as multiple subfields of the field of power, for example, the economic, artistic, academic and political fields (Bourdieu 1984, 1998). We can also envision fields that are much more restricted in size and scope than these; teenage girls in schools (Haines *et al.* 2009) and members of a boxing gym (Paradis 2012) may also constitute elements of identifiable fields, for example. Each field has its own logic (including the capitals that are at stake in the field), the habitus and doxa evident in the people who occupy the field and the practices that emerge within the field that must be comprehended by the researcher.

Having identified a field of interest, the construction of a topographical model of the field requires an a priori general understanding of the logic of the field being studied (habitus, doxa, capitals). This necessitates having a theoretical and intuitive[5] understanding of the social forces and factors that are believed to be the most relevant representations of positions within the field (Bourdieu and Wacquant 1992). The goal is:

> … To link the pertinent data in such a manner that they function as a self-propelling program of research capable of generating systematic questions … which can be put to the test. (Bourdieu and Wacquant 1992: 231)

A preliminary understanding of the underlying logic of a field helps to avoid tautological kinds of explanation. This means, however, that a researcher cannot simply identify and select a new field for inquiry and then leap into an examination of it with a rigorously defined empirical research strategy – time must be spent first apprehending the logic and contours of the field and the people who frequent it.

In the absence of an a priori identification or understanding of a field within which a practice is made manifest, beginning an empirical investigation of the logic of a health practice with the society-wide field of power is unlikely to be a poor choice. Other scholars have already investigated these fields, in various national contexts, providing valuable insights into their character, especially in regards to the array of capitals at stake within them. For example, the sum total of economic capital in the form of wealth and institutionalised cultural capital in the form of educational credentials appears to structure the primary dimension of the field of power, the dimension along which social classes are presumably arrayed, in France of the 1960 to 1970s (Bourdieu 1984), Canada of 1998 (Veenstra 2010), France of 2003 (Coulangeon and Lemel 2009) and the UK in 2003 (Le Roux *et al.* 2008). The relative composition of wealth and educational credentials also seemingly contributed to structuring the French field of power of the 1960 and 1970s (Bourdieu 1984) and Canada in 1998 (Veenstra 2010) but not the contemporary fields of power of France and the UK. Some of the work on the characteristics of these particular fields has already been done.

Nevertheless, it is possible, even probable, that smaller fields than these are the more appropriate arenas for investigating specified health practices; if so, each will have its own logic that must be intuitively identifiable by the researcher and empirically explored on its own terms. In addition, a given health practice might emerge within multiple fields, which means that a researcher might have to investigate several fields in order to fully understand the logic of a health-related practice. Practically speaking, studying only one of the fields would mean that not all aspects of the habitus and doxa that inform the health practice would be illuminated. Identifying the right field and comprehending its logic prior to an empirical examination of its properties are obstacles that are not easily surmounted.

One of us has variously embraced substantialism (Garnett *et al.* 2008, Veenstra 2005, 2007b, Veenstra and Patterson 2012) and relationalism (Veenstra 2007a, 2009, 2010) in previous empirical implementations of aspects of Bourdieu's theory of practice and found the substantialist perspective and its associated methods by far the more familiar and straightforward. This indicates that upturning one's taken-for-granted ontological world-view and departing from prevailing doxa in health research is not easily accomplished. Indeed, eschewing substantialism for relationalism may be asking for too much from health promotion and public health researchers, let alone from their diverse publics. If this is true, then scholars like Cockerham (2005, 2007), Frohlich *et al.* (2001) and Abel and Frohlich (2012), who have adopted selected concepts from Bourdieu and merged them with concepts from other theoretical schemas, have done health promotion and public health an important service by translating relational concepts into substantialist frameworks. Newly substantial concepts, including the social capital of places (for example, Kawachi *et al.* 2004), cultural capital (for example, Abel 2007, 2008, Khawaja and Mowafi 2006) and capital interactions (Abel *et al.* 2011, Abel and Frohlich 2012, Veenstra and Patterson 2012), inspired by Bourdieu's concepts but inhabited by subtly different ideas, may produce useful insights into the logic of health practices for a substantially inclined research community. That said, we revisit Williams' (1995) claim that there remains a pressing need to theorise the structure–agency problem with regard to health practices. To the degree that this still is and continues to be the case, we may find instead that the audience for a relational approach to understanding health practices is large and growing.

Notes

1   The degree to which Bourdieu's theory of practice short-changes agency in favour of determining structures is a huge debate in social theory. See Jenkins (1982), Alexander (1995) and Vandenberghe (1999) for allegations of determinism and Potter (2000), Crossley (2001), Dillabough (2004), Fowler (2006), Catt (2006) and Mills (2008) for counter-arguments.

2   Many classical and contemporary social theorists have utilised relational conceptions of the social in order to transcend the restrictions and contradictions of dualities such as agency–structure and material–ideal. Examples include ideas pertaining to social forms of interactional contexts (Simmel 1910), dynamism and multiplicity in time and space (Bergson 1910), types and typical relations of types (Schütz 1959), sociality and emergence of the social self (Mead 1972), inter-psychology and social interplay (Tarde 1903), social relations of interdependence (Foucault 1986), social processes of interdependent individuals in society (Elias 1992) and dynamics of interpersonal relations (Tilly 2001).

3   In the substantialist universe, causality in the social world resembles causality on the billiard table (Martin 2003). On the billiard table, one ball impels movement in another by striking it and transferring to it some kind of force. In the social sciences, the hard substance of billiard balls is replaced not by the substance of individuals but by variables measuring characteristics of individuals or collectives. Causality exists when a change in state in one variable impels a change in state in another. Mechanisms are then invoked to explain the causal relationship, taking the form of other characteristics of individuals or collectives that connect the independent variable to the dependent variable in some linear-causal linkage or pathway. Causal factors or forces can be local (proximal) or at a distance (distal). The more proximal factors identified when attempting to causally link a distal factor to a dependent variable the more plausible the explanation. In addition, multiple particularities are needed in order to begin to understand a generality in the substantialist universe. If a relationship holds in Texas in one study, in Nairobi in another and in northern Scotland in yet another, we can then begin to discern the nature of a general relationship – the results of any one study can be no more than suggestive of generalities. Needless to say, causality operates very differently from a relational perspective. See Martin (2003) for an extensive discussion of the nature of causal explanation in social fields.

4   Capital interactions of the kind described by Abel and Frohlich (2012) can be understood in relational terms, however. For example, Bourdieu (1986) extensively described processes within fields whereby one form of capital is converted into another.

5   'Ordinary intuition is quite respectable; only, one must be sure to introduce intuitions into the analysis in a conscious and reasoned manner' (Bourdieu and Wacquant 1992: 108).

References

Abel, T. (2007) Cultural capital in health promotion. In McQueen, D., Kickbusch, I., Potvin, L., Pelikan, J.M. *et al.* (eds) *Health and Modernity: the Role of Theory in Health Promotion.* New York: Springer.

Abel, T. (2008) Cultural capital and social inequality in health, *Journal of Epidemiology and Community Health*, 62, 7, e13. doi:10.1136/jech.2007.066159.

Abel, T. and Frohlich, K. (2012) Capitals and capabilities: linking structure and agency to reduce health inequalities, *Social Science & Medicine*, 74, 2, 236–44.

Abel, T., Fuhr, D.C., Bisegger, C., Ackermann Rau, S. *et al.* (2011) Money is not enough: exploring the impact of social and cultural resources on youth health, *Scandinavian Journal of Public Health*, 39, 6, 57–61.

Alexander, J.C. (1995) *Fin de Siècle Social Theory: Relativism, Reduction, and the Problem of Reason.* London and New York: Verso.

Bergson, H. (1910) *Time and Free Will, an Essay on the Immediate Data of Consciousness.* New York: Macmillan.

Bourdieu, P. (1977) *Outline of a Theory of Practice.* Cambridge University Press.

Bourdieu, P. (1984) *Distinction. A Social Critique of the Judgement of Taste.* Cambridge: Harvard University Press.

Bourdieu, P. (1985) Social space and the genesis of groups, *Theory & Society*, 14, 6, 723–44.

Bourdieu, P. (1986) The forms of capital. In Richardson, J.G. (ed.) *Handbook of Theory and Research for the Sociology of Education.* New York: Greenwood Press.

Bourdieu, P. (1988) *Homo Academicus*. Stanford: Stanford University Press.

Bourdieu, P. (1989) Social space and symbolic power, *Sociological Theory*, 7, 1, 14–25.

Bourdieu, P. (1990) *The Logic of Practice*. Stanford: Stanford University Press.

Bourdieu, P. (1998) *Practical Reason*. Stanford: Stanford University Press.

Bourdieu, P. (2000) *Pascalian Meditations*. Stanford: Stanford University Press.

Bourdieu, P. (2008) *Sketch for a Self-Analysis*. Chicago: University of Chicago Press.

Bourdieu, P. and Wacquant, L. (1992) *An Invitation to Reflexive Sociology*. Chicago: University of Chicago Press.

Catt, E.A. (2006) Pierre Bourdieu's semiotic legacy: a theory of communicative agency, *American Journal of Semiotics*, 22, 1–4, 31–54.

Cockerham, W.C. (2005) Health lifestyle theory and the convergence of agency and structure, *Journal of Health and Social Behavior*, 46, 1, 51–67.

Cockerham, W.C. (2007) *Social Causes of Health and Disease*. Cambridge: Polity Press.

Cockerham, W.C., Ruuten, A. and Abel, T. (1997) Conceptualizing contemporary health lifestyles: moving beyond Weber, *Sociological Quarterly*, 38, 2, 321–42.

Coulangeon, P. and Lemel, Y. (2009) The homology thesis: *Distinction* revisited. In Robson, K. and Sanders, C. (eds) *Quantifying Theory: Pierre Bourdieu*. Berlin: Springer.

Crossley, N. (2001) The phenomenological habitus and its construction, *Theory & Society*, 30, 1, 81–120.

Dépelteau, F. (2008) Relational thinking: a critique of co-deterministic theories of structure and agency, *Sociological Theory*, 26, 1, 51–73.

Dillabough, J. (2004) Class, culture and the 'predicaments of masculine domination': encountering Pierre Bourdieu, *British Journal of Sociology of Education*, 25, 4, 489–506.

Eagleton, T. and Bourdieu, P. (1992) Doxa and common life, *New Left Review*, 191, 111–121.

Elias, N. (1992) *Time: An Essay*. Oxford: Blackwell.

Emirbayer, M. (1997) Manifesto for a relational sociology, *American Journal of Sociology*, 103, 2, 281–317.

Emirbayer, M. and Mische, A. (1998) What is agency?, *American Journal of Sociology*, 103, 4, 962–1023.

Foucault, M. (1986) Of other spaces, *Diacritics*, 16, 1, 22–7.

Fowler, B. (2006) Autonomy, reciprocity and science in the thought of Pierre Bourdieu, *Theory, Culture & Society*, 23, 6, 99–117.

Frohlich, K.L., Corin, E. and Potvin, L. (2001) A theoretical proposal for the relationship between context and disease, *Sociology of Health & Illness*, 23, 6, 776–97.

Garnett, B., Guppy, N. and Veenstra, G. (2008) Careers open to talent: educational credentials, cultural talent, and skilled employment, *Sociological Forum*, 23, 1, 144–64.

Haines, R.J., Poland, B.D. and Johnson, J.L. (2009) Becoming a smoker: cultural capital in young women's accounts of smoking and other substance use, *Sociology of Health & Illness*, 31, 1, 66–80.

Jenkins, R. (1982) Pierre Bourdieu and the reproduction of determinism, *Sociology*, 16, 2, 270–81.

Kawachi, I., Kim, D., Coutts, A. and Subramanian, S.V. (2004) Commentary: reconciling the three accounts of social capital, *International Journal of Epidemiology*, 33, 4, 682–90.

Khawaja, M. and Mowafi, M. (2006) Cultural capital and self-rated health in low income women: evidence from the Urban Health Study, Beirut, Lebanon, *Journal of Urban Health*, 83, 3, 444–58.

Korp, P. (2008) The symbolic power of healthy lifestyles, *Health Sociology Review*, 17, 1, 18–26.

Le Roux, B., Rouanet, H., Savage, M. and Warde, A. (2008) Class and cultural division in the UK, *Sociology*, 42, 6, 1049–71.

Martin, J.L. (2003) What is field theory?, *American Journal of Sociology*, 109, 1, 1–49.

Marx, K. (1973) [1939]) *Grundrisse: Foundations of the Critique of Political Economy*. London: Penguin.

Marx, K. (1990 [1867]) *Capital: a Critique of Political Economy*, Vol. 1. London: Penguin.

Mead, G.H. (1972) *Mind, Self, and Society: From the Standpoint of a Social Behaviorist*. Chicago: University of Chicago Press.

Mills, C. (2008) Reproduction and transformation of inequalities in schooling: the transformative potential of the theoretical constructs of Bourdieu, *British Journal of Sociology of Education*, 29, 1, 79–89.

Mische, A. (2011) Relational sociology, culture, and agency. In Scott, J. and Carrington, P. (eds) *Sage Handbook of Social Network Analysis*. London: Sage.

Paradis, E. (2012) Boxers, briefs or bras? Bodies, gender and change in the boxing gym, *Body & Society*, 18, 2, 82–109.

Potter, G. (2000) For Bourdieu, against Alexander: reality and reduction, *Journal for the Theory of Social Behaviour*, 30, 2, 229–46.

Schinkel, W. (2007) Sociological discourse of the relational: the cases of Bourdieu & Latour, *Sociological Review*, 55, 4, 707–29.

Schütz, A. (1959) Tiresias, or our knowledge of future events, *Social Research*, 26, 1, 71–89.

Simmel, G. (1910) How is society possible?, *American Journal of Sociology*, 16, 3, 372–91.

Somers, M.R. (1994) Rights, rationality, and membership: rethinking the making and meaning of citizenship, *Law & Social Inquiry*, 19, 1, 63–112.

Tarde, G. (1903) Inter-psychology, the inter-play of human minds, *International Quarterly*, 7, 59–84.

Tilly, C. (2001) Relational origins of inequality, *Anthropological Theory*, 1, 3, 355–72.

Vandenberghe, F. (1999) 'The real is relational': an epistemological analysis of Pierre Bourdieu's generative structuralism, *Sociological Theory*, 17, 1, 32–67.

Veenstra, G. (2005) Can taste illumine class? Cultural knowledge and forms of inequality, *Canadian Journal of Sociology*, 30, 3, 247–79.

Veenstra, G. (2007a) Social space, social class and Bourdieu: health inequalities in British Columbia, Canada, *Health & Place*, 13, 1, 14–31.

Veenstra, G. (2007b) Who the heck is Don Bradman? Sport culture and social class in British Columbia, Canada, *Canadian Review of Sociology*, 44, 3, 319–44.

Veenstra, G. (2009) Transmutations of capitals in Canada: a 'social space' approach. In Robson, K. and Sanders, C. (eds) *Quantifying Theory: Pierre Bourdieu*. Berlin: Springer.

Veenstra, G. (2010) Culture and class in Canada, *Canadian Journal of Sociology*, 35, 1, 83–111.

Veenstra, G. and Patterson, A.C. (2012) Capital relations: mediating and moderating effects of cultural, economic, and social capitals on mortality in Alameda County, *California, International Journal of Health Services*, 42, 2, 277–91.

Wacquant, L.J.D. (1998) Pierre Bourdieu. In Stones, R. (ed.) *Key Sociological Thinkers*. Basingstoke: Macmillan.

Williams, G.H. (2003) The determinants of health: structure, context and agency, *Sociology of Health & Illness*, 25, 3, 131–54.

Williams, S.J. (1995) Theorising class, health and lifestyles: can Bourdieu help us?, *Sociology of Health & Illness*, 17, 5, 577–604.

5

Environmental justice and health practices: understanding how health inequities arise at the local level
Katherine L. Frohlich and Thomas Abel

Introduction

The literature on social inequalities in health behaviour is vast. Within the last 10 years or so, the interest in this area has moved from a general concern to one of considering these same inequalities in local or neighbourhood areas (Chow *et al.* 2009, Ellaway and Macintyre 2009, Frohlich *et al.* 2002). While extremely important, this research has mostly focused on detailing the extent of the inequality (understood in statistical terms). Normally this is undertaken by studying the effect of the inequality of specific social determinants, such as socioeconomic status, on the inequality of outcomes (in our case, behaviour). The study of health inequality has therefore largely focused on the distribution of primary goods (mostly money, but often also education), rather than on the inequality of opportunity or the impact that this differential distribution of social determinants has on people's ability to engage, or not, in healthy behaviour.

In order to take a different approach, we start with a critique of epidemiological approaches to health behaviour, arguing that their focus on the individual and neglect of context is a major problem when it comes to understanding how behaviour comes to be socially differentiated. As a solution, we suggest moving from health behaviour, as medically defined risk factors, to health practices, as sociologically defined features of context-specific social differentiation. The move from health behaviour to health practices is discussed as a prerequisite for another substantial change necessary in inequalities research; the move from the study of the inequality of outcomes to the inequity of opportunities.

In so doing we focus on two theoretical concepts we think may offer some novelty to the current debate on the production of health inequalities with regard to health behaviour: capital interaction and capabilities. We discuss Pierre Bourdieu's capital interaction theory (Bourdieu 1977, 1986) in order to explain the importance of the distribution of structurally based resources as the basis for social inequality in health practices. We then explore Amartya Sen's capability approach (Sen 1985, 1999, 2009), which draws attention to the range of options for health-relevant agency. In bringing together Bourdieu's capital theory with the capability theory of Sen we come to see that social inequalities in health behaviour are not natural or inherent, but are unfairly socially structured and therefore mutable. This moral dimension leads us to speak of inequities rather than inequalities. Beyond a question

From Health Behaviours to Health Practices: Critical Perspectives, First Edition. Edited by Simon Cohn. Chapters © 2014 The Authors. Book Compilation © 2014 Foundation for the Sociology of Health & Illness / Blackwell Publishing Ltd.

of semantics, this change of focus helps us understand that social inequalities are not naturally occurring but socially structured and unfair phenomena. We conclude with a concrete application of these ideas in a framework from the 'Interdisciplinary study of inequalities in smoking' (ISIS), which applies these ideas to explain social inequities in health practices at the local level.

Moving from inequalities in health behaviour to inequities in health practices

Much empirical research on social inequalities in health behaviour is firmly entrenched in the social epidemiological approach; the unequal distribution of unhealthy behaviour (like smoking, drinking, eating habits and lack of exercise) is linked to unequal social conditions (most often operationalised with variables such as income, education and social support). The inability of public health to change individual behaviour on a large scale, however, despite expensive and labour-intensive large-scale interventions (for example, the multiple risk factor intervention trial), has given epidemiologists reason to pause with regard to how they view behaviour and its causes and their ability to modify it.

Indeed, certain fundamental characteristics of the epidemiological approach require rethinking social inequalities in health behaviour. Here we focus on two features most relevant for our argument; (i) epidemiologists' focus on individuals as passive disease hosts instead of active agents and (ii) the basic neglect in social epidemiology of unequal choices as a key element in the distribution of health practices.

First, we describe the problem inherent in epidemiologists' sole focus on disease. Disease can be defined as a biomedical process occurring inside the human body. Epidemiologists study its distribution and set out to identify factors that increase its probability of occurrence. Social epidemiology, by extension, can be defined by its focus on the social (risk) factors in disease causation. In social, as well as general epidemiology, the meaning attributed to individuals – as part of the complex processes in disease distribution – goes back to the established concept of humans as hosts. By defining individuals as hosts, agency is ascribed to individual biology (or at least, the ultimately decisive active part). Consequently, epidemiological approaches tend to pay little or no attention to individuals or groups of individuals as social agents in the production and reproduction of health behaviour and social inequalities. Instead (social) epidemiological research focuses on the study of individuals as being exposed to risk or as carriers of risks. The fact that people actively manage their lives, including health issues, does not receive particular attention.

The term and concept of health practices, rather than health behaviour, is critical if we are to reintroduce agency as a social concept. A discussion of health practices allows us to focus on context-specific human agency as a key factor in understanding social inequality in health (Frohlich *et al.* 2001). In contrast, the term and concept of health behaviour, defined as individuals' actions relevant for medically defined outcomes and (potentially) causal for pathological processes inside the human body, does not fit well with such a sociological perspective.

The second problem revolves around the treatment of health inequality in the epidemiological paradigm. Health inequality research in public health took off in an important way with the first results of the legendary 1978 article entitled 'Employment grade and coronary heart disease in British civil servants' (Marmot *et al.* 1978). The Whitehall I study, begun in 1967, found, as has the subsequent Whitehall II study, a strong association between grade levels of civil servant employment and morbidity and mortality rates from a range of causes. Importantly, this gradient was only very partially explained through health behaviour.

The results from the Whitehall studies created a flurry of excitement in the nascent world of social epidemiology. The focus of these studies remained, however, on the outcome side of the equation; much emphasis was (and still is) placed on describing how unequal people are with regard to their health behaviour, morbidity and mortality, with less attention being paid to the inequitable processes leading to these health inequalities (Frohlich *et al.* 2006). This is not entirely surprising, given that epidemiology is the study of the determinants and distribution of disease, and not an area of inquiry that seeks to understand why the gradient exists.

Some of these oversights are debated in the day-to-day work of political philosophers and ethicists. These thinkers discuss issues of social inequality under the purview of equity and choice. Political philosophers concerned with issues of social inequality, for instance, have addressed the problem of the voluntariness or otherwise of behavioural choices. Many of them have suggested that this focus clouds an important consideration in the normative analysis of these 'choices'; namely, the unequal background conditions against which individuals from different social groups make decisions about what they do. These suggest that a host of external factors affects whether or not individuals start to, for instance, smoke, whether or not they attempt to quit and whether or not any such attempts are successful (Viehbeck *et al.* 2011).

The issue of choice brings us to a fundamental distinction often neglected in epidemiology; the difference between (in)equality and (in)equity. Health inequality has been defined by Margaret Whitehead (1992) as: 'measureable differences in health experience and health outcomes between different population groups – according to socioeconomic status, geographical area, age, disability, gender or ethnic group'. Health inequity, on the other hand, has a moral and ethical dimension. It refers to differences in health that are unnecessary and avoidable and in addition, are also considered unfair and unjust. Inequities include differences in opportunity for different population groups that result in, for example, unequal life chances, nutritious food and adequate housing.

But judgements on which situations are unfair will vary from place to place and time to time. One widely used criterion, however, is the degree of choice involved. Where people have little to no choice in their living and working conditions, the resulting health conditions are likely to be considered particularly unjust. Social inequities, of course, can make certain choices easy and accessible for some, but costly and difficult for others. Even if we think that individuals' choices can, in principle, justify unequal health outcomes, we must still ask whether different people's choices were made against roughly equitable background conditions (Viehbeck *et al.* 2011).

Because epidemiologists focus on the outcome side of the gradient effect they only really emphasise the unfairness of the outcome. By turning the lens from the issue of inequality to one of equity, we begin to ask why some people are better able to be healthy than others. Precisely these issues are what Marmot and the Whitehall researchers missed until they began to consider issues of distributive justice, largely through the influence of Amartya Sen (Commission on Social Determinants of Health [CSDH] 2008).

We conclude that we need a new theoretical grounding for our discussion about health practices that no longer relies solely on an epidemiological paradigm but rather, considers individuals as having agency for change. Furthermore, rather than detailing inequality in outcomes, we need to better understand how society creates inequitable chances for people based on its distributive practices. In the next section we discuss how one can apply capital and capability theory to help make such a shift.

A structure-agency perspective on health practices

There is widespread recognition today that concern with the production and reproduction of health inequalities must take into account both the social structure and individual agency to be given credence (Cockerham 2005, Frohlich *et al.* 2002, Popay *et al.* 2003, Williams 2003). Yet we suggest that this literature, while helpful in moving forward by underlining and explicating the importance of both, has left some questions open on how structure and agency are linked in the production, reproduction or reduction of inequities in health practices (Abel and Frohlich 2012). Bourdieu argues for a strong link between the possession of different forms of capital, a class-specific habitus, and the choices individuals have. The significant advancement in Bourdieu's work for our argument is that it allows us to analyse key components of social inequity that are directly relevant to agency. We argue that a closer consideration of the different forms of capital and their interactions opens a gateway to the role of the individual in the production and reproduction of inequities in health practices, thereby underscoring the relationship between structure and agency.

According to Bourdieu the inequitable distribution of structurally based resources (capitals) can be understood as part of the fundamental system of inequity in a given society; it is both the result and a key mechanism of the social reproduction of power and privilege. His concept of capital is based on distinguishing three forms: social, economic and cultural capital. These three forms of capital are interrelated and inextricably linked. A major thrust of Bourdieu's theory is his elaborate account of the interaction between these three forms of capital in everyday life and the ways in which this interaction process contributes to the reproduction of social inequities and power distribution in society (Bourdieu 1984, Swartz 1997). Since this interaction has been given little attention in health research (Abel 2008), we concentrate here on their different forms. Prior to this we briefly discuss Bourdieu's notion of economic, social and cultural capital (for more see Abel 2007, Bourdieu 1986, Williams 1995).

Bourdieu (1986) describes capital as:

> Accumulated labour (in its materialized or its 'incorporated', embodied form … It is a
> force inscribed in objective or subjective structures, but it is also the principle
> underlying the immanent regularities of the social world. (Bourdieu 1986: 241)

A critical aspect of Bourdieu's theory of capital is that no single one of the three forms of capital alone can fully explain the reproduction of social inequalities; it takes all three, and importantly, the interaction between the three to permit social inequalities to endure over time.

Economic capital (or the lack thereof) in the form of money and material assets (income, property, financial stocks), is a decisive factor in social advantage and disadvantage. It is also 'the root of all the other types of capital' (Bourdieu, 1986: 252). Social capital, from a Bourdieusian perspective, is located at the inter-individual level. As such, it refers to material and non-material resources that can be mobilised by virtue of many different kinds of social relationships. Social capital is thus understood as the:

> Aggregate of the actual or potential resources which are linked to possession of a
> durable network of mutual acquaintance and recognition or membership in a group
> which provides each of its members with the backing of the collectively-owned capital.
> (Bourdieu 1986: 248)

Lastly, cultural capital can be broadly defined as people's symbolic and informational resources for action (Bourdieu 1986, Wacquant 1992). Cultural capital exists in three different forms: incorporated (such as skills and knowledge); objectivised (such as books, tools and bicycles) and institutionalised (such as educational degrees and vocational certificates) (Bourdieu 1986). It is acquired mostly through social learning, with learning conditions varying across social classes, status groups or milieux (Abel 2007, Swartz 1997, Veenstra 2007, Williams 1995). In the form of knowledge and skills, cultural capital is a precondition for most individual action and, as such, is a key component in people's capacity for agency, including that for health practices.

There is a high degree of complexity among capitals in their different forms. Three of these relationships (conversion, accumulation and transmission) have been discussed by Bourdieu (1986) and here we add a fourth principle of interaction we call conditionality. All four forms of interaction are important for the purposes of our argument. Firstly, the different forms of capital can be converted one into another; economic capital, in the form of money, can be invested in order to improve one's education or cultural capital. Secondly, capital in these different forms can be accumulated; money can be invested in the stock market, for instance, in order to make more money. Thirdly, the different forms of capital can be transmitted; children can inherit financial assets from parents and/or capital can be received through family socialisation; for example, when knowledge and social skills are passed on from parents to their children. Lastly, different forms of capital, in their acquisition and use, are dependent and conditional on each other. For instance, cultural capital is essential in the acquisition of social capital; certain values, communication styles and behavioural skills are expected from all those who want to belong to, and participate in, powerful social networks. The gainful use of economic capital might depend on the authorising properties of higher educational degrees and the knowledge that comes with it.

The decisive meaning of the three forms of capital and their interactions leads us to acknowledge the active role of individuals who (beyond simply owning or consuming such resources) acquire and use, in some active way, health-relevant capital. The active acquisition and development of such capital is part of agency, as is making a health-relevant use of them. In other words, in order for cultural, social and economic capital to become health promoting, individuals have to actively use them. For instance, money is spent on health-relevant practices (such as involvement in physical activity classes), support in health matters is sought out (such as by participating in self-help groups), and knowledge is applied by individuals in order for it to function actively to engender health (for instance, by making decisions about what one eats).

What is missing from Bourdieu's argument, however, is a deeper analysis, beyond a discussion of resources (or capitals), of the inequity in choice that arises from these social inequities. In the last 10 years or so, Sen's capability theory has been proposed as being potentially important for public health action concerned with the reduction of social inequalities in health. This has recently been spearheaded by the World Health Organization (WHO) CSDH 2008 and the writings of experts like Ruger (Marmot 2010, Ruger 2010). The capability theory puts the emphasis on the empowerment of individuals to be active agents of change in their own terms both at the individual and collective levels (Ruger 2004). Central to the capability theory is the idea of 'the public as an active participant in change, rather than as a passive and docile recipient of instructions of dispensed assistance' (Sen 1999: 281). This perspective on collective activity for change allows us to link the capability theory to Bourdieu's capital theory.

The core characteristic of the capability theory is its focus on what people are effectively able to do and be; that is, on their capabilities (Robeyns 2005). Individuals' effective opportunities to undertake the actions and activities that they want to engage in are what matter. These actions and activities ('doings') together with the 'beings', or what Sen calls 'functionings', constitute a valuable life. Functionings include, but are not limited to, being healthy, being active as a community member, working, resting and being literate. The distinction between realisable and realised functionings is crucial to the capabilities approach. 'A functioning is an achievement, whereas a capability is the ability to achieve' (Sen 1987: 36). Sen puts much emphasis on the distinction between functionings and capabilities because he believes that wellbeing should not only include realised functionings, but that the ability to choose from a set of alternative functionings is a freedom sui generis (Sen 1999).

Sen puts great emphasis on freedom. Freedom is important to equity issues for Sen for at least two different reasons. Firstly, more freedom gives people more opportunity to pursue their objectives. It helps, for example, in their ability to decide to live as they would like and to promote the ends that they may want to advance. This aspect of freedom is concerned with people's ability to achieve what they value, no matter what the process is through which that achievement comes about (Sen 2009). Secondly, we may attach importance to the process of choice itself. We may, for example, want to make sure that people are not being forced into health practices, or are not able to behave in the way they wish, because of particular constraints.

Sen distinguishes between two types of freedom; opportunity and process (Sen 2009). When describing opportunity freedom, Sen draws on the structural constraints and opportunities that people have to make choices. The ability to be a certain way and live a certain life is confined, or not, by the options that are available for people to choose from. The process aspect, on the other hand, focuses on the true agency that people have to make their choices.

The focus of the capability approach is not just on what a person actually ends up doing (or achieving), but also whether or not she chooses freely to make use of that opportunity and what her overall options are. The focus is therefore on the ability of people to choose to live different kinds of lives within their reach, rather than confining attention only to what may be described as the culmination – or aftermath – of choice. In this sense, freedom is both structured (having collective/shared aspects) and individual. It is this inequity in capability, understood as an inequity in choice, that Sen argues is at the core of inequality in society.

Consequently, and in relation to health inequities, evaluations of social and health interventions based on the capability theory should include, on the structural side, not only the quality and quantity of available resources (or in Bourdieu's language, capitals), or the realised doings and beings on the agency side, but also the range of capabilities available to people. People's capitals will determine the range of options for health practices by shaping their capabilities. In other words we must take into account the capability sets from which individuals can draw (Sen 1993) in order to understand how inequities in health practices come about.

Environmental justice and its link to health practice inequity

Up until here our discussion has been purely theoretical. The case of environmental injustice, however, can help explain what these issues look like in our everyday lives by focusing on modern urban conditions. Urbanisation is probably the single most important demographic shift worldwide during the past and in the new century, and it represents a sentinel change from how most of the world's population has lived throughout history (Galea and Vlahov 2005). Cities such as Los Angeles, New York, London, Hong Kong, Mumbai and Rio de Janeiro now have income disparities that rank among the highest in the world. Although resources are made available to urban residents through private, public and volunteer conduits in these cities, socioeconomic inequities in cities are linked to differential access to these resources. These inequities suggest that people at different ends of the socioeconomic spectrum may have different opportunities to benefit from the resources available in cities, resulting in differentials in health practices.

One area of urban studies of particular importance to social inequities in health is that of neighbourhoods. There is increasing evidence that health practices tend to be substantially more damaging to health in areas characterised by high levels of social and economic disadvantage, relative to areas characterised by social and economic advantage (Drewnowski 2009, Pearce *et al.* 2010, Pabayo *et al.* 2011). Because where people live is the basis for health practices, their experiences of engaging in them are to a certain extent constrained or encouraged by several aspects of these areas: the physical environment, the cultural expectations about appropriate behaviour and the social experiences possible there (Fitzpatrick and LaGory 2011). Physical and social qualities of place therefore make some health practices more possible than others.

Despite this growing area of work in neighbourhoods and health, the spatial dimension has hitherto tended to be treated as a kind of fixed background, a physically formed environment that has some influence on our lives (and health) but that remains external to the social world as well as to efforts to make the world more socially just (Soja 2010). However, for certain segments of the population it seems that being in an unhealthy place is not a matter of timing or accident, but rather a function of the social structure (Fitzpatrick and Lagory 2011, Macintyre 2007); a structure that is amenable to change if the political will is present. It is also now recognised in the environmental justice literature that marginalised populations face a double burden: being individually socially marginalised and being subject to the inequities resulting from being located in poor social and physical environments (Masuda *et al.* 2010). Since cities are artificially constructed environments, that is, intentional, built environments, they should as easily be engineered to promote more desirable health outcomes (Fitzpatrick and Lagory 2011).

One area of research and advocacy that has developed to confront these issues is the environmental justice movement. In its early stages environmental justice was defined as the disproportionate exposure to and burden of harmful environmental conditions experienced by people in low socioeconomic positions (Taylor *et al.* 2006). This movement, which has since its humble beginnings become global in scope, now involves a theoretical positioning linking environmental research to debates around human rights and social equity (Masuda *et al.* 2010). In this sense, environmental justice offers a remarkably important framework for thinking about the inequitable distribution of health practices across areas.

Within this framework, cities and neighbourhoods can be considered resource spaces where the goods and services capable of protecting and enhancing the health of their residents can be more or less equitably distributed (Fitzpatrick and LaGory 2011). Urban spaces are home to various social groups, sorted and sifted according to political and economic resources. Those with the greatest social, economic and cultural resources generally reside in areas containing the most health-promoting resources while those with the least personal resources find their access restricted to less desirable areas with the fewest health-promoting resources. As a logical conclusion, these same groups with the least exposure to health-promoting resources have health practice choices that are constrained by reduced life chances. And indeed, studies continue to show that the most socially disadvantaged neighbourhoods lack the resources necessary to promote healthy health practices (Drewnoski 2009, Fitzpatrick and LaGory 2011, Pabayo *et al.* 2011, 2012).

A new approach: ISIS

Drawing on the principles of the environmental justice movement, along with our earlier theoretical argument regarding Bourdieu and Sen, we propose a framework that moves towards an operationalisation of how inequities in health practices come about in neighbourhoods. In the past, attempts to conceptualise how neighbourhoods influence health outcomes inequitably tended to fall into the traditional epidemiological trap of treating neighbourhoods as units of analysis, rather than areas that themselves can explain how inequities arise:

> Seldom … does location itself play a real part in the analysis; it is the canvas on which events happen but the nature of the locality and its role in structuring health status and health related behaviour is neglected. (Jones and Moon 1993: 515)

The ISIS framework, developed in Montreal, Canada, is concerned with this neighbourhood canvas, how it can differentially make available and accessible resources, and how this social inequity can lead to inequities in health practices. Crucially, our framework examines inequity at work in two different ways; at an aggregate neighbourhood level, what others have called environmental injustice, and at an individual level (through the capital stock of individuals). We argue that it is at the interface of both the inequitable distribution of capitals and the inequities in neighbourhood resources that individuals' capabilities become shaped. As such, we argue, similarly to Masuda, Poland, and Baxter (2010), that marginalised populations often face a double burden: being personally socially marginalised as well as being subjected to poor quality living environments. Our framework describes how neighbourhoods can unfairly structure capabilities due to the inequitable constraints and opportunities at both the individual and collective levels. We then develop the argument as to how they interact to create inequitable health practices.

In the framework the geographical patterning of health inequities is linked to inequities in health-related resources available in one's immediate environment, the neighbourhood. In other words, neighbourhoods make available resources with a positive and/or negative valence for producing, in the case of the ISIS study, social inequities in smoking. We do not view health inequities to be a result of the inequitable distribution of resources understood as differences in the amount of resources alone. Instead we have expanded on what is meant by distribution of resources. We do not view this distribution to be an outcome understood in terms of variation in a statistical sense, but as the set of processes through which resources are spread out among neighbourhoods (Bernard et al. 2007). Furthermore, we argue that this inequitable distribution influences people's capabilities to access and use freely these resources for health, as described by Sen.

How resources are distributed at the neighbourhood level

In order to help operationalise how resources at the neighbourhood level might come to be inequitably distributed, we call upon a complementary theorist to the ideas of Bourdieu and Sen. In Jacques Godbout's theory of informal reciprocity (Godbout 2000) he contends that many resources are procured and exchanged outside the interventions of markets or the state. He suggests that there are three distinct sets of rules for the circulation of resources: market rules, states and networks within which informal reciprocity occurs. We extend Godbout's theory and develop the idea that availability of, and access to, resources are regu-

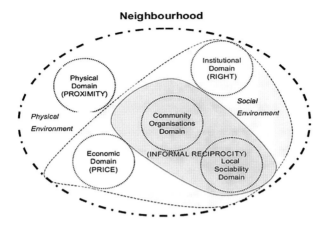

Figure 1 *Neighbourhood environments and rules of access (Bernard et al. 2007). Four sets of rules (in brackets) determine access to neighbourhood resources coming from the physical as well as the social environment. The latter influence comprises four domains. Two of these domains (dark grey) obey the rule of reciprocity*

lated by four rules: proximity, price, rights and informal reciprocity. These rules further give rise to five interrelated domains through which residents may acquire resources influencing smoking: the physical, economic, institutional, local sociability and community organisation domains (Bernard *et al.* 2007, Frohlich *et al.* 2008). The variable configurations of these domains in neighbourhoods, we argue, lead to the local production of inequities in smoking. Figure 1.

Specifically, the physical domain includes features of the natural and built environments such as air quality and the presence of buildings and open spaces, as well as their condition and cleanliness. Access and exposure to these resources is ruled by what we have termed proximity: people living in the same area share the same physical environment and they are thus basically exposed to the same positive and negative resources. The economic domain is ruled by the market through price mechanisms. This domain and its rules function under the economic hypothesis that parties are presumed to seek the maximisation of their own utility. Resources in this domain can therefore be obtained only if people pay for them. In the case of the ISIS study, resources such as cigarettes sold through tobacco-selling outlets would be a prime example of a market-regulated resource.

Resources made available through the institutional domain are accessed through the state via rights' mechanisms. Institutional rules regulate access to resources which citizens are entitled to according to publicly enacted rules; such entitlements are balanced against the fulfilment of citizen obligations. There is a recognised relationship between citizens who have rights and the state, which has some measure of authority. General examples of resources offered through this domain are schools, health clinics, shelters and childcare centres. An example of a resource provided through the institutional domain in the case of ISIS are publicly funded smoking cessation services.

The local sociability domain involves resources that can be mobilised through informal networks formed by the social links that people share. These involve non-contractual exchanges of resources outside markets and state interventions. In this domain social relationships are explicitly engaged in gift-giving, which creates obligations of reciprocity that are not specific to the contents, the target or the time frame of what has to be given back. Such resources include smoking-related norms.

Finally, the community organisation domain follows the informal reciprocity rule but includes resources provided through formally organised collective entities such as charity groups. Many of these organisations are involved in some form of collective action. Resources offered by community organisations are normally given freely by groups or individuals to other individuals, such as when community organisations organise local support groups for residents wanting to quit smoking. The critical difference between the local sociability and community organisations domains are that the former procure individuals benefits only, whereas the latter is mobilised in view of pursuing collective goals.

A final component to our framework is an understanding of the social processes that permit the transformation of these resources into health outcomes, or in our case, health practices. We argue that health is produced not only with (or without) the structural constraints and opportunities offered at the local level but, harking back to Bourdieu's and Sen's theories, through individuals' capital stock as well as their capabilities, which permit them to identify, access and choose to utilise (or not) resources in neighbourhoods to their health advantage. Essentially health practice outcomes at a local level are a function of both individuals' capitals and capabilities and the demands and opportunities of the environment (Abel 2008). Social inequities in health practices are therefore a function of the quantity, quality and accessibility of local resources and their correspondence with the forms of capital that residents have at their disposal, the interaction of which will yield inequitable capabilities. Figure 2.

We therefore suggest that inequity goes beyond just the unequal distribution of capital. Social inequity also exists in the chances, choices and ability for people to have the different forms of capital consistently support and complement each other with the end result of their interaction being a health advantage. And this is where the two levels of inequity become of critical importance. At the individual level, capitals provide the agency potential for health when matched with capability. However, this potential is contingent on resources being available and accessible within a neighbourhood. So, for instance, an individual might have the cultural capital that would lead you to value jogging, but if your neighbourhood is too dangerous to jog in (whether this be due to traffic, stray dogs or human-caused violence), your capital may not be actualised due to your reduced capability.

Conclusion

Our chapter began with a critique of current social epidemiological approaches to studying social inequalities in health behaviour. We argue that if we desire to understand how health practices come to be inequitably distributed we need to have a greater theoretical understanding of two things: (i) what social factors are inequitably distributed that lead people to behave in differential ways and (ii) how these social factors interact with people's agency to bring about differential capabilities to act in health promoting ways. We turned to Pierre Bourdieu's capital theory to give guidance on the composition of social inequality, the three capitals, and we explored how these capitals interact to lead to differential abilities to act. We then discussed the role that Amartya Sen's CA could have in helping us focus on the inequity involved in the freedom afforded people to engage in health-enhancing health practices. The focus of CA is the gamut of choices and freedom to choose and the importance of this when considering issues of distributive justice and inequity.

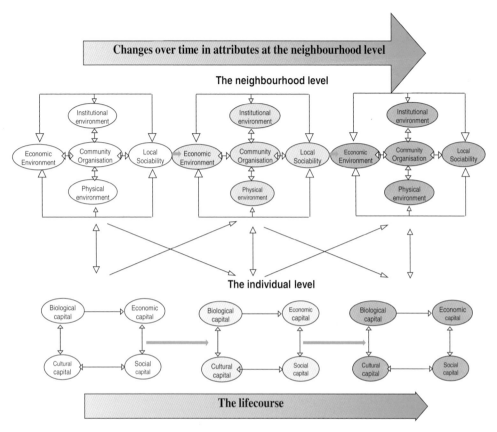

Figure 2 *The ISIS framework: explaining how inequities in health practices are produced in neighbourhoods*

We then turned to a discussion of environmental justice and the specific case of inequities in health practices across urban neighbourhoods. Epidemiological approaches to social inequalities in health across neighbourhoods, we argue, tend to neglect individual agency and focus on the outcome side of inequities. Neighbourhoods tend to be conceived of as geo-spatial structures relevant to health inequality primarily because of the particular distribution of risks, including risk behaviour, found among people living there. This more epidemiological approach to this area of enquiry pays less attention to inequalities in the distribution of resources for health and health behaviour.

In contrast, if neighbourhoods are understood as social contexts in which the resources for health-enhancing behaviour are inequitably provided and therefore inequitably available to be chosen, we reintroduce individuals as social agents back into the discussion of health inequity. In such a perspective, structural conditions for health relevant agency become the focus of understanding the links between neighbourhood and people's health-relevant action. This we explored using Bourdieu's capital and Sen's CA theories. We discussed how neighbourhoods differ with regard to their physical and social structures (what we call domains) and how these structures interact with people's capital stock, thereby yielding differential freedoms to choose health-promoting health practices. Thus inequity exists at three levels; in differential levels of capitals (economic, social and cultural), differential levels of neighbourhood resources (available or not through the domains) and through the differential capabilities that result from the interaction of these two.

These arguments are, of course, as relevant in neighbourhood research as they would be in any other environment. Most importantly, we bring to the fore the importance of understanding the socially structured and inequitable shaping of choice. People do not have equal choices to act, and this lies at the basis of inequity in society. A firmer understanding of this, at both the individual and societal level, should help us make a much needed move from discussions about the inequality in health behaviour to inequities in health practices.

Acknowledgement

This work was partially funded through an operating grant and a New Investigator Award from the Canadian Institutes of Health Research to K.L. Frohlich. K.L. Frohlich would like to acknowledge the Humboldt Foundation and the Wissenshaftszentrum Berlin for making this work possible during her sabbatical year in Berlin.

References

Abel, T. (2007) Cultural capital in health promotion. In McQueen, D.C. and Kickbusch, I. (eds) *Health and Modernity. The Role of Theory in Health Promotion*. Berlin: Springer.

Abel, T. (2008) Cultural capital and social inequality in health, *Journal of Epidemiology and Community Health*, 62, 7, e13. doi:10.1136/jech.2007.066159.

Abel, T. and Frohlich, K.L. (2012) Capitals and capabilities: linking structure and agency to reduce health inequalities, *Social Science & Medicine*, 74, 2, 236–44.

Bernard, P., Charrafedine, R., Frohlich, K.L., Daniel, M., *et al.* (2007) Health inequalities and place: a theoretical conception of neighbourhood, *Social Science & Medicine*, 65, 9, 1839–52.

Bourdieu, P. (1977) *Outline of a Theory of Practice*. Cambridge: Cambridge University Press.

Bourdieu, P. (1984) *Distinction: a Social Critique of the Judgement of Taste*. Cambridge, MA: Harvard University Press.

Bourdieu, P. (1986) The forms of capital. In Richardson, J.G. (ed.) *Handbook of Theory and Research for the Sociology of Education*. Westport: Greenwood Press.

Chow, C.K., Lock, K., Teo, K., Subramanian, S.V., *et al.* (2009) Environmental and societal influences acting on cardiovascular risk factors and disease at a population level: a review, *International Journal of Epidemiology*, 38, 6, 1580–94.

Cockerham, W.C. (2005) Health lifestyle theory and the convergence of agency and structure, *Journal of Health and Social Behavior*, 46, 1, 51–67.

Commission on Social Determinants of Health (2008) *Closing the Gap in a Generation: Health Equity through Action on the Social Determinants of Health*. Final report of the Commission on Social Determinants of Health. Geneva: World Health Organization.

Drewnowski, A. (2009) Obesity, diets, and social inequalities, *Nutrition Reviews*, 67, Suppl. S1, S36–9.

Ellaway, A. and Macintyre, S. (2009) Are perceived neighbourhood problems associated with the likelihood of smoking?, *Journal of Epidemiology and Community Health*, 63, 1, 78–80.

Fitzpatrick, K. and LaGory, M. (2011) *Unhealthy Cities. Poverty, Race and Place in America*. New York: Routledge.

Frohlich, K.L., Corin, E. and Potvin, L. (2001) A theoretical proposal for the relationship between context and disease, *Sociology of Health & Illness*, 23, 6, 776–97.

Frohlich, K.L., Potvin, L., Gauvin, L. and Chabot, P. (2002) Youth smoking initiation: disentangling context from composition, *Health and Place*, 8, 155–66.

Frohlich, K.L., Ross, N.A. and Richmond, C. (2006) Health disparities in Canada today: evidence and pathways, *Health Policy*, 79, 2–3, 132–43.

Frohlich, K.L., Bernard, P., Charafeddine, R., Daniel, M., *et al.* (2008) L'émergence d'inégalités de santé dans les quartiers: Un cadre théorique. In Frohlich, K., DeKoninck, M., Demers, A. and Bernard, P. (eds) *Les Inégalités Sociales de Santé au Québec*. Montréal: Presses Universitaires de Montréal.

Galea, S. and Vlahov, D. (2005) Urban health: evidence, challenges and directions, *Annual Review of Public Health*, 26, 341–65.

Godbout, J.T. (2000) *Le Don, la Dette et l'Identité: Homo Donator Versus Homo Economicus*. Paris and Montréal: Editions La Découverte et Editions du Boréal.

Jones, K. and Moon, G. (1993) Medical geography: taking space seriously, *Progress in Human Geography*, 17, 4, 515–24.

Macintyre, S. (2007) Deprivation amplification revisited: or, is it always true that poorer places have poorer access to resources for healthy diets and physical activity?, *International Journal of Nutrition and Physical Activity*, 4, 32. doi:10.1186/1479-5868-4-32.

Marmot, M. (2010) Fair society, healthy lives 2010. In Marmot, M. (ed.) *The Marmot Review*. Available at http://www.instituteofhealthequity.org/projects/fair-society-healthy-lives-the-marmot -review (accessed 19 October 2013).

Marmot, M.G., Rose, G., Shipley, M. and Hamilton, P.J. (1978) Employment grade and coronary heart disease in British civil servants, *Journal of Epidemiology and Community Health*, 32, 4, 244–9.

Masuda, J.R., Poland, B. and Baxter, J. (2010) Reaching for environmental health justice: Canadian experiences for a comprehensive research, policy and advocacy agenda in health promotion, *Health Promotion International*, 25, 4, 453–63.

Pabayo, R.A., Belsky, J., Gauvin, L. and Curtis, S. (2011) Do area characteristics predict change in moderate-to-vigorous physical activity from ages 11 to 15 years?, *Social Science & Medicine*, 72, 3, 430–8.

Pabayo, R.A., Gauvin, L., Barnett, T.A., Morency, P., *et al.* (2012) Understanding the determinants of active transportation to school among children: Evidence of environmental injustice from the Quebec longitudinal study of child development, *Health and Place*, 18, 2, 163–71.

Pearce, J.R., Richardson, E.A., Mitchell, R.J. and Shortt, N.K. (2010) Environmental justice and health: the implications of the socio-spatial distribution of multiple environmental deprivation for health inequalities in the United Kingdom, *Transactions of the Institute of British Geographers*, 35, 4, 522–39.

Popay, J., Thomas, C., Williams, G., Bennett, S., *et al.* (2003) A proper place to live: health inequalities, agency and the normative dimensions of space, *Social Science & Medicine*, 57, 1, 55–69.

Robeyns, I. (2005) The capability approach: a theoretical survey, *Journal of Human Development*, 6, 1, 93–114.

Ruger, J.P. (2004) Ethics of the social determinants of health, *The Lancet*, 364, 9439, 1092–7.

Ruger, J.P. (2010) Health capability. Conceptualization and operationalization, *American Journal of Public Health*, 100, 1, 41–9.

Sen, A. (1985) *Commodities and Capabilities*. Amsterdam: Elsevier.

Sen, A. (1987) The standard of living. In Hawthorn, G. (ed.) *The Standard of Living*. Cambridge: Cambridge University Press.

Sen, A. (1993) Capability and well-being. In Nussbaum, M. and Sen, A. (eds) *The Quality of Life*. Oxford: Clarendon Press.

Sen, A. (1999) *Development as Freedom*. New York: Random Books.

Sen, A. (2009) *The Idea of Justice*. Cambridge: Belknap Press.

Soja, E.W. (2010) *Seeking Social Justice*. Minnesota: University of Minnesota Press.

Swartz, D. (1997) *Culture and Power: the Sociology of Pierre Bourdieu*. Chicago: University of Chicago Press.

Taylor, W.C., Poston, W.S.C., Jones, L. and Kraft, M.K. (2006) Environmental justice: obesity, physical activity, and healthy eating, *Journal of Physical Activity and Health*, 3, S30–54.

Veenstra, G. (2007) Social space, social class and Bourdieu: health inequalities in British Columbia, Canada. *Health and Place*, 13, 1, 14–31.

Viehbeck, S., Melnychuk, R., McDougall, C.W., Greenwood, H., *et al.* (2011) Population and public health ethics in Canada: a snapshot of current national initiatives and future issues, *Canadian Journal of Public Health*, 102, 6, 410–2.

Wacquant, L.J.D. (1992) Toward a social praxeology: the structure and logic of Bourdieu's sociology. In Bourdieu, P. and Wacquant, L.J.D. (eds) *An Invitation to Reflexive Sociology*. Chicago: University of Chicago Press.

Whitehead, M. (1992) The concepts and principles of equity and health, *International Journal of Health Services*, 22, 3, 429–45.

Williams, G.H. (2003) The determinants of health: structure, context and agency, *Sociology of Health & Illness*, 25, 3, 131–54.

Williams, S.J. (1995) Theorising class, health and lifestyles: can Bourdieu help us?, *Sociology of Health & Illness*, 17, 5, 577–604.

6

Why behavioural health promotion endures despite its failure to reduce health inequities

Fran Baum and Matthew Fisher

Introduction

Although average life expectancy has doubled over the past two centuries (Williams 2004), people with a low health status, including those with chronic disease, are concentrated in disadvantaged areas and towards the lower end of the social gradient. Health inequities closely follow this gradient (Banks *et al.* 2006, Commission on the Social Determinants of Health 2008, Crombie *et al.* 2005, Mackenbach 2005, Turrell *et al.* 2006). There is also mounting evidence in developed nations that disparities in health status have begun to widen in response to changing social and economic conditions (Draper *et al.* 2004, Kroll and Lampert 2011, Stamatakis *et al.* 2010) and that inequities between rich and poor countries are also increasing (Labonté *et al.* 2007, Sanders *et al.* 2005). The persistence of health inequities has been the focus of policy concern for decades and most recently has been highlighted by the World Health Organization (WHO) Commission on the Social Determinants of Health (CSDH) which concluded that 'social injustice is killing people on a grand scale' (2008: 26). The CSDH made a series of recommendations on ways in which health inequities could be reduced both between and within countries. However, it did not call for measures to directly change behaviour that is known to be risky to health. Instead it emphasised the need to change environments and introduce regulations.

The history of public health policy is characterised by a chasm between two central views of how population health may be improved through action to prevent ill health and promote health. On the one hand there is a focus on unhealthy behaviour (for example, the US Department of Health, Education and Welfare 1979) and on the other are the views that underlying social and economic factors are the primary determinant of health outcomes (CSDH 2008). This tension has existed since at least the 19th century, when public health reformers such as Virchow in Silesia, Engels and Chadwick in the UK, and Villermé in France pointed to the impact of industrialisation and urbanisation on health among the working class and promoted structural and political reforms accordingly, while others claimed that the poor health of the working class was the product of their own behaviour and 'immorality' (Porter 1999).

These differences foreshadowed tensions that are still evident in public health policy and policy debates today (Nutbeam and Boxall 2008). While public health advocates continue to call for healthy public policy to address the social factors shaping health and health

From Health Behaviours to Health Practices: Critical Perspectives, First Edition. Edited by Simon Cohn. Chapters © 2014 The Authors. Book Compilation © 2014 Foundation for the Sociology of Health & Illness / Blackwell Publishing Ltd.

behaviour, governments and international agencies are still inclined to direct their policy actions at changing risky behaviour directly through social marketing and other means of exhorting individuals to change (Alvaro *et al.* 2011, Bryant *et al.* 2010, Glass and McAtee 2006).

This chapter examines why behavioural forms of health promotion are an inadequate strategy for addressing social inequities in health and are unlikely to resolve social differences in risky health behaviour. It then considers why, despite these inadequacies and increasing evidence on the social determinants of health (SDH), behavioural approaches may be appealing to governments and thus come to dominate health promotion policy. The chapter concludes with a discussion of health promotion strategies consistent with addressing the SDH and health inequities, and why these are more likely to improve population health and health behaviour.

Behavioural health promotion and its limitations in reducing inequities in health and health behaviour

Behavioural health-promotion strategies are typically aimed at addressing widely recognised behaviour known to increase health risks, including tobacco smoking, excessive use of alcohol, consuming a high-fat diet or being physically inactive (Davies and Macdowall 2006). A basic example is disseminating information about health and lifestyle risks or benefits associated with different behaviour, on the assumption that this will motivate individuals to modify their behaviour (Lefebvre and Flora 1988).

Behavioural approaches to health promotion have drawn on theories of behavioural change and health behaviour stemming from social psychology, such as social cognitive theory (Bandura 2004), the health belief model (Becker 1974), reasoned action and planned behaviour theory (Ajzen 1991) and social marketing (Egger *et al.* 1990). While some such theories do take account of the potential influence of wider social factors, the main focus has been on individual action and choice as the key mechanisms for improving health behaviour (Nutbeam and Harris 2004). The idea that providing knowledge of health risks and benefits to people will lead them to change their unhealthy behaviour has an inherently logical appeal, and certainly in some circumstances behavioural strategies can influence individual health behaviour, especially among those with a high socioeconomic status (SES) (for example, Montague *et al.* 2001, Powles and Gifford 1993). There are, however, a range of reasons why this approach will have only a limited effect on the health status of a population, and why the more unfavourable the social and economic conditions of a population group, the less effective behavioural change strategies are likely to be.

Contemporary behavioural-health promotion strategies fall into two broad types; those applied across a large population (universal), and those implemented in a local area or in an identified at-risk group (targeted). Universal strategies such as social marketing campaigns tend to work best with people who have access to a range of social and economic resources, and they are therefore more likely to decrease prevalence of risky behaviour in high SES groups (Slama 2010). They may also help to decrease the overall rate of a form of behaviour in a population, especially when used with a mix of complementary strategies and sustained over time (Gordon *et al.* 2006, Lefebvre and Flora 1988, Randolph and Viswanath 2004). However, there is also evidence that they tend to generate significantly less or little improvement with low SES or other disadvantaged groups (Alvaro *et al.* 2011, Layte and Whelan 2009, Lee *et al.* 1991). The overall effect, therefore, may be to entrench or exacerbate inequality in health behaviour and so in health outcomes, as has been found with a number of tobacco control campaigns (Baum 2007, Layte and Whelan 2009, Slama 2010). This is despite the fact that most tobacco control involves both behavioural strategies and restrictive policies and regulations.

A similar pattern of outcomes has been found in the strongly behaviourally oriented US Healthy People 2010 strategy. A US Health and Human Services (2005) mid-course review of the strategy notes that health performance targets had been less successful for a number of disadvantaged groups, including those with a low income or education, than for more advantaged groups (p. 8).

Several large-scale, targeted behaviour-change interventions of the 1970s and 1980s, which sought to address smoking and other health behaviour, also failed to produce sufficient evidence to support their value (Glass 2000, Syme 2004). Evidence showing the limitations or failure of behavioural health-promotion strategies appears to inform policy rarely. If it did, then it would follow that there would be much less tendency to adopt behavioural strategies (See also Baum 2008: 460–5, Egger *et al.* 1983).

Small-scale targeted strategies such as intensive behaviour-change interventions with highrisk individuals have produced some limited positive results (for example, Laatikainen *et al.* 2007). These trials require significant resources and may produce benefits for a small group, usually those with other aspects of their life are going well. However, this form of evidence is not helpful in terms of changing risk factors across a whole population because even a large change in such a small proportion of the population will not have any significant effect on overall population health (Chapman 1985, Rose 1992), and the intensive intervention methods required are not feasible on a large scale.

Behavioural health-promotion strategies tend to assume that people are blank sheets ready to be receptive to health promotion messages. The reality is that people's lives reflect a range of factors, including their current social and economic resources, and risk factors are accumulated over the life span, with negative conditions in early life being particularly damaging (Lantz *et al.* 2007, Lindsay 2010). This means that peoples' abilities both to respond to health promotion messages and improve their health and risk factor status as a result of the messages vary significantly, and the overall impact is likely to be greater in economically advantaged groups (Link and Phelan 2005).

This point is illustrated by the experience of Aboriginal people in Australia who as a group face overwhelming structural impediments to their ability to act on health promotion messages, including poverty, a low education, high rates of incarceration, sub-standard or crowded housing (Thomson *et al.* 2010), and racism (Ziersch *et al.* 2011). Thomas *et al.* (2008) report that Aboriginal people removed as children from their families under a previous government policy (Human Rights and Equal Opportunity Commission 1997) are twice as likely to be a current smoker as those who were not removed, indicating the powerful impact of social factors on health behaviour.

This example is consistent with evidence that exposure to psychosocial stressors can increase engagement in risky health behaviour as a form of seeking relief (Krueger and Chang 2008). These stressors often co-exist with a low SES and exposure to environments where risky health behaviour such as smoking are encouraged by social norms or corporate sales promotion (Smith *et al.* 2004). When people behave in ways that are not good for their health it is generally not because they are unaware of the risk but rather that the constraints of their life and accumulated dispositions over the life-course means they are unable or unwilling to change their behaviour (Anthony *et al.* 2004).

Bourdieu (1984) bridges the agency–structure divide with his theory that explains how individuals accumulate durable and transposable values and dispositions through socialisation and then adapt their ambitions and actions to the social circumstances and context of their lives. He maintains that values, beliefs and worldviews are created through the *habitus* (Bourdieu 1986), which reflects and helps to maintain class, gender or cultural position, and can be more or less supportive of health-promotion practices in everyday life. Bourdieu sees that economic capital is maintained and reproduced through cultural, social and symbolic capital and these capitals are crucial in determining opportunities to adopt healthy lifestyles over the life course.

What is the appeal of behavioural health promotion to governments and others?

Despite the limitations of behavioural health promotion, especially in relation to addressing inequities in health and health behaviour, it has come to dominate recent governments' health promotion policy in a number of Organisation for Economic Co-operation and Development countries including Canada (Bryant *et al*. 2010), the USA (Lantz, Lichtenstein, and Pollack 2007), the UK (Popay *et al*. 2010) and Australia (Baum 2011, Nutbeam and Boxall 2008).

In this section we suggest a variety of reasons why behavioural health promotion may be attractive to governments. Contemporary governments shape policies that privilege behavioural health promotion despite the considerable information available about SDH. Such information is evident in many background or policy papers on health promotion but is then often subject to lifestyle drift; namely a 'tendency for policy to start off recognising the need for action on upstream social determinants of health inequalities only to drift downstream to focus largely on individual lifestyle factors' (Popay *et al*. 2010: 148). Carter *et al*. studied the extent to which cancer control policies in six OECD countries incorporated information on SDH. They concluded that these documents 'foregrounded SDH as significant for cancer control in rhetoric but their recommendations for prevention centred almost entirely on generating individual behaviour change' (2009: 1454). We consider lifestyle drift as a by-product of the appeal of behavioural health promotion, particularly in relation to the several factors considered below.

Historical factors

The history of public health policy reviewed above that stresses the importance of improving living conditions in order to improve population health status (McKeown 1976) is usually overlooked in favour of accounts that stress medical and behavioural intervention, reflecting the power of medicine. Health education in high-income countries emerged in the early 20th century, firstly as part of efforts to control infectious diseases and later with a greater focus on chronic disease and the health behaviour which increased the risk of these conditions (Nutbeam 2000). The dominant public discourse that has since developed has portrayed chronic diseases as an outcome of poor individual 'lifestyle' choices, from which it is an easy step to see them as preventable through lifestyle changes encouraged by behavioural messages. Thus programmes of health promotion that directly target behaviour linked to chronic conditions have been normalised and easily gain public acceptance. Also, the previous limited successes of some behavioural health-promotion campaigns (albeit, often in combination with other strategies) may lead to assumptions that more of the same is all that is required (Alvaro *et al*. 2011, de Leeuw 1993).

Ideological factors

From the early 1980s the political character of several Western countries underwent a marked shift from welfare liberalism to a neoliberal stance in favour of reduced government intervention in markets, privatisation, the deregulation of labour markets and trade, and reduced welfare programmes. Underlying these policy stances is an ideology that regards free markets as self-regulating systems, and differences in individual attributes and choices as the primary determinants of variation in economic status (Harvey 2005). The individualism of neoliberal theory offers little space to support a view that health is primarily created by the structures which powerfully shape peoples' lives, including the dominant economic structure. Tesh (1988) has described how neoliberal individualism underpins public health policy in the USA. Similar tendencies are evident in Australia (Baum 2008) and Canada (Bryant *et al.* 2010).

A strong ethos of individualism is likely to lead to blaming the victim (Crawford 1977) and the treatment of social inequalities in health behaviour as merely the cumulative result of individual choice (Levinson 1998); so paving the way for policies that exhort individuals to change their behaviour. The dominant biomedical model of disease and treatment that drives most health policy also reinforces individualism and directs the bulk of resources to medical services and research (Lantz, Lichtenstein, and Pollack 2007). Such policies are likely to be more acceptable to political actors sympathetic to a neoliberal worldview because they define health in terms of individual biology and risky health behaviour as primarily a product of individual choice. Navarro argues that the implications of neoliberal politics for the health sector include:

> [T]he need to reduce public responsibility for the health of populations … [to increase] individuals' personal responsibility for health improvements … [and] an understanding of health promotion as behavioral change. (Navarro 2009: 425)

The fact that changes in health promotion policies have often accompanied changes in the political orientation of governments in countries such as the USA, the UK, Australia and Canada also reinforces the view that underlying political beliefs and values are exerting a significant influence on public health and health promotion policy (Baum 2008, Bryant *et al.* 2010, Nutbeam and Boxall 2008).

A further consideration is on the ways in which class and its underlying power are maintained. Bourdieu (1984) argues that this happens through both institutional structures of social and economic power and the subjective structuring of beliefs and dispositions in systems of classification that serve to define and promote the acceptance of social position. He suggests (1997) this process is most effective when the correspondence between the objective and subjective elements of power engenders a tacit or explicit belief among people that the social structure they inhabit is just the natural way of things; a taken-for-granted 'reality' which he describes as the doxa (Bourdieu 1997). Furthermore, he suggests, a crucial part of the effectiveness of this 'self-evident' reality lies in the fact that it can also, in effect, serve to maintain social silences about the perpetuation of power itself and about alternative ways of understanding the world (1997: 183–9).

From this perspective, the popular acceptance of individualised, biomedical or behavioural views of health and illness (Robert *et al.* 2008), and the ways these are institutionalised in health policies and systems, can be seen as elements of the dominant ideology of individualism in some high-income free market societies. Furthermore, individualised views of health may also, in effect, serve to protect certain power relations by helping to maintain a form of social silence around alternative views of health that challenge the normality of everyday social, economic and cultural inequalities in such societies; including the view that these inequalities cause and perpetuate inequities in health, and need not do so.

Practical factors
There is a strong inherent logic to behavioural change strategies. If the problem of smoking is seen as one of people choosing to smoke and obesity as one of people over-eating, then telling them not to do this seems to make sense. This is a powerful, simple logic for politicians and does not involve upsetting corporate donors to political parties (see below) or require legislative change that will inevitably attract complaints about a nanny state. It is also true that Rose's prevention paradox (1992) is somewhat counter-intuitive, as on face value, changing the behaviour of high-risk individuals appears as if it will change the health status of the population (Baum 2007). Rose (1985) points out that treating high-risk or diseased individuals does not have much impact on population health, but changing a risk factor across a whole population by just a small amount (which may be clinically insignificant at the individual level) can have a great impact on the overall incidence of a disease or problem. For example, reducing salt content in manufactured food by a small proportion (at a level individuals would not notice) would reduce blood pressure levels across the population and in time reduce death rates from cardiovascular disease (Cobiac *et al.* 2010). This latter option is politically more problematic for politicians as it involves regulating the behaviour of corporations.

It is also true that most other approaches to health promotion call for action across sectors to achieve health goals. However, without strong leadership from above, competition or ideological differences between departments can make these inter-sectoral approaches difficult to implement (Alvaro *et al.* 2011, de Leeuw 1993). It is also easier to establish evaluation mechanisms for behaviour change and time-limited interventions with easily measurable outputs. These fit more easily with demands for evidence-based policy than the use of legislation and long-term community development health promotion, which are harder to measure (Baum 2010, Kavanagh *et al.* 2002).

Policymakers are also likely to be influenced by public perceptions of factors influencing health; which appear to favour both individual behavioural choices and access to medical treatment (Robert *et al.* 2008).

Corporations and health promotion
The power of corporations in shaping population health and wellbeing has been receiving greater attention (Hastings 2012, Korten 2006) as shown by the role of big tobacco companies in resisting the attempts by governments or international agencies to restrict the supply of tobacco (Saloojee and Dagli 2000, Ullrich *et al.* 2004). The industry's strategy was to portray smoking as a purely individual choice and so downplay the impact of their advertising and encourage governments to adopt behavioural change strategies, placing the onus on individuals rather than industry. Similarly, while it is extremely unlikely that the recent rise in overweight and obesity is merely a result of a spontaneous change in eating habits, a surprisingly large number of policy responses promote individual behaviour change in eating and exercise habits. Such a response does not challenge the practices of multinational food corporations who make large profits from the sale of cheap, easily available high-fat and sugar content food (Egger and Swinburn 2010). Hawkes *et al.* (2009) have shown that the rapid increase in international trade has influenced a change in dietary patterns in India and the Pacific Islands from local, 'healthy' diets to the consumption of fattier diets. Corporations make large donations to political parties around the world (Saloojee and Dagli 2000) and can be expected to influence national health policies to shift attention away from the influence of food supply and marketing to that of consumption. There is increasing evidence that corporations invest directly in research and lobbying to persuade government and international organisations to adopt policies that do not threaten their interests. Ullrich

et al. (2004) note that when the 2004 WHO resolution on diet, physical activity and health was being formulated, the food industry lobbied heavily to water down recommendations on maximum levels of dietary sugar and on the contribution of soft drinks to the obesity epidemic. They also noted that:

> [S]everal countries wanted to see the Global Strategy paying more attention to the roles of individuals in determining their lifestyle, and criticised the approach of seeking environmental changes as a key role for governments. (Ullrich *et al.* 2004: 254)

As Egger and Swinburn (2010: 8) note of the corporate food interests:

> there is little doubt that ... it is in the best interests of governments ... as well as big business ... for individuals to see obesity as merely the product of sloth and gluttony, and hence as solely an individual responsibility.

This representation of individual responsibility is an example of the exertion of power through Bourdieu's social silences that we discussed earlier. It illustrates the political advantages involved in not talking about health in a structural way, because to do so presents a critical, de-normalising perspective on the socioeconomic status quo and on the actions of some powerful corporations (Hastings 2012).

Conclusions: implications for policy

WHO has produced a succession of initiatives leading up to the CSDH which emphasise the important of SDH, including the Alma Ata Declaration on Primary Health Care (WHO 1978) and the Ottawa Charter for Health Promotion (WHO 1986), leading to a settings approach to health promotion, including 'Healthy Cities' (WHO 1996). The SDH approach recognises that individual and population health outcomes are affected not only by behavioural and biological factors but by the environmental, social, cultural, economic and political settings in which people live (Baum 2008, Kickbusch 2009). There are central lessons that emerge from the accumulated WHO work to guide action to address the SDH and health behaviour.

Firstly, it is important for jurisdictions to adopt broad-based measures to improve overall population health within a 'healthy public policy' (International Union for Health Promotion and Education 2007: 200) or a 'health in all policies' framework (Kickbusch 2009: 1), where the health impact of each sector is considered and measures taken to minimise adverse effects and promote positive health benefits. There is also increasing evidence supporting the use of universal regulatory, taxation or planning measures to address structural factors influencing the prevalence of risky health behaviour or the degree of risk involved, including price incentives, controls on advertising or sales or regulation of food standards; for example, in relation to alcohol use (Cobiac *et al.* 2009), physical exercise (Giles-Corti and Donovan 2002, MacDougall 2007), smoking (Levy *et al.* 2004) and salt intake (Cobiac, Vos, and Veerman 2010).

Such risk factor-specific initiatives need to be underpinned by measures that tackle the root causes of inequities. Three are vital: firstly, broad-based strategies to reduce socioeconomic disadvantage and introduce redistributive mechanisms in education, housing, employment and income and wealth; secondly, targeted interventions to address proximal structural factors disproportionately affecting disadvantaged groups – for example in Australia, the exploitative sale of alcohol in some Aboriginal communities; and thirdly, sustained community development strategies in disadvantaged areas to alleviate the effects of exposure to SDH and build local capabilities for wellbeing (Labonté et al. 2008, Tesoriero 2010).

These measures would also improve health for those often regarded as being hard to reach (Lefebvre 1992). In looking at overall population health gains achieved in different countries, Navarro has shown that socially and economically redistributive policies and full employment policies have led to greater health gains (Navarro and Shi 2001). An analysis by Lundberg et al. (2008) concluded that the universal nature of Nordic welfare systems had improved population health. Yet support for such welfare regimes has been under intensive attack since the days of Reagan in the USA and Thatcher in the UK, acting on the neoliberal principle of a smaller, non-interventionist government. The global financial crisis is now seeing such arguments intensify in Europe and the USA, where there is growing pressure to cut social spending despite the arguments by some economists for a return to expansionary growth budgets. Marmot (2012) notes, however, that the economic argument is always about a return to economic growth and not about the welfare of the population as the outcome measure. He points to the report of the Commission on the Measurement of Economic Performance and Social Progress (Stiglitz et al. 2009) that argues for broader measures of social and economic progress than simply gross domestic product. Gaining commitment to action on SDH to reduce health inequities will require the use of such social measures of progress (Baum and Fisher 2010, Hamilton and Saddler 1997, New Economics Foundation 2010) and the political will to drive policies that are based on achieving these measures. Evidence and arguments of the limits to growth, sustainability and climate change must also figure in how progress in society is defined and measured (Jackson 2009).

We have shown that there are strong incentives for governments to base their health-promotion policies on behaviourism. Yet the accumulating evidence on SDH is very clear that achieving health equity will require policies that change the conditions in which people make their unhealthy choices. Our review also indicates that ideology is a powerful driver of policy and political actors with a strong commitment to neoliberalism and individualism are very likely to be to drawn to behavioural solutions and to use power over the representation of social issues to maintain this stance. Evidence is not likely to change the ideology of these actors. While we acknowledge that evidence is a crucial part of the public health jigsaw, perhaps too little attention has been paid by public health actors to the importance of ideology in their efforts to translate evidence on the SDH into practical policy. The progressive 19th century public health activists were well aware that challenging the idea that the poor health of poor people resulted from their behaviour required direct attention to political will – Virchow became a politician and Engels co-authored The Communist Manifesto with Karl Marx. Political will, in significant part, draws on popular support and we conclude that public health researchers should pay more attention to ways of discussing their research evidence with people at the grassroots. As economic and health inequities grow, people's movements around the world are questioning the economic structures that have given rise to them. The People's Health Movement, for example, has adopted a People's Health Charter (2000) which explicitly challenges existing power structures and the ideology of individualism and argues that achieving health equity will require a redistribution of power and resources and the adoption of structural reforms. It sees itself as speaking truth to power and opening up areas of social silence to critical examination. Public health, then, has a clear role to highlight the lack of evidence for much behavioural health promotion and promote the evidence that supports the value of action on the social and economic determinants of health in order to force the hand of governments to adopt effective means of promoting health equity.

Acknowledgement

Fran Baum's time was supported by an Australian Research Council Federation Fellowship.

References

Ajzen, I. (1991) The theory of planned behaviour, *Organizational Behaviour and Human Decision Processes*, 50, 2, 179–211.

Alvaro, C., Jackson, L.A., Kirk, S., McHugh, T.L., *et al.* (2011) Moving governmental policies beyond a focus on individual lifestyle: some insights from complexity and critical theories, *Health Promotion International*, 26, 1, 91–9.

Anthony, A.C., Gatrell, C., Popay, J. and Thomas, C. (2004) Mapping the determinants of health inequalities in social space: can Bourdieu help us?, *Health and Place*, 10, 3, 203–91.

Bandura, A. (2004) Health promotion by social cognitive means, *Health Education and Behaviour*, 31, 2, 143–64.

Banks, J., Marmot, M., Oldfield, Z. and Smith, J.P. (2006) Disease and disadvantage in the United States and in England, *JAMA*, 295, 17, 2037–45.

Baum, F. (2007) Cracking the nut of health equity: Top down and bottom up pressure for action on the social determinants of health, *Promotion and Education*, 14, 2, 90.

Baum, F. (2008) *The New Public Health*. Melbourne: Oxford University Press.

Baum, F. (2010) Overcoming barriers to improved research on the social determinants of health, *MEDICC Review*, 12, 3, 36–8.

Baum, F. (2011) From Norm to Eric: Avoiding lifestyle drift in Australian health policy (editorial), *Australian and New Zealand Journal of Public Health*, 35, 5, 404–6.

Baum, F. and Fisher, M. (2010) Health equity and sustainability: extending the work of the Commission on the Social Determinants of Health, *Critical Public Health*, 20, 3, 311–22.

Becker, M.H. (1974) The health belief model and personal health behaviour, *Education Monographs*, 2, 4, 324–508.

Bourdieu, P. (1984) *Distinction: A Social Critique of the Judgement of Taste*. London: Routledge.

Bourdieu, P. (1986) The forms of capital. In Richardson, J. (ed.) *Handbook of Theory and Research for Sociology of Education*. New York: Greenwood Press.

Bourdieu, P. (1997) *Outline of a Theory of Practice*. Cambridge: Cambridge University Press.

Bryant, T., Raphael, D., Schrecker, T. and Labonté, R. (2010) Canada: a land of missed opportunity for addressing the social determinants of health, *Health Policy*, 101, 1, 44–58.

Carter, S.M., Hooker, L.C. and Davey, H.M. (2009) Writing social determinants into and out of cancer control: an assessment of policy practice, *Social Science & Medicine*, 68, 8, 1448–55.

Chapman, S. (1985) Stop smoking clinics: a case for their abandonment, *Lancet*, 1, 8434, 918–20.

Cobiac, L.J., Vos, T., Doran, C. and Wallace, A. (2009) Cost-effectiveness of interventions to prevent alcohol-related disease and injury in Australia, *Addiction*, 104, 10, 1646–55.

Cobiac, L.J., Vos, T. and Veerman, J.L. (2010) Cost-effectiveness of interventions to reduce dietary salt intake, *Heart*, 96, 23, 1920–5.

Commission on the Social Determinants of Health (2008) *Closing the Gap in a Generation: Health Equity through Action on the Social Determinants of Health*. Geneva: World Health Organization.

Crawford, R. (1977) You are dangerous to your health: the ideology and politics of victim blaming, *International Journal of Health Services*, 7, 4, 663–80.

Crombie, I.K., Irvine, L., Elliot, L. and Wallace, H. (2005) *Closing the Health Inequalities Gap: an International Perspective*. Copenhagen: WHO Regional Office for Europe.

Davies, M. and Macdowall, W. (eds) (2006) *Health Promotion Theory*. Maidenhead: Open University Press.

de Leeuw, E. (1993) Health policy, epidemiology and power: the interest web, *Health Promotion International*, 8, 1, 49–52.

Draper, G., Turrell, G. and Oldenburg, B. (2004) *Health Inequalities in Australia: Mortality. Health Inequalities Monitoring Series No. 1*. Canberra: Queensland University of Technology, Australian Institute of Health and Welfare.

Egger, G. and Swinburn, B. (2010) *Planet Obesity*. Sydney: Allen and Unwin.

Egger, G., Fitzgerald, W., Frape, G., Monaem, A., *et al.* (1983) Results of large scale media antismoking campaign in Australia: North Coast 'Quit for Life' programme, *BMJ*, 287, 6399, 1125–28.

Egger, G., Spark, R. and Donovan, R.J. (1990) *Health Promotion Strategies and Methods*. Sydney: McGraw-Hill.

Giles-Corti, B. and Donovan, R.J. (2002) The relative influence of individual, social and physical environment determinants of physical activity, *Social Science & Medicine*, 54, 12, 1793–812.

Glass, T.A. (2000) Psychosocial interventions. In Berkman, L.F. and Kawachi, I. (eds) *Social Epidemiology*. New York: Oxford University Press.

Glass, T.A. and McAtee, M.J. (2006) Behavioural science at the crossroads in public health: extending horizons, envisioning the future, *Social Science & Medicine*, 62, 7, 1650–71.

Gordon, R., McDermott, L., Stead, M. and Angus, K. (2006) The effectiveness of social marketing interventions for health improvement: what's the evidence?, *Public Health*, 120, 12, 1133–9.

Hamilton, C. and Saddler, H. (1997) The genuine progress indicator: a new index of changes in well-being in Australia. *Discussion Papers*. Canberra: The Australia Institute.

Harvey, D. (2005) *A Brief History of Neoliberalism*. New York: Oxford University Press.

Hastings, G. (2012) Why corporate power is a public health priority, *BMJ*, 345, e5124. doi:10.1136/bmj.e5124.

Hawkes, C., Chopra, M. and Friel, S. (2009) Globalization, trade, and the nutrition transition. In Labonté, R., Schrecker, T., Packer, C. and Runnels, V. (eds) *Globalization and Health: Pathways, Evidence and Policy*. New York: Routledge.

Human Rights and Equal Opportunity Commission (1997) *Report of the National Inquiry into the Separation of Aboriginal and Torres Strait Islander Children from Their Families*. Sydney: Commonwealth of Australia.

International Union for Health Promotion and Education (2007) Shaping the future of health promotion: priorities for action, *Promotion and Education*, 14, 4, 199–202.

Jackson, T. (2009) *Prosperity Without Growth: Economics for a Finite Planet*. London: Earthscan.

Kavanagh, A., Daly, J. and Jolley, D. (2002) Research methods, evidence and public health, *Australian and New Zealand Journal of Public Health*, 26, 4, 337–42.

Kickbusch, I. (ed.) (2009) *Policy Innovation for Health*. New York: Springer.

Korten, D. (2006) *The Great Turning. From Empire to Earth Community*. San Francisco: BerrettKoehler.

Kroll, L.E. and Lampert, T. (2011) Changing health inequalities in Germany from 1994 to 2008 between employed and unemployed adults, *International Journal of Public Health*, 56, 3, 329–39.

Krueger, P.M. and Chang, V.W. (2008) Being poor and coping with stress: health behaviors and the risk of death, *American Journal of Public Health*, 98, 5, 889–96.

Laatikainen, T., Dunbar, J.A., Chapman, A., Kilkkinen, A., *et al.* (2007) Prevention of type 2 diabetes by lifestyle intervention in an Australian primary health care setting, *BMC Public Health*, 7, doi:10.1186/1471-2458-7-249.

Labonté, R., Blouin, C., Chopra, M., Lee, K., *et al.* (2007) *Towards Health-Equitable Globalisation: Rights, Regulation and Redistribution*. Geneva: Commission on the Social Determinants of Health.

Labonté, R., Sanders, D., Baum, F., Schaay, N., *et al.* (2008) Implementation, effectiveness and political context of comprehensive primary health care: preliminary findings of a global literature review, *Australian Journal of Primary Health*, 14, 3, 58–67.

Lantz, P.M., Lichtenstein, R.L. and Pollack, H.A. (2007) Health policy approaches to population health: the limits of medicalization, *Health Affairs*, 26, 5, 1253–7.

Layte, R. and Whelan, C.T. (2009) Explaining social class inequalities in smoking: the role of education, self-efficacy, and deprivation, *European Sociological Review*, 25, 4, 399–410.

Lee, A.J., Crombie, I.K., Smith, W. and Tunstall, H.D. (1991) Cigarette smoking and employment status, *Social Science & Medicine*, 33, 11, 1309–12.

Lefebvre, R. (1992) The social marketing imbroglio in health promotion, *Health Promotion International*, 7, 1, 61–4.

Lefebvre, R. and Flora, J. (1988) Social marketing and public health interventions, *Health Education Quarterly*, 15, 3, 299–315.

Levinson, R. (1998) Issues at the interface of medical sociology and public health. In Scambler, G. and Higgs, P. (eds) *(eds) Modernity, Medicine, and Health: Medical Sociology Towards 2000*. London: Routledge.

Levy, D.T., Chaloupka, F. and Gitchell, J. (2004) The effects of tobacco control policies on smoking rates: A Tobacco Control Scorecard, *Journal of Public Health Management and Practice*, 10, 4, 338–53.

Lindsay, J. (2010) Healthy living guidelines and the disconnect with everyday life, *Critical Public Health*, 20, 4, 475–87.

Link, B.G. and Phelan, J.C. (2005) Fundamental sources of health inequalities. In Mechanic, D., Rogut, L., Colby, D. and Knickman, J. (eds) *Policy Challenges in Modern Health Care*. Chapel Hill: Ruthers University Press.

Lundberg, O., Yngwe, M., Stjarne, M., Elstad, J., *et al.* (2008) The role of welfare state principles and generosity in social policy programmes for public health: an international comparative study, *Lancet*, 372, 9650, 1633–40.

MacDougall, C. (2007) Reframing physical activity. In Keleher, H., MacDougall, C. and Murphy, B. (eds) *Understanding Health Promotion*. Melbourne: Oxford University Press.

McKeown, T. (1976) *The Role of Medicine: Dream, Mirage or Nemesis*. London: Nuffield Provincial Hospital Trust.

Mackenbach, J.P. (2005) *Health Inequalities: Europe in Profile*. Rotterdam: European Commission.

Marmot, M. (2012) Policy making with health equity at its heart, *JAMA*, 307, 19, 2033–4.

Montague, M., Borland, R. and Sinclair, C. (2001) Slip! Slop! Slap! And SunSmart, 1980–2000: Skin cancer control and 20 years of population-based campaigning, *Health Education and Behaviour*, 28, 3, 290–305.

Navarro, V. (2009) What we mean by social determinants of health, *International Journal of Health Services*, 39, 3, 423–41.

Navarro, V. and Shi, L. (2001) The political context of social inequalities and health, *Social Science & Medicine*, 52, 481–91.

New Economics Foundation (2010) *Happy Planet Index*. Available at http://www.happyplanetindex. org/ (accessed 10 February 2010).

Nutbeam, D. (2000) Health literacy as a public health goal: a challenge for contemporary health education and communication strategies into the 21st century, *Health Promotion International*, 15, 3, 259–67.

Nutbeam, D. and Boxall, A.M. (2008) What influences the transfer of research into health policy and practice? Observations from England and Australia, *Public Health*, 122, 8, 747–53.

Nutbeam, D. and Harris, E. (2004) *Theory in a Nutshell: a Guide to Health Promotion Theory*. Sydney: McGraw-Hill.

People's Health Movement (2000) *The People's Charter for Health*. Available at http://www.phmovement.org/ (accessed 8 February 2013).

Popay, J., Whitehead, M. and Hunter, D.J. (2010) Injustice is killing people on a large scale – but what is to be done about it?, *Journal of Public Health*, 32, 2, 148–9.

Porter, D. (1999) *Health, Civilization and the State: a History of Public Health from Ancient to Modern Times*. London: Routledge.

Powles, J. and Gifford, S. (1993) Health of nations: Lessons from Victoria, Australia, *BMJ*, 306, 6399, 125–7.

Randolph, W. and Viswanath, K. (2004) Lessons learned from public health mass media campaigns: marketing health in a crowded media world, *Annual Review of Public Health*, 25, 419–37.

Robert, S.A., Booske, B.C., Rigby, E. and Rohan, A.M. (2008) Public views on determinants of health, interventions to improve health, and priorities of government, *Wisconsin Medical Journal*, 107, 1, 16–22.

Rose, G. (1985) Sick individuals and sick populations, *International Journal of Epidemiology*, 14, 1, 32–8.

Rose, G. (1992) *The Strategy of Preventive Medicine*. Oxford: Oxford University Press.

Saloojee, Y. and Dagli, E. (2000) Tobacco industry tactics for resisting public policy on health, *Bulletin of the World Health Organization*, 78, 7, 902–10.

Sanders, D., Todd, C. and Chopra, M. (2005) Confronting Africa's health crisis: more of the same will not be enough, *BMJ*, 331, doi: http://dx.doi.org/10.1136/bmj.331.7519.755.

Slama, K. (2010) Tobacco control and health equality, *Global Health Promotion*, 13, 1, 3–6.

Smith, T.W., Orleans, C.T. and Jenkins, C.D. (2004) Prevention and health promotion: decades of progress, new challenges, and an emerging agenda, *Health Psychology*, 23, 2, 126–31.

Stamatakis, E., Wardle, J. and Cole, T.J. (2010) Childhood obesity and overweight prevalence trends in England: evidence for growing socioeconomic disparities, *International Journal of Obesity*, 34, 1, 41–7.

Stiglitz, J.E., Sen, A. and Fitoussi, J. (2009) *Report by the Commission on the Measurement of Economic Performance and Social Progress*. Paris: CMEPSP.

Syme, S.L. (2004) Social determinants of health: the community as an empowered partner. *Preventing Chronic Disease*. Available from http://www.cdc.gov/pcd/issues/2004/ (accessed 26 October 2013).

Tesh, S. (1988) *Hidden Arguments: Political Ideology and Disease Prevention Policy*. New Brunswick: Rutgers University Press.

Tesoriero, F. (2010) *Community Development: Community-based Alternatives in an Age of Globalisation*. Sydney: Pearson Education.

Thomas, D.P., Briggs, V., Anderson, I.P. and Cunningham, J. (2008) The social determinants of being an Indigenous non-smoker, *Australian and New Zealand Journal of Public Health*, 32, 3, 110–6.

Thomson, N., MacRae, A., Burns, J. and Catto, M. *et al.* (2010) *Overview of Australian Indigenous health status*. Perth: Australian Indigenous HealthInfoNet. Available at http://www.healthinfonet.ecu.edu.au/health-facts/overviews (accessed 16 February 2011).

Turrell, G., Stanley, L., de Looper, M. and Oldenburg, B. (2006) *Health Inequalities in Australia: Morbidity, Health Behaviours, Risk Factors and Health Service Use*. Canberra: Australian Institute of Health and Welfare.

US Department of Health, Education and Welfare (1979) *Healthy People: the Surgeon General's Report on Health Promotion and Disease Prevention*. Washington: US Government Printing Office.

US Department of Health and Human Services (2005) *Healthy People 2010 Midcourse Review: Executive Summary*. Washington: USDHHS.

Ullrich, A., Waxman, A., Luiza da Costa e Silva, V. and Bettcher, D. *et al.* (2004) Cancer prevention in the political arena: the WHO perspective, *Annals of Oncology*, 15, 4, iv249–56.

Williams, J. (2004) *50 Facts that Should Change the World*. Cambridge: Icon Books.

World Health Organization (WHO) (1978) Declaration of Alma Ata. International Conference on Primary Health Care. 6–12 September. Available at www.who.int/publications/almaata_declaration_en.pdf (accessed 25 October 2013).

WHO (1986) Ottawa Charter for Health Promotion. *Health Promotion*, 1, 4, i–v.

WHO (1996) *Creating Healthy Cities in the 21st Century*. Geneva: WHO.

Ziersch, A., Gallaher, G., Baum, F. and Bentley, M. (2011) Racism, social resources and mental health for Aboriginal people living in Adelaide, *Australian and New Zealand Journal of Public Health*, 35, 3, 231–7.

7

Behaviour change and social blinkers? The role of sociology in trials of self-management behaviour in chronic conditions

Bie Nio Ong, Anne Rogers, Anne Kennedy, Peter Bower, Tom Sanders, Andrew Morden, Sudeh Cheraghi-Sohi, Jane C. Richardson and Fiona Stevenson

Introduction

Individual-focused self-management interventions have been one response to an ageing society and purported increase in chronic conditions in most western countries. In the UK health policy documents appear to promote self-management approaches that are underpinned by behavioural change theories, for example, in the expert patient programme (EPP) that has been adapted from the USA model (Lorig *et al.* 1993, 1999). While advances have been made in behaviour change theory and practice, the question of social context remains under-theorised and under-explored empirically. This is particularly the case in trials of self-management, which have tended to focus solely on the individual and individual attributes that require modification.

In this chapter we argue for modifications to both trial design and interventions to change behaviour that make constructive use of the concept of social context. We start by outlining the policy drivers for self-management approaches, followed by discussing some behaviour change models underpinning self-management approaches that inform current UK health policy, and examine their implications for change in patients and healthcare professionals. This is followed by a discussion of the use of trials to amass evidence about the effectiveness of interventions. To conclude, two examples of theory-based self-management trials for chronic conditions are presented. These highlight the complex nature of self-management and the necessity of better integrating the social into behaviour change models.

Health policy and self-management

Since the late 1990s successive governments in the UK and elsewhere have promoted self-management. The Labour Government (1997–2010) embarked on a wide-ranging reform of the English National Health Service (NHS). Moreover, it endorsed upstream changes promulgated in the Wanless report (2002: 9) which defined 'the fully-engaged scenario' whereby

From Health Behaviours to Health Practices: Critical Perspectives, First Edition. Edited by Simon Cohn. Chapters © 2014 The Authors. Book Compilation © 2014 Foundation for the Sociology of Health & Illness / Blackwell Publishing Ltd.

the state and citizens share responsibility for health and wellbeing. This translated into the government's leitmotiv of fostering greater patient choice and involvement in decision-making. The patient was placed at the centre of health care within a system that was a quasi-consumer resource for patients to manage their own health (Department of Health 2000).

The first outline of the new way of managing long-term conditions appeared in a keynote report: 'The expert patient: a new approach to chronic disease management for the 21st century' (Department of Health 2001). It argued that patient knowledge and experience was an underused asset and made the case for an approach that promoted engagement with patient's psychological needs and social context (Department of Health 2001). One key route to ensuring the optimised self-management of chronic conditions was the EPP. The EPP was deemed an essential tool for empowering patients to have the motivation and self-efficacy to manage their condition effectively, and to enhance their ability to engage with professionals and reclaim control their lives (Department of Health 2001, Donaldson 2003). However, the endorsement given to the EPP and embedding patient-centred self-management in primary care was also driven by an economic rationale. The EPP was heralded as a way to reduce the economic burden associated with chronic illness and the financial pressures on the NHS and the welfare state (Department of Health 2001, 2005, Donaldson 2003). There was little underlying these general aspirations that specified the mechanisms of behavioural change: instead there was a reliance on idealised identities which were presumed to emerge:

> [W]hilst previous policies focused on what patients should do to maintain their health, the new policy approach to self-management is focused on what sort of person the patient should become … There has been a proliferation of terms representing an idealized self-managing individual ('empowered', 'autonomous', 'future', 'expert', 'activated', 'wireless', 'co-producer' or 'flat pack patient'). The ideal type notion of patienthood demands the capacity of being confident, in control, able to monitor and manage a condition, engage with technological innovations, whilst at the same time allowing constraints on the demands made on services. (Rogers 2009: 173)

In 2010 the Conservative–Liberal coalition government set in motion a radical reform of the NHS in England that destabilised the infrastructure of the NHS against the backdrop of financial austerity and reductions in public sector funding (Timmins 2012). Despite a reduced emphasis on EPP, the drive to increase self-management remains central to health policy. This is reflected in the new NHS outcomes framework 2012–2013 (Department of Health 2011) that defines five domains, the second of which being entitled 'enhancing quality of life for people with long-term conditions'. The first improvement area is described as: ensuring people feel supported to manage their condition. Thus, self-management remains at the top of the health agenda.

Individual behaviour change models in self-management interventions

Behaviour change is clearly a key issue for psychology. The role of the social has, however, changed over time. Lewin coined the equation $B = f(P,E)$, to encapsulate the notion that behaviour is a function of the person (P) and their environment (E), and early debates in the discipline concerned the relative priority of P and E as determinants of behaviour. The influence of the social has waxed and waned in psychological models, with behaviourist models contending that the environment was a necessary and potentially sufficient explanation for behaviour (Davison 2007). The rise of cognitive approaches to understanding behaviour and emotion have increasingly focused interest and behaviour change technologies on the intrapsychic processes of belief and attitude formation, cognitive styles and mental models. Such approaches have a relatively dominant position in current guidance around certain aspects of behaviour change (British Psychological Society 2008).

A large number of psychological models of behaviour change exist which differ in their exact formulation. The commonsense illness model (McAndrew *et al.* 2008) and the transtheoretical stages of change (Prochaska *et al.* 1992) have unique features, but many of these models have significant similarities, for example, the theory of planned behaviour (Conner and Norman 2005, Conner and Sparks 1996) and the health belief model (Schwarzer and Fuchs 1996). These postulate a basic set of social-cognitive variables that may account for most of the variance in behavioural outcomes (Fishbein *et al.* 2001):

- Environmental constraints that impact on the ability to carry out the behaviour
- Intention to conduct the behaviour and an evaluation of the skills that are required to carry out the behaviour.

Other concepts that may have either a direct impact on behaviour or indirect impact through intention are:

- Self-discrepancy (gap between internalized representations of the self)
- Emotional reactions such as fear, anxiety, stress, dissatisfaction or guilt.

Based on a detailed review of behaviour change interventions Michie *et al.* (2011) developed an integrated model, entitled the behaviour change wheel, which characterises interventions and policies to change behaviour. It places individual behaviour at the centre, encircled by intervention functions and policy categories that include a number of social and contextual issues. Environmental constraints are seen as a key determinant that may act directly on the likelihood of a type of behaviour occurring, while social psychological processes can impact on the formation of intention to change through social pressures and perception of the social norms surrounding activities. Although this model acknowledges the social, it is fundamentally built upon notions of self-efficacy and the technologies adopted remain individually focused.

Behaviour change in self-management interventions is frequently viewed as mediated through increases in the psychological attribute of self-efficacy (Bandura, 1977). Self-management technologies, which present the processes of change in terms of modelling persuasive communication by health professionals and the reinterpretation of physiological symptoms (Barlow *et al.* 2000) tend to propose standardised ways of responding to patients and clients. Consequently, interventions are designed to move an individual from one stage to the next, even in the face of the observation that where change does occur it does not necessarily follow the theoretical stages of change incorporated into models of health behaviour (O'Connor *et al.* 1997). This view of cognitive processes and stages of change and outcome measures may detract from a focus that views change in relation to the complexities of patients' existing ways of behaving and responding to chronic illness. Detailed examination of existing behaviour and activities in context are more usually ignored or viewed as maladaptive, requiring reform. The latter is evident in the normative assumptions underlying theories of planned action about the desirability of changing one form of behaviour for another. While such assumptions may be appropriate in behaviour such as smoking, arguably this is less applicable to chronic illness self-management, given the variety of strategies adopted in coping with illness.

Prioritising a focus on beliefs rather than practices in self-management is problematic for three reasons. Firstly, it tends to exclude a fine-grained view of patient agendas and potentially fails to engage with those from marginalised groups. Moreover, explanations about the causes of the problems may not relate primarily to behavioural explanations, but rather to structural issues (for example, Hodgins *et al.* 2006). Secondly, theories predicated on changing beliefs are not designed to evaluate the everyday components of patient practices and strategies in the broader social context (Balfe 2007, Seear 2009). Thirdly, identifying the points of intervention most likely to change behaviour in causal modelling may not be as relevant as the priorities that individuals hold about managing a chronic condition. For example, symptom management may not be as important to maintain as preserving valued social roles, coherent identities and a normal life (Morden *et al.* 2011, Townsend *et al.* 2006).

Behaviour change interventions and health professionals

Health professionals are expected to promote and support self-management. It is therefore equally important when considering the promotion of behaviour change interventions in health settings to take account of how they respond to a change in their own role and its potential effects on their relationships with patients. The assumption underlying self-management is that health professionals adopt a patient-centred approach, tailor their support to individual patients and relinquish a degree of power. This requires behaviour change in professionals. A growing body of literature covers this issue and we draw on the concepts most relevant to this chapter.

Interventions aimed at changing the behaviour of clinicians have had limited success (Post *et al.* 2009, Vollmar *et al.* 2010). There is an assumption that rationalistic approaches to behaviour change, such as encouraging uptake of clinical guidelines, are self-evidently adopted in practice (Sackett *et al.* 2000). Yet it is clear that this view does not reflect the everyday work of clinicians, who may prefer to manage patients in accordance with established clinical routines. Checkland *et al.* (2007), following Weick (1995), claim that health professionals engage in sense-making to assign meaning to their role and changes to the content of work, both of which involve an evaluation of the impact of change on tasks and relationships. Armstrong and Ogden (2006) reported that general practitioners (GPs) engaged in experimentation to try out new medications and their impact on routines before introducing alterations to their work. Looked at in this way, innovations that 'make sense' are more likely to succeed by virtue of their positive impact on clinical routines. The introduction of new innovations in health care may also demand a proactive response so that professionals engage in what might be called transition work. Consequently, health professionals may need to become convinced of the benefits of a new approach, in terms of what is 'practical' or 'relevant', and what may be professionally desirable.

The implementation literature suggests that coercive drivers alone, such as indicators in the NHS outcomes framework, are unlikely to be successful in bringing about change (Baus 2004). Addressing the different layers of implementation at the level of health professionals is needed to understand its complexity. However, tensions may arise between the different components of change. Wider policy promoting self-management and behaviour change technologies may conflict with the priority to maintain the self–other relationship between clinicians and patients (Blakeman *et al.* 2010). The alignment of self-management interventions with local or personal priorities is central to their adoption. To further complicate matters, professionals may not simply apply abstract evidence to their own context, but engage in the active interpretation and reconstruction of its local validity and usefulness (Lave and Wenger 1991, Wood *et al*. 1999). Thus, translation involves testing out a new approach in daily practice (Armstrong and Ogden 2006, Berg 1999, Doolan *et al*. 2003).

Trials of behaviour change interventions

Current policy has influenced the growing interest in implementation and why interventions work, and evidence from the trials literature has figured prominently. A UK trial of the EPP, a programme designed to improve self-efficacy for self-management, revealed that the EPP produced modest effects on self-efficacy and did not result in reduced healthcare utilisation (Kennedy *et al*. 2007). Suggested reasons for this centred on the idea that people's expectations and problems were not adequately dealt with by the course because the self-management skills training prioritised improvements in self-efficacy and did not engage with patients' material and social needs (Rogers *et al*. 2008). In other words, changing behaviour may not be a priority for the individuals being targeted.

The effects of trials of self-management in musculoskeletal pain have been assessed in a systematic review (Miles *et al*. 2011), but behaviour change in both patients and professionals has not previously been addressed systematically. In the two examples below we discuss a range of issues relating to these processes. Firstly, we highlight a few concerns, relevant to these case examples, about the appropriateness of the trial design to test self-management interventions.

The traditional randomised controlled trial (RCT) aims to measure the clinical effectiveness of a trial intervention rather than the real-world change and impact once an intervention is rolled out. Yet what works under ideal trial conditions may have less than the desired effect when implemented in routine practice. Such limitations have precipitated the move towards pragmatic trials that assess the benefit of the intervention in an everyday context (Roland and Torgerson 1998). Moreover, assessing behaviour change is a complex and multifaceted phenomenon with multiple levels of influences (Miles *et al*. 2011). While RCTs are often adopted in this field, they present an important limitation in that they rely on a positivist worldview. This assumption of a closed system ignores field effects, such as the complex political, social and economic currents that permeate the social world (Burawoy 1998) which is an open system; fluid, interactive and with permeable boundaries. As a consequence, RCTs can tell us which interventions are most successful or not under controlled circumstances but they cannot, on their own, tell us why or how success or failure has occurred and what role social context has played in achieving particular results.

Qualitative research has been used to address the contextual and sense-making issues in RCTs. While qualitative methods are not synonymous with a sociological approach the role that can be played by both in the context of RCTs is similar. Lewin *et al*. (2009) outline the three areas in which qualitative methods can be used alongside RCTs: before (to generate hypotheses, to develop interventions and outcome measures); during (to explore the delivery of and responses to the intervention, to explore processes of change) and after (to explore reasons for findings, including variations in effectiveness, to examine the appropriateness of the underlying theory or to generate further hypotheses). Despite the wide range of possibilities for the use of qualitative methods alongside trials, the largest group of studies identified by Lewin *et al*. was the studies carried out before trials. These, and studies carried out alongside or after a trial, reported little integration of findings and suffered from poor reporting of methods. In the examples below we aim to show how researchers from different disciplines have worked together successfully at all stages of a trial in order to fully explore the social context of behaviour change.

Example 1   *The whole system informing self-management engagement (WISE) patient normalisation: self-management interventions and assumptions about change in complex interventions*

WISE is a conceptual model that is used to guide a portfolio of studies on complex interventions in the area of self-management for chronic conditions. The WISE approach set out to work with a view of the everyday, relational and embodied ways that patients can and do behave. People are viewed as having the capacity to creatively reformulate practices that meet local situations and the individual's own situation. It incorporates a focus on three domains relevant to integrating self-management within a broad environment:

- Lay/patient arena
- Consultation
- Health service organisational level.

The model suggests that creating interactions within and between these domains is the most likely way of providing effective self-management support (Kennedy and Rogers 2001). Within the patient/lay domain three key components are identified relating to integration and effectiveness: firstly, a recognition of patients' pre-existing experiences and way of living with a chronic condition; secondly, lay social support networks and resources and thirdly, interpersonal interaction at the level of the professional–patient consultation.

How people experience and manage illness beyond the realms of professional health care is intrinsic to the first two components. The sociology of chronic illness provides insights into the workability of self-management interventions. The literature on the experience of chronic illness points to the way in which people develop strategies for managing, as a naturalistic response to being diagnosed with a chronic illness. This provides a point of reference for explaining what happens to people's management of their condition when technologies designed to change illness behaviour or improve their knowledge are introduced. Implicit to WISE has been illness work and a recursive relationship with services.

In relation to illness, Corbin and Strauss (1985) identified three types of work:

- Illness work (concerned with symptom management)
- Everyday life work (the practical tasks such as housework, caring, paid employment)
- Biographical work (the reconstruction of the ill person's biography).

The parameters of change with regard to complex self-management interventions can be viewed as a continued search for meaning and legitimacy of a chronic condition and the negotiation of a new personal and social equilibrium. An essential part of this process necessarily draws upon the various coping mechanisms, strategies and styles of adjustment that individuals develop over time (Bury 1991). Additionally as Faircloth *et al.* (2004) note, while biographical work tends to be associated with biographical histories, the future also emerges as a concern in the experience of illness.

The role played by services has at times been separated out from people's own efforts to manage illness. For example, self-management has been viewed as something that is marginalised in the consultation in favour of medical instruction (Stevenson *et al.* 2003). This picture of a failure of medicine to engage with the life-worlds of patients has encouraged a view in which living with chronic illness is conceptualised as a reactive flight into normalisation rather than being connected to the clinical settings that provide access to resources for self-management. It is this body of work that has utility for contextualising component three (interpersonal interaction at the level of the professional–patient consultation). Contacts with a variety of resources, services and expert knowledge have been viewed as invoking a process whereby individuals bring into play frequent internal contestation and revision of what constitutes legitimate expert knowledge about the best way to manage health and illness (Giddens 1991). The framing of illness in such settings has been shown to be highly differentiated, depending on the negotiated relationship between professional and patient. The role played by contact and utilisation with the health service has at times been viewed as separated from people's own efforts to manage illness, for example, by viewing these efforts as a purposive action that stops at the outset of the consultation in which 'proper' medicine takes over. Rather, contact with services or technologies can be seen as a recursive relationship that reinforces or changes illness identities and illness-related activities (Rogers *et al.* 1999) and contextualises complex self-management interventions.

Narrative analysis of respondents' accounts from an early study of WISE introduces the notion of change as a process of continuity and accelerated change. We have shown how this can be seen as relating to patients' work in self–management in terms of perceptions and experience of previous relationships, perceptions about authority to change matters (for example, appointments) and perspectives over what counts as patients' self-management (Rogers *et al.* 2007). A new technology for self-management must fit an actual or realisable set of roles within the patients' division of labour. Simultaneously, it must be capable of integration within existing patterns of service utilisation and contact with professionals. Therefore, the advantage to patients must be tangible and evident to their everyday illness work and contact with services is crucial to the evaluation of new interventions and practices.

A training intervention has been developed for delivery in primary care incorporating the WISE approach (as part of a RCT). The intervention contains a patient-centred approach where practitioners are trained to consider the patient's current ability to self-manage, their priorities and what they are able and prepared to work on, and what support they need to manage their condition. In order to focus attention on patient needs and experiences, information resources were developed in partnership with patients incorporating lay experiences and views on self-management.

WISE envisages a changed professional response and the training intervention is focused on providing clinicians with the skills and knowledge to assess patients' needs and priorities, to share decisions and increase patient participation in management decisions and to support patients in any changes they need to make. A simple questionnaire tool called patient response informing self-management support (PRISMS) jointly created by patients and professionals assists in this process. The training has a behavioural change basis and has been refined over time. At the level of the health system, WISE envisages more joined-up support where practice staff work together to develop systems and resources to provide information and access to appropriate support for patients, ideally, set in a wider health and social system where resources are available and accessible.

In the pragmatic trial of the WISE approach, we aimed to test whether patient outcomes can be improved through a training intervention that gives practice staff the skills and tools to support their patients to manage their illness themselves in the context of a supportive health economy. Many self-management interventions have focused on patient behaviour change or professional training only, but each level has a different function in encouraging and supporting self-management behaviour and effects are maximised when interventions occur at all levels and include attention to patient action outside health service contexts. This affects trial design (Bower *et al.* 2012, Kennedy *et al.* 2010).

We aimed to recruit practices and patients from within one health economy and to offer the training intervention to all eligible practices in this area. The trial took place in a primary care trust (PCT) with the active provision of community activities and groups to support it. The PCT employed and supported two trained facilitators who delivered the training and created and maintained a web-based directory of local self-management support organisations. In order to measure the impact of this whole systems approach on patient outcomes, a cluster randomised trial was considered appropriate, with randomisation at the level of the practice. The trial intervention development and process of recruitment was set in a normalisation framework, that is, we aimed to implement the WISE approach in such a way that self-management support behaviour could be integrated into everyday clinical practice (Murray *et al.* 2010). When recruiting practices we were aware that training had to be arranged to fit everyday working behaviour and priorities, for example, at certain times of the year, practices prioritised meeting the pay-for-performance targets of the quality outcomes framework, so were unavailable for training. Providing self-management support may require clinicians to challenge current patient behaviour and risk disrupting existing relationships. During the recruitment of the practices the emphasis was on the benefits of the training, including development of practical strategies and improving skills to benefit patient care. The training intervention itself was put across in a pragmatic and flexible way to allow the practices to own and shape the approach. Patients were recruited to the trial by practices that contacted all those on their lists with the conditions of interest to the trial (diabetes, chronic obstructive pulmonary disease and irritable bowel syndrome). Changes in behaviour at the patient level were expected to come through better support during consultations and signposting what community groups could be of help to patients. As part of the trial process, we sent all patients in the intervention group a leaflet including a PRISMS form to inform them to expect a different approach from their practice: 'Your doctor or nurse can find the best type of support to help you make changes to the way you manage your life with your condition'.

Example 2   *The management of osteoarthritis in consultations study (MOSAICS) pilot trial of implementing a new model of osteoarthritis consultation in primary care*

The National Institute for Health and Clinical Excellence (NICE 2008) has formulated osteoarthritis (OA) guidelines that define a set of core treatments for use in primary care to support self-management alongside other recommended treatments with evidence of efficacy. Research has shown that patients with OA are not optimally treated (Jinks *et al.* 2007, Porcheret *et al.* 2007) and a trial has been designed to implement a new approach to OA management based on the NICE recommended core treatments in eight general practices. The intervention is a model OA consultation delivered by GPs and practice nurses, developed by researchers in close collaboration with primary care clinicians and patients (Dziedzic 2012a, Porcheret 2012). It contained an important element of WISE concerned with improving professionals' response to patients' need. GPs in the eight practices use a computer-based template that prompts and enables GPs to code aspects of a consultation for OA (Edwards *et al.* 2011). In the four general practices randomised to deliver the intervention the GP can offer the patient an OA guidebook specifically written by professionals and patients for use in the consultation (Grime and Dudley 2011) and refer them, if appropriate, to a nurse-led OA clinic. This clinic is staffed by specially trained practice nurses who can see patients for up to four sessions and tailor their advice and support to individual needs (Dziedzic 2012b). The four control practices continue with usual treatment.

For the purpose of this chapter we focus on the practice nurses who, through their training, were introduced to new behaviour change technologies such as use of the specific, measurable, appropriate, realistic, time-based tool for goal setting with patients, but in the context of the WISE approach (Dziedzic 2012b). Thus, the training emphasised the fact that patients' own experience of living with chronic joint pain had to be the starting point and that advice and support about using the NICE core treatments to self-manage needed to make sense to the individuals concerned. The adaptive nature of the intervention, by locating it within people's own meaning-making frame of reference and social roles and relationships, allowed the adoption of behaviour change technologies to be flexible and evolve over time. Early indications from current observations of the nurse clinics are that the personal, embodied knowledge of the practice nurses is important in that they mesh their expertise (often gained from running other special clinics such as for diabetes or asthma) with the learning from the OA training. Thus, they appear to be confident in embracing a patient-centred consultation style that is responsive and adaptive.

This approach to implementing a complex intervention and system change poses a challenge to the traditional cluster RCT design with an often fixed timing of training and of intervention delivery within the researchers' control. In response, our pragmatic design adopts a realist perspective in that it reflects the everyday contexts of both patients and health professionals and the real-world primary care setting where the practitioners, rather than the researchers, control the implementation of the intervention. The WISE model already states that the social world of patients represents an open setting, and primary care may be similarly denoted because of the variability between and within practices and health professionals operationalising the intervention in individualised ways. The MOSAICS trial recognises this reality and adjusts its behaviour change interventions by taking the individual and the practice within their social context as a starting point, and also builds the social into the trial design. Counterbalancing the potential threat of compromising the interventional–control comparison of an RCT, the MOSAICS cluster trial carefully documents the implementation of the intervention (through interviews with professionals and patients and observations of clinics and feedback meetings) in each of the four practices. Insights into the interaction between the model OA consultation, its interpretation by individual practice nurses and its application to the patient's needs, circumstances and illness work can thus be highlighted and recognised. In some ways, this can be understood as a sociological theory-based iteration of the behaviour change wheel, adding more depth and meaning to the intervention in action.

With regard to behaviour change in practice nurses, early indications from their feedback about implementing the model OA consultation are that they perceive it as increasing their skills and repertoire of options, thus enhancing professionalism. The continued adoption of the new approach may be realised as it fits the practice nurses' image of themselves as a learning profession.

Conclusion

Self-management is expected to remain a dominant feature of health policy, and the belief in the benefits of behaviour change technologies continues to underpin many government initiatives. A constructive sociological critique, however, has the ability to enhance current approaches and this chapter has offered examples of the way forward. We build on the analysis of Taylor and Bury who argue that trialists of EPP-type interventions have presented their evidence without adequately contextualising their findings against the socioeconomic background of the participants, thus leading to an unsophisticated promulgation of the benefits of the approach (Taylor and Bury 2007). Critical commentators also observe the positive virtues of patient self-management interventions that use behaviour change technologies. They recognise that jettisoning them would reduce the options open to patients and be detrimental to those who may benefit from behaviour change approaches (Bury *et al.* 2005, Redman 2010). Taylor and Bury suggest that, rather than rejecting psychological approaches outright, it will be fruitful to integrate their strengths with sociological work that recognises context and the everyday lives and strategies of individuals living with chronic illness. They argue that this can facilitate the robust use of evidence and provide comprehensive and responsive health services (Taylor and Bury 2007).

Our discussion of the policy drivers, the contextualisation of behaviour change approaches and the responsive trial design used in WISE and MOSAICS points to a way forward to produce effective interventions for self-management. By re-emphasising the social and its constituent components – individuals' illness work, clinician–patient negotiation and sense-making by both patients and health professionals – and integrating these in the overall design of interventions a more complex understanding can be achieved of why certain interventions work and for whom, and under what circumstances they are accomplished. Consequently, it will be possible to improve support for self-management in ways that are meaningful to patients and professionals in their everyday life and work.

Acknowledgements

We would like to thank Krysia Dziedzic and Mark Porcheret for their input in the section on the MOSAICS study. We would like to acknowledge the funders of the WISE programme of work at the National Primary Care Research and Development Centre and the National Institute for Health Research (NIHR) under its programme grants for applied research funding scheme (grant no. RP-PG-0407–10136). The MOSAICS element of this chapter presents independent research funded by the NIHR under its programme grants for applied research funding scheme (grant no. RP-PG-0407–10386). The views expressed in this chapter are those of the authors and not necessarily of the NHS, the NIHR or the Department of Health.

References

Armstrong, D. and Ogden, J. (2006) The role of etiquette and experimentation in explaining how doctors change behaviour: a qualitative study, *Sociology of Health & Illness*, 28, 7, 951–68.
Balfe, M. (2007) Diets and discipline: the narratives of practice of university students with type 1 diabetes, *Sociology of Health & Illness*, 29, 1, 136–53.
Bandura, A. (1977) Self-efficacy: towards a unifying theory of behaviour change, *Psychological Review*, 84, 2, 191–215.
Barlow, J., Turner, A. and Wright, C. (2000) A randomized controlled study of the arthritis self-management programme in the UK, *Health Education Research*, 15, 6, 665–80.
Baus, A. (2004) *Literature Review: Barriers to the Successful Implementation of Healthcare Information Systems.* Office of Health Services Research: West Virginia University Department of Community Medicine.
Berg, M. (1999) Patient care information systems and health care work: a sociotechnical approach, *International Journal of Medical Informatics*, 55, 2, 87–101.
Blakeman, T., Bower, P., Reeves, D. and Chew-Graham, C. (2010) Bringing self-management into clinical view: a qualitative study of long-term condition management in primary care consultations, *Chronic Illness*, 6, 2, 136–50.

Bower, P., Kennedy, A., Reeves, D., Rogers, A., *et al.* (2012) A cluster randomised controlled trial of the clinical and cost-effectiveness of a 'whole systems' model of self-management support for the management of long-term conditions in primary care: trial protocol, *Implementation Science*, 7, 1, 1–13.

British Psychological Society (2008) *Improving Health: Changing Behaviour. NHS Health Trainer Handbook.* London: Department of Health.

Burawoy, M. (1998) The extended case method, *Sociological Theory*, 16, 1, 4–33.

Bury, M. (1991) The sociology of chronic illness: a review of research and progress, *Sociology of Health & Illness*, 13, 4, 451–68.

Bury, M., Newbould, J. and Taylor, D. (2005) *A Rapid Review of the Current State of Knowledge Regarding Lay-Led Self-Management of Chronic Illness.* London: National Institute for Health and Clinical Excellence.

Checkland, K., Harrison, S. and Marshall, M. (2007) Is the metaphor of 'barriers to change' useful in understanding implementation? Evidence from general medical practice, *Journal of Health Services Research and Policy*, 12, 2, 95–100.

Conner, M. and Norman, P. (2005) Predicting health behaviour: a social cognition approach. In Conner, M. and Norman, P. (eds) *Predicting Health Behaviour: Research and Practice with Social Cognition Models*, 2nd edn. Maidenhead: Open University Press.

Conner, M. and Sparks, P. (1996) The theory of planned behaviour and health behaviours. In Conner, M. and Norman, P. (eds) *Predicting Health Behaviour: Research and Practice with Social Cognition Models*. Buckingham: Open University Press.

Corbin, J. and Strauss, A. (1985) Managing chronic illness at home: three lines of work, *Qualitative Sociology*, 8, 3, 224–47.

Davison, G. (2007) Behaviour therapy. In Ayers, S., Baum, A., McManus, C., Newman, S., *et al.* (eds) *Cambridge Handbook of Psychology, Health and Medicine*, 2nd edn. Cambridge: Cambridge University Press.

Department of Health (2000) *The NHS Plan: a Plan for Investment, a Plan for Reform.* London: The Stationary Office.

Department of Health (2001) *The Expert Patient: a New Approach to Chronic Disease Management for the 21st Century.* London: Department of Health.

Department of Health (2005) *Self Care – a Real Choice. Self Care Support – a Practical Option.* London: Department of Health.

Department of Health (2011) *The NHS Outcomes Framework 2012–2013.* London: Department of Health.

Donaldson, L. (2003) Expert patients usher in a new era of opportunity for the NHS, *British Medical Journal*, 326, 7402, 1279–80.

Doolan, D., Bates, D. and James, B. (2003) The use of computers for clinical care: a case series of advanced U.S. sites, *Journal of the American Medical Association*, 10, 1, 94–107.

Dziedzic, K. (2012a) An overview of best practices in OA care, *Annals of the Rheumatic Diseases*, 71, Suppl 3, 5.

Dziedzic, K. (2012b) Self management in OA: evidence for the role of the multidisciplinary team, *Annals of the Rheumatic Diseases*, 71, Suppl 3, 20.

Edwards, J., Khanna, M., Jordan, K., Jordan, J., *et al.* (2011) A systematic review of quality indicators in the primary care of osteoarthritis, *Annals of the Rheumatic Diseases*, 70, Suppl 3, 388.

Faircloth, C., Boylstein, C., Rittman, M., Young, M., *et al.* (2004) Sudden illness and biographical flow in narratives of stroke recovery, *Sociology of Health & Illness*, 26, 2, 242–61.

Fishbein, M., Triandis, H.C., Kanfer, F.H. and Becker, M. *et al.* (2001) Factors influencing behaviour and behaviour change. In Baum, A., Revenson, T.A. and Singer, J.E. (eds) *Handbook of Health Psychology*. Mahwah: Lawrence Erlbaum Associates.

Giddens, A. (1991) *Modernity and Self-Identity*. Cambridge: Polity Press.

Grime, J. and Dudley, B. (2011) Developing written information on osteoarthritis for patients: facilitating user involvement by exposure to qualitative research, *Health Expectations*, doi:10.1111/j.1369-7625.2011.00741.x.

Hodgins, M., Millar, M. and Barry, M. (2006) '… it's all the same no matter how much fruit or vegetables or fresh air we get': traveller women's perceptions of illness causation and health inequalities, *Social Science & Medicine*, 62, 8, 1978–90.

Jinks, C., Ong, B.N. and Richardson, J. (2007) A mixed methods study to investigate needs assessment for knee pain and disability: population and individual perspectives, *BMC Musculoskeletal Disorders*, 8, doi:10.1186/1471-2474-8-59.

Kennedy, A. and Rogers, A. (2001) Improving self-management skills: a whole systems approach, *British Journal of Nursing*, 10, 11, 734–7.

Kennedy, A., Reeves, D., Bower, P., Lee, V., *et al.* (2007) The effectiveness and cost effectiveness of a national lay led self care support programme for patients with long-term conditions: a pragmatic randomised controlled trial, *Journal of Epidemiology and Community Health*, 61, 2, 254–61.

Kennedy, A., Chew-Graham, C., Blakeman, T., Bowen, A., *et al.* (2010) Delivering the WISE (Whole Systems Informing Self-Management Engagement) training package in primary care: learning from formative evaluation, *Implementation Science*, 5, 1, 7. doi:10.1186/1748-5908-5-7.

Lave, J. and Wenger, E. (1991) *Situated Learning: Legitimate Peripheral Participation.* Cambridge: Cambridge University Press.

Lewin, S., Glenton, C. and Oxman, A. (2009) Use of qualitative methods alongside controlled trials of complex healthcare interventions: methodological study, *British Medical Journal*, 339, doi: \http://dx.doi.org/10.1136/bmj.b3496.

Lorig, K., Mazonzon, P. and Holman, H. (1993) Evidence suggesting that health education for self management in patients with chronic arthritis has sustained health benefits while reducing health care costs, *Arthritis and Rheumatism*, 36, 4, 439–46.

Lorig, K., Sobel, D., Stewart, A., Brown, B., *et al.* (1999) Evidence suggesting that a chronic disease self-management program can improve health status while reducing hospitalization, a randomized trial, *Medical Care*, 37, 1, 5–14.

McAndrew, L., Musumeci-Szabo, T., Mora, P., Vileiktye, L., *et al.* (2008) Using the common sense model to design interventions for the prevention and management of chronic illness threats: from description to process, *British Journal of Health Psychology*, 13, 2, 195–204.

Michie, S., van Stralen, M. and West, R. (2011) The behaviour change wheel: a new method for characterising and designing behaviour change interventions, *Implementation Science*, 6, 42. doi:10.1186/1748-5908-6-42.

Miles, C., Pincus, T., Carnes, D., Homer, K., *et al.* (2011) Can we identify how programmes aimed at promoting self-management in musculoskeletal pain work and who benefits? A systematic review of sub-group analysis within RCTs, *European Journal of Pain*, 15, 8, 1–11.

Morden, A., Jinks, C. and Ong, B.N. (2011) Lay models of self-management: how do people manage knee osteoarthritis in context?, *Chronic Illness*, 7, 3, 185–200.

Murray, E., Treweek, S., Pope, C., MacFarlane, A., *et al.* (2010) Normalisation process theory: a framework for developing, evaluating and implementing complex interventions, *BMC Medicine*, 8, 63. doi:10.1186/1741-7015-8-63.

National Institute of Health and Clinical Excellence (NICE) (2008) Osteoarthritis: the care and management of osteoarthritis in adults. Available online at http://www.guideline.gov/content .aspx?id=14322 (accessed 27 October 2013).

O'Connor, P., Crabtree, B. and Yanoshik, M. (1997) Differences between diabetic patients who do and do not respond to a diabetes care intervention: a qualitative analysis, *Family Medicine*, 29, 6, 424–8.

Porcheret, M. (2012) Self management for OA: the role of the GP, *Annals of the Rheumatic Diseases*, 71, Suppl 3, 20.

Porcheret, M., Jordan, K., Jinks, C. and Croft, P. (2007) Primary care treatment of knee pain – a survey in older adults, *Rheumatology*, 46, 11, 1694–700.

Post, E., Kilboure, A., Bremer, R., Solano, F., *et al.* (2009) Organizational factors and depression management in community-based primary care settings, *Implementation Science*, 4, 84. doi:10.1186/1748-5908-4-84.

Prochaska, J., DiClemente, C. and Norcross, J. (1992) In search of how people change, *American Psychologist*, 47, 9, 1102–4.

Redman, B. (2010) Patient self-management: potential harms to control, *Chronic Illness*, 6, 2, 151–3.

Roland, M. and Torgerson, D. (1998) What are pragmatic trials?, *British Medical Journal*, 316, 7127, 285.

Rogers, A. (2009) Advancing the expert patient, *Primary Health Care Research & Development*, 10, 3, 167–76.

Rogers, A., Lee, V. and Kennedy, A. (2007) Continuity and change?: Exploring reactions to a guided self-management intervention in a randomised controlled trial for IBS with reference to prior experience of managing a long term condition, *Trials*, 8, doi:10.1186/1745-6215-8-6.

Rogers, A., Hassell, K. and Nicolaas, G. (1999) *Demanding Patients? Analysing the Use of Primary Care*. Buckingham: Open University.

Rogers, A., Kennedy, A., Bower, P., Gardner, C., *et al.* (2008) The United Kingdom expert patients programme: results and implications from a national evaluation, *Medical Journal of Australia*, 189, 10, S21–4.

Sackett, D., Straus, S., Richardson, W., Rosenberg, W., *et al.* (2000) *Evidence-Based Medicine: How to Practise and Teach EBM*. Edinburgh: Churchill Livingstone.

Schwarzer, R. and Fuchs, R. (1996) The health belief model. In Conner, M. and Norman, P. (eds) *Predicting Health Behaviour: Research and Practice with Social Cognition Models*. Buckingham: Open University Press.

Seear, K. (2009) 'Nobody really knows what it is or how to treat it': why women with endometriosis do not comply with healthcare advice, *Health, Risk and Society*, 11, 4, 367–85.

Stevenson, F., Britten, N., Barry, C., Bradley, C., *et al.* (2003) Self-treatment and discussion in medical consultations: how is medical pluralism managed in practice?, *Social Science & Medicine*, 57, 3, 513–27.

Taylor, D. and Bury, M. (2007) Chronic illness, expert patients and care transition, *Sociology of Health & Illness*, 29, 1, 27–45.

Timmins, N. (2012) *Never Again? The Story of the Health and Social Care Act 2012*. London: King's Fund and Institute for Government.

Townsend, A., Wyke, S. and Hunt, K. (2006) Self-managing and managing self: practical and moral dilemmas in accounts of living with chronic illness, *Chronic Illness*, 2, 3, 185–95.

Vollmar, H., Mayer, H., Ostermann, T., Butzlaff, M., *et al.* (2010) Knowledge transfer for the management of dementia: a cluster-randomised trial of blended learning in general practice, *Implementation Science*, 5, 1. doi:10.1186/1748-5908-5-1.

Wanless, D. (2002) *Securing Our Future Health: Taking a Long-Term View*. London: HM Treasury.

Weick, K. (1995) *Sensemaking in Organisations*. London: Sage.

Wood, M., Ferlie, E. and Fitzgerald, L. (1999) Achieving clinical behaviour change: a case of becoming indeterminate, *Social Science & Medicine*, 47, 11, 1729–38.

8

Thinking about changing mobility practices: how a social practice approach can help

Sarah Nettleton and Judith Green

The problem: insufficient mobility

Our hyper-mobile world is, paradoxically, one in which many human actors are increasingly sedentary. A growing anxiety has arisen over the health implications of inactive lifestyles (Department of Health 2004), perhaps most evident in alarm about a threatened obesity epidemic (Gard, 2010). Policy and practice in the UK and many other countries has addressed this lack of active mobility (Department of Health 2011, Pate *et al.* 1995), with two main arenas as the focus: encouraging sports participation and, more recently, encouraging active transport, such as cycling and walking (de Nazelle *et al.* 2011).

The policy gains from these promotional efforts have been modest at best (Hillsdon *et al.* 2001, Killoran *et al.* 2006), reflecting to some extent limitations in the evidence base underpinning policy approaches and interventions. Much of this expanding research literature on the problem of how to encourage active mobility maps onto two theoretical approaches. Behaviourist perspectives address the existence of individual barriers to undertaking more exercise and structural approaches focus on the material and social environments that limit opportunities for taking up healthier habits. The literature has been disappointing on identifying which environments do foster more exercise, with findings being difficult to generalise and taking insufficient account of the cultural factors that mediate how far, for instance, access to green space or well-connected streets might impact on the amount of walking or cycling done (Steinbach *et al.* 2012: 917). A review by the National Institute for Health and Clinical Excellence (NICE) on interventions to increase physical activity found insufficient evidence to recommend popular individual level interventions, such as exercise referral or organised walking/cycling schemes (NICE 2006), and a systematic review found little evidence for population interventions to achieve changes to more active modes of transport (Ogilvie *et al.* 2004).

In this chapter we draw upon Bourdieu's (1977) *Outline of a Theory of Practice*, which offers a route beyond this theoretical dualism and the potential for making a sociological contribution to public health debates. We begin with a sketch of Bourdieu's theory of practice, paying particular attention to the epistemological and methodological implications for sociological analyses of changing health behaviour. As a case study, we then explore three modes of transformations in practice that we label: unthinkable, thwarted and resisted, which are drawn from secondary analysis of two empirical studies (on cycling and on

From Health Behaviours to Health Practices: Critical Perspectives, First Edition. Edited by Simon Cohn. Chapters © 2014 The Authors. Book Compilation © 2014 Foundation for the Sociology of Health & Illness / Blackwell Publishing Ltd.

running) to demonstrate the potential of a Bourdieusian approach to the analysis of mobility as social practice.

Mobility as social practice

Bourdieu (1977) opens his book, *Outline of a Theory of Practice*, with a critique of sociological theory. The problem, for him, is that sociologists align themselves to either objectivist or subjectivist approaches to the study of social life. The former seeks to identify the social structures (or social facts) that shape human action, while the latter focuses on the ways in which individuals' interpretative actions collectively construct social realities. As an alternative, he proposes a dialectical approach that seeks to synthesise both social and mental structures. Perceptions and actions are not purely determined by social structures and, conversely, perceptions and actions do not create social realities; instead they might be more productively understood as mutually constituting. Thus a science of society must attend to the '*dialectical* relations' (p. 3 emphasis in the original) between subjective and objective structures in order to:

> [C]onstruct the theory of practice, or, more precisely, the theory of the mode of generation of practices, which is the precondition for establishing an experimental science of the *dialectic of the internalization of externality and the externalisation of internality*, or, more simply, of incorporation and objectification. (Bourdieu 1977: 72 emphasis in the original).

Bourdieu offers a set of conceptual tools to facilitate this science of social practice including (among others): habitus, field and doxa. Habitus he defines as the 'subjective but not individual system of internalized structures, schemes of perception, conception, and action common to all members of the same group or class' (1977: 86). These schemes of perception are malleable and as people move through varying social spaces or fields their perceptions are likely to alter. These social fields are structured social spaces such as sport, leisure, art, science and academic settings, which mark out the parameters of the more or less implicit norms and regulations that individuals intuitively come to live by. Relations between habitus and field generate social practice with neither determining the other. Furthermore, and important to the arguments we develop here, the degree of congruence between habitus and field determines doxa, that is, the taken-for-grantedness of the social world. As Bourdieu puts it:

> The stabler the objective structures and the more fully they reproduce themselves in agents' dispositions, the greater the extent of the field of doxa, of that which is taken for granted. (Bourdieu 1977: 165–6)

This has important consequences for understanding how and why practices may change, not least because how and why people act as they do is likely to be beyond their cognitive and rational understanding. In those circumstances where people are most at home in any given social space – where habitus meshes with field – their apprehension of their social environment is more practical than it is theoretical and more tacit than it is explicit. This practical comprehension (1977: 80) implies that how we act is pre-reflective; with social traditions, expectations, classifications and so on appearing to be so natural and self-evident that their arbitrariness is misrecognised. Thus, the most profound influences and constraints on our actions remain implicit. Consequently, sociologists should seek to look beyond informants' accounts and examine the interplay between context, circumstance and practice in order to decipher the informants' implicit assumptions, which may be hinted at or left unsaid. In other words, the social analyst should attempt to grasp practical knowledge, because practical (rather than cognitive or intellectual) reasoning underpins action. As Bourdieu (1977) points out, when:

> [I]nvited by the anthropologist's questioning to effect a reflexive and quasi-theoretical return on to his own practice, the best informed informant produces a discourse *which compounds two opposing systems of lacunae*. Insofar as it is a *discourse of familiarity*, it leaves unsaid all that goes without saying. (Bourdieu 1977: 18, italics in the original)

In essence: 'It is because subjects do not, strictly speaking, know what they are doing, that what they do has more meaning than they know' (p. 79). Of course, examining what remains unsaid and seeking to decipher meanings that remain beyond the ken of participants represents a challenge. We suggest, however, that the challenge is surmountable and a useful starting point when looking at physical mobility, for example, might be a shift in focus; to think of physical activity not as a form of health behaviour but as a mode of social practice.

Researching changing social practice

To explore how a focus on social practice might inform a sociology of health that can usefully address questions on the conditions of possibility for change, we reflect on data derived from empirical studies of two deliberately contrasting practices, namely, cycling and fell running, that are located (in our particular case studies) across the different fields of transport, leisure and sport. Our analysis focuses specifically on the data from these studies that relate to questions of transformation in practice. These data were generated from two studies: one designed to examine why women and some minority ethnic groups are underrepresented among those cycling for transport in London (Steinbach *et al.* 2011), which included a study of adults learning to cycle; and one which explored the experiences of accomplished veteran fell runners in the English Lake District. The data on learning to cycle were in the form of interviews and participant observation (Green *et al.* 2012, Steinbach, Green, and Edwards 2012). The data on fell running were generated from an ethnographic study comprising participant observation, informal conversations and formal qualitative interviews with 14 men and five women; the youngest being 55-years old and the oldest 85. All were living in the Lake District and have been running on the fells for at least three to six decades. All are white British and at the time of the interview were still running. In all data reported in this chapter, names are pseudonyms and some place and other identifiers have been changed to maintain anonymity. In terms of transformations of practice these empirical data represent instances of change that we conceptualise here as unthinkable, thwarted and resisted.

Changing social practice: unthinkable

As a first illustration of a social practice approach, we turn to a study that sought to identify why women and those from minority ethnic groups are underrepresented among those cycling for transport in London (Steinbach *et al.* 2011). In a group discussion with Asian parents, the participants' first response to a question about whether they cycle is to laugh, with one man saying, 'What a ridiculous question'. Only once the laughter subsides can they contribute a number of reasons for the inappropriateness of cycling, given their particular circumstances:

Shila: So, if you're using the bicycle, what about the children? How are you going to bring them to school? You have to ride the bicycle, and where are the kids? [All laugh] Where do you put them? So, that's not a good idea!

Deepa: And another thing is that, because everyone lives in a flat, and there's not enough space, so where would you put your bike?

Anjali: And it's not useful for us because we, if we wear a jilbab, how are we going to ride a bike? (Steinbach *et al.* 2011)

There is a seductive reading of this as a list of barriers to cycling, suggesting their own mitigating solutions. Indeed, this is what a number of health promotion and other campaigns do explicitly in their advice to women on overcoming barriers, including technological adaptations (ever more complex carriers for children; a clothes peg for holding long clothes) and advice on building confidence. However, such a reading misses the ways in which the practice of riding a bicycle is not the result (or not only the result) of rational assessments of the possibilities and limitations of particular modes of transport in particular circumstances. As a practice, cycling is also both embodied and embedded social action, clearly articulated within particular social and material environments from which it derives its meaning. Here is a classic example of one type practical, tacit knowledge: the ways in which the dispositions of a particular group exclude a particular practice as 'unthinkable' (Bourdieu 1977: 77).

The conditions of possibility that make cycling inherently ridiculous, rather than merely inconvenient, are hinted at not in the content of individual contributions ('I can't carry the children') but rather the context in which these are offered. That is, following uproarious and universal laughter, these participants finally take pity on the facilitator and attempt to answer the ridiculous question. It is the laughter, and the interaction, which provide the insight into the shared, taken-for-granted, tacit knowledge which frame the rationales offered later in response to the interviewer's question. This laughter was echoed in many informal interviews in this same study. Asking whether people considered cycling to work was met by the frequent assumption that the question was a joke: clearly, respondents were obviously 'not the sort' to cycle. The absurdity of the question is derived from the way in which it articulates the implicit – what goes without saying – and is recognised through the humour that it generates. In formal interviews, however, where the framing was already one in which the respondent has been primed to discuss, in an abstract and theoretical way, their choices about transport behaviour, rationales were offered thoughtfully: cycling is too much hassle; it is too dangerous; it is too difficult to do when wearing clothes appropriate for the working day.

Changing social practice: thwarted
While our first example focuses on those for whom cycling as a mode of transport was unimaginable, our second illustration offers an interpretation of a second mode of transformation: that which has been attempted but thwarted. This case is also taken from the study of cycling, but here it comes from the narratives of two women who intended a change in practice, in that they proactively attended an adult cycling course. For many, learning to cycle is an iconic milestone achievement of childhood. The physical skills required, once achieved, are proverbial examples of embodied tacit knowledge, in that you never forget

how to ride a bike, yet the formal principles of balance and locomotion are (for most riders) not only difficult to articulate but also problematic in transmitting the ability to ride a bike to others. Indeed, theorists of tacit knowledge have taken bicycle-riding as illustrative of the irreducibility of human behaviour to a set of codified protocols or rules of social life (Collins 2010, Polanyi 1966). That learning has to be embodied is one essential element of its tacitness: skills, once habituated in the body, become taken-for-granted. This is not, of course, to say that the process of learning those physical skills is not amenable to exposition. Candy, a Black British woman in her late thirties living in inner London, and Rosalind, a White British woman in her late fifties living in outer London, interviewed just after they attended the training course, can articulates this process adeptly:

Candy:	So [my friends used to ask me] 'Can you ride a bike?' No, I can't do it, that's just my handicap in sort of a way, do you know what I mean? ... I just thought me and two wheels just don't go. ...
Interviewer:	So what changed?
Candy:	I think the sessions, I think his [trainer's] approach to it ... he would say, 'Well, just the fact that you walked here or you ran is more complicated than a bike', so I'm like, 'Ah, huh!' and just the way he, the analogies that he puts together and just how he breaks it down as well, made me see it more that I'm the one who's stopping myself from doing it, and he's like, 'Yeah, you are going to be falling and you're always constantly falling but it's the way that you balance and counterbalance and the faster you go the more you'll ride smoothly' and just different things that have actually stuck with me from when he said them ... I couldn't believe I was cycling by the end of the session ... I like being able to master something that I thought I could never do.
Rosalind:	It's the first time in my life that I've ever cycled, because I couldn't cycle. Well, I'd convinced myself I couldn't cycle ... I was quite scared about starting the cycle classes ... they just, within half an hour, because I, they just showed me how to stop. ... They said well they can't give you training wheels or that they can't, push you and run behind you. But they didn't need to do any of that, they're just very, very good at showing me how to start, which was, to use the brakes and it just, I think it worked ... It was brilliant ... I felt incredibly proud.

These two accounts of learning to cycle have a similar redemptive narrative arc: psychological barriers overcome with the intervention of a skilled instructor; physical techniques acquired; and resolution, with the emotional and physical pleasure of achievement to come from accomplished cycling. However, interviewed a few months later, the stories of Rosalind and Candy diverge radically. Clearly, the embodied knowledge both attest to in the first interview proves insufficient to enable the social practice of cycling. In contrast to the fluid account of the successes of the training scheme in an initial interview, Candy's follow-up interview is punctuated throughout with hesitations, and talk about her frustrations in enacting her fledgling skills:

Candy:	I've only done it once ... And a friend gave me a bike as well, she said I could have a bike, but I've just been seeing some horrible things with buses and bikes, and I'm just like, I think I'm really quite frightened to

go on the road, so that's probably what's stopping me from doing it. I was finding it difficult to start off, once I start I hope I can pedal and get around ...

Interviewer: Because when you were at cycle training you were learning actually how to ride, right?

Candy: ... So it was like, actually you know, 'You can ride, you just can't ride well', so I'm like, 'OK'. So yeah, so we trained and everything, but I just found it difficult to start off, just to get the, get my head and my feet working together. Do you know what I mean? But a friend of mine gave me a bike, so we went out once, and again I found it difficult to, you know?

Rosalind's follow-up interview, however, is an enthusiastic catalogue of successful cycle rides, including a 16-mile ride with her family while on holiday, regular leisure cycling around the park with friends and gaining the confidence to cycle on the roads to go to the shops and other local amenities. Her enthusiasm is such that others have been enrolled:

Rosalind: The friend who hadn't cycled for 10 years, now she's thinking of getting a bike ... and my Yoga teacher ... she said, 'Oh, I will definitely sign up for it'.

So how and why does this transformation from the unthinkable (in this case because there is no physical capital in the field of cycling) to potential practice happen in one case, but get thwarted in another? The acquisition of the skill may be a necessary condition (one cannot be a cyclist if one cannot, literally, perform cycling), but this is not enough.

A comparison of individual motivations is not particularly enlightening. The initial interviews with Candy and Rosalind reveal rather similar themes in terms of potential motivators: both were keen to learn a new skill, had friends who cycled, explicitly mentioned health motivations and noted their environmental concerns. That these similar incentives led to different outcomes is not, at one level, surprising. The divergent trajectories of their cycling practice six months after we met them at cycling training reflect, of course, the complicated interrelationships of opportunity and constraint that any individual faces. It is not inevitable that a set of motivations in combination with a set of novice skills will lead to some behavioural change. However, beyond merely noting the contingencies of these interrelationships, it may be instructive to also consider how a different habitus within (crucially) rather different overlapping social fields, differentially constitute cycling as more or less possible for these two women.

To illustrate, if we take one environmental possible predictor of walking and cycling, access to green space, and one motivator, friends who cycle, both women had access to both. However, whereas Rosalind speaks with pleasure about a group of what she calls cycling ladies with whom she 'cycled around Tiverton Park and over to Cleveleys and had a drink in a pub and cycled back', Candy's attempts to practise the new skill in her local park have a completely different valence:

Interviewer: It's harder than you thought it was going to be?

Candy: A lot harder, because I just thought, 'Well, gosh if they can do it, a kid can do it, I can do it', and then getting there and realising, actually no I can't ... and just thinking, 'Well, I need to get it to the park', and you know? And then, 'Well I haven't got the time to go to the park, and if I get home it'll be like six and stuff'. So it's not too bad now, but I think

> also with the kids, round my area there's a lot of kids who take over the park and I don't want to be the adult trying to learn how to ride a bike, you know what I mean? It's all these factors, no I'll go on a bus instead, or go out instead.

For Rosalind, a social, material and environmental network has coalesced to enable cycling to happen: her physical ability; time and energy; a working bicycle; supportive husband, family and friends with time to encourage her fledgling skills; local places (park, quiet roads) where not only is cycling theoretically possible, but culturally appropriate for a female, middle-aged and less than fluidly competent practitioner to do it. For Candy, despite her best efforts to mobilise these elements, they do not quite coordinate in a way that enables a transformation from novice to accomplished practitioner. She has acquired a bike, a lock-up near her flat to keep her bike, somewhere to practise (the park) and friends who can accompany her, and she maintains a motivation to cycle ('It would be nice to be on a bike and just whip through ... its nicer ... it's cheaper') but in the context of a busy job, low energy at the end of the day, the visible dangers of inner-city roads and the less than welcoming environment of her local park, these are not possible to bring together in the process of embedding newly acquired embodied skills: that is, learning to ride on the road.

The different contingencies of Candy's and Rosalind's accounts are embedded in particular material environments that may both include what is described as green space but are socially and culturally very different: the suburban parks of Rosalind's neighbourhood are indeed full of cycling ladies, where her fledgling efforts will be unremarkable. Candy's local park, however, is one in which a novice, in the after-work dusk, will be visible and potentially uncomfortable (see Horton 2007). Crucially, class and ethnic habitus may not be explicitly referenced in their accounts of practice, but they nonetheless constitute tacit underpinnings; the resonances of inclusion (the cycling ladies) or exclusion (kids who take over the park) that reflect these differing social circumstances. It is not that social class (or indeed ethnicity or other social categories) explains or in itself predicts their differing likelihood of cycling – but that these ethnic and social parameters constitute the conditions of what is possible and normal, on the one hand, or unusual and idiosyncratic, on the other.

One way to frame Candy's particular challenge is to note that leisure cycling – which has been a way for Rosalind to accomplish a move from novice to practitioner – is less available as a field. Both Candy and Rosalind, at the point of the second interview, are acutely conscious of the additional embodied tacit skills that are needed to accomplish cycling. As Candy notes: 'There's quite a lot more to master with the cycling as well as the cycling, you know'. Both articulate what is needed: additional skills in balancing, placing oneself at an appropriate point on the road and so on. Again, what they do not explicitly articulate but hint at in their very different descriptions of both the local park as an environment for acquiring these skills and the local streets as an environment of potential risk to be managed, is the way that the conditions of possibility for achieving cycling, as practice, are shaped by both habitus (the specific constellations of class, gender, ethnicity and so on that frame each life), but also the field in which the practice is enacted.

Learning to cycle involves both embodied skills and a cultural and social fluency appropriate to a specific field. The lack of such skills, including such as how to maintain eye contact with drivers, where on the road to place the bike, culturally appropriate styles of physical deportment, clothing and so on (Aldred and Jungnickel 2012, Green, Steinbach, and Datta 2012) – the hexis of the fluent cycling body – are an overwhelming signification of the dislocation between habitus and field for the novice. To cycle in a contemporary city requires considerable refinement of both somatic and social skills. A habitus in which the network of people, environments and technologies can be articulated to incorporate the role of novice is one in which these can be developed, as Rosalind notes:

> My husband comes with me because I'm still not so steady doing hand signals and things … I can now go to the park on my own … we go shopping … I've got practice on lots of different terrains.

Significantly, these have been acquired within a field of leisure cycling, which seems unavailable for Candy. Where there are fewer resonances between the personal transformation and the cultural habitus, the conditions of possibility for changing practice may be reduced and the practice may be less easily transposed from one field (leisure) to another (transport). Conversely, where strong resonances between habitus and social field are in place then there is scope to consolidate social practice. Cycling, it seems, has become a practice which meshes easily with Rosalind's various social fields, such that at one point in the second interview she says, 'I consider myself a cyclist now', whereas Candy, when asked if she considers herself a cyclist answers: 'Not really, no'.

Changing social practice: resisted
The third mode of transformation we address is that of a change urged in the name of health and normatively appropriate ageing, but resisted. An ethnography of fell runners, which included interviews with men and women who have been running on the fells for at least three and up to six decades, found that the participants were able to describe the embodied skills required for negotiating mountainous terrains. They were eloquent on their proficiency of navigation, reading the ground, understanding changes in vegetation, knowing how to hold the body when running up hill, understanding techniques of relaxing the body when running downhill and so on. Albert's account of the skills and pitfalls of running in response to questions about the expertise needed for fell is typical:

> You study maps, and also you learn through experience. For example, once there was a checkpoint at Black Sale, at the head of Ennerdale, and the next one was on the far side of Scafell. Now, you could go up and over Scafell, which was a very steep climb, very difficult, but you might look at the map and think, 'I could contour around the mountain', which I tried to do, but I didn't know that bit of the mountain, and it was a great disaster because it was head-high bracken and huge blocky boulders, so it was a disastrous mistake. Very depressing. Now, in theory, you know, a contour around would be the sensible thing, but I'd never been around there before I'd guessed that it would be safe and it wasn't. That's the sort of difficult challenge that comes in, and perhaps if I'd been in a better sort of frame on the day I might have realised what I was getting into and cut back on to another route, but I think you tend to get rather dispirited, you know, or switch off and follow somebody in front rather than make a decision yourself, and that can be, you know, a disaster. (Albert 80–85-years)

Albert's theory of practice reveals an explicitly theorised knowledge of bodily expertise required in a particular physical environment and an understanding of the rules of running (it is well established that following other runners is foolish). The fell runner's body hexis, 'a whole system of techniques involving the body and tools, and charged with a host of social meanings and values' (Bourdieu 1977: 87) is sustained through prolonged participation in the field. The runners gain an existential enrichment, an embodied intoxication (Shilling and Mellor 2011) that, although beyond articulation, is hinted at by comments such as: 'only a runner could understand'. The existential capital of experiential gains from running serve to cement the social relations within – what therefore becomes – a bounded, relatively autonomous social field (Nettleton 2013). These older runners then are embedded in a field that those outwith this social space might find difficult to comprehend, to the extent that only those unacquainted with the field of fell might be shortsighted enough to suggest that they should change their practice.

Throughout the fieldwork a puzzle emerged. When asked during interviews about times when they had not been able to run, the participants deftly avoided addressing the question. Across the data set, respondents were, it seems, unable to articulate the explanatory answers that were being called for. For example, when the interviewer asked Jack, who is in his seventies, 'How do you feel when you can't run?' he replied:

Jack: It's not nice. [Pause] But I just accept it, I know where the problem is, and that. Sometimes, after an hour or so I start to go better like, you know, start to climb better. But you haven't got to look at the clock when you come back you know.
Interviewer: So when you say it's not nice, you just accept it, but I get the feeling you're still going out then?
Jack: Oh aye, I still go out.

Somehow, during this exchange the point of the question is lost. Jack sidesteps the issue and reformulates the conversation to talk about running with an injury. This is curious because it was apparent earlier in the interview that he has had invasive surgery and extended periods of hospitalisation. Ed (aged 65–70 years) too, was asked the same question, to which he replied:

I mean, I have days when I don't run, I feel absolutely awful, I mean I go out for a walk or I go out on the bike, so I do something. (Ed, aged 65–70 years)

He then went into elaborate detail about technical aids (such as strapping his Achilles) that enabled him to run when injured. Deirdre (aged 65–70 years) when asked: 'How do you feel when you can't run?' replied, 'Well it's happened so little'. Rather floored by this response in the light of her medical history, the interviewer prompts: 'I mean, presumably when you had the hip replacement you couldn't run for a while?' to which she responds:

No, but you know, you just sort of, you've just got to get through it, haven't you, there's lots of good reports of people running and orienteering, I did a lot of walking after that, and a bit of cycling; what you don't want to do is fall. (Deirdre, aged 65–70 years)

Why, then, do the runners not speak about times when they can't run? It seems that although the runners are able to offer explicit theorised accounts of their running, it was difficult, and at times virtually impossible, to elicit clear accounts of times when they were unable to run. In fact, descriptions of not being able to run (for example, after a hip replacement or having a pace-maker fitted) comprised accounts of physical activities that approximated to running. Or cautions, such as taking care 'not to fall' and 'you mustn't look at the clock'. Expectations that running might be curtailed were resisted, perhaps because they risk 'imposing different definitions of the impossible, the possible, and the probable' Bourdieu (1977: 78).

Tussles about age, or generationally acceptable behaviour were also evident in the data, indicating the participants' awareness that other social groups might find their activity to be age inappropriate. For example, they participants hinted that those outwith the field of fell running 'don't get it', as Yvonne reveals:

> [They] say, aren't you getting a bit old for this, you know, and family sort of said, 'Are you sure all of this is good for you? but it's not done any harm, so far, so you know, nonrunners and non-fell runners do perhaps think you should be slowing down, but people in fell running, no. (Yvonne, aged 60–65 years)

Exhortations to stop were more overt in formal healthcare settings. Recollections of exchanges with health professionals were accompanied by laughter, indicating that doctors did not understand the absurdity of their advice. For example, Albert laughs when recalling a visit to GP: 'The doctor, he said "you'll do your hips and do your knees no good, you want to pack that up"' (Albert 80–85 years). Such explicit negative sanctions by those with no grasp of the running habitus simply reinforced their resolve. For example, Oscar is candid about his non-compliance in his mid-fiftiess, reflected:

> In 1973 I had a serious illness and they said I had never to run again, and I ignored it. I used to run quietly without telling anybody. Well I was depressed really because I'd run all my life, and so that was why I ran without telling the doctor. (Oscar, aged 85–90 years)

We see then that, rather like the novice cyclists, these expert runners are able to articulate a theory of practice when describing their somatic skills but, unlike the novice cyclists, their running habitus is congruent with a relatively autonomous social field with which they are comfortable. Furthermore, the nature of the sport – the skills required, the hardships, the exhilaration and the intensity of the experience – in combination embeds a fundamentally embodied habitus. This visceral quality makes it all the more difficult to change. Running as a social practice was critical not only to identity but also to their body and soul (Wacquant 2004). This form of mobility, it seems, is not a behaviour undertaken in the pursuit of health but an embodied social practice not readily amenable to change.

Discussion

We have sought to illustrate that a fruitful approach to examining transformations of practice (such as to make more people undertake healthy mobility practices) needs to be attuned to the ways in which practical or tacit knowledge frames the conditions for possibility of transformation. This framing issue has methodological implications: if we want to further our understanding of social practices that have relevance for health, we cannot rely on naive readings of interview data that merely document articulated theories of practice and, crucially we must not take at face value insiders' explicit rationales for their action. More fundamentally, if sociology is to make a contribution to understanding what is useful for public health, in outlining the most productive possibilities for changing practice or helping to identify what the conditions of possibility for change might be, we need to move beyond merely noting that practice is contingent and complex, and start building new more theoretical models of where, how, and when change is more or less likely to happen.

Bourdieu described a doxa of traditional societies in which 'the social and natural world appears self-evident' (1977: 164) and there can be no awareness of orthodoxy or heterodoxy: practice is the taken-for-granted way in which the habitus is reproduced in the physical and social body; only ever revealed when it comes up against what Bourdieu calls the field of opinion. Whether or not this is (or was ever) true of much practice in traditional society, one could argue that contemporary cosmopolitan societies are marked by a fragility of the boundary between doxa and the field of opinion. All practice is potentially contestable and it may be inappropriate to think of individuals inhabiting one habitus. Instead, practice is negotiated within multiple, overlapping fields, in which plural identities may be understood as relating to a number of sites of habitus. In researching practice, there is often then a sense of dislocation; for each practitioner is also an anthropologist, forced from time to time to confront different sites of habitus, at times overtly (as in the case of social researchers asking, 'Why do you do this'?), but also routinely, in the minutiae of real or implied interactions, such as those between Candy and the 'kids' in the park, or the fell runners and their medical advisers. The doxa, apparently, has all but disappeared in cosmopolitan society, with all practice up for at least the implication of debate.

However, this disappearance is illusory and (methodologically) a dangerous chimera. In cosmopolitan societies where all are called to engage in health practices, all are obligated to account for their practices (or lack of them). But these accountings belong to the world of theories of practice, not the habitus, which remains only partly, at best, explicated. Given the overlapping sites of habitus, rationales may be offered in one field, but impossible in another, where tacit knowledge shapes dispositions. Thus, for the fell runners, the ageing habitus is one in which running may be contestable; yet within the field of practice of fell running itself, it is unquestionably necessary. For novice cyclists in London, the acquisition of somatic skills may be explicable, but accounting for a thwarted transformation to cyclist relies on a difficult to articulate dislocation of habitus and field.

This is what accounts for the contradictory accounts of practice that have been identified in recent ethnographic accounts of, for instance commuting as a social practice, which is explained in terms of the 'messiness and multiplicity of everyday life' (Guell et al. 2012: 233). While our case studies support this contingency, and the need to understand individual practices in the context of the quotidian, we also suggest that more attention to tacit knowledge of various kinds might make sense of what is apparently contradictory. Beneath the rationales that our methodological obsession with formal interviewing generates are the rather less easy to document tacit, somatic and collective forms of knowledge that shape what is done and why in rather more regular ways. Understanding practice as being shaped by habitus within particular fields provides some purchase on why, despite (for instance) similar accounts of learning to cycle, Candy and Rosalind have different experiences, or why (for instance) fell runners apparently have such difficulties in answering questions about when health problems stopped them running. Methodologically, the point is not that interviews per se, or any other form of data generation technique, is necessarily the problem. Rather, the issue relates to how we handle our data. We must avoid literal readings and analysis that simply reproduce actors' accounts and instead we must pay attention to what is not said and be attuned to the interactional responses to questions or informal exchanges; and be aware of the more structural patterning of utterances and practices, which reflect habitus and doxa, and collective tacit knowledge.

Conclusion

Instead of accepting the premise inherent in much public health research that seeks to identify barriers to change, we need to first undertake a 'rigorous science of practice ... [asking] what are the conditions which make such knowledge possible' (Bourdieu, 1977: 4). A key element of this, we argue, is to take various elements of practical, tacit knowledge more seriously as part of these conditions of possibility. Then, it may be possible to more fruitfully identify how and why such practices are transformed and, thus, what might be the conditions of possibility for change or resistance. Beginning with questions of behaviour, and taking accounts of barriers as unproblematic evidence for why people do (or don't) do what they do, risks finding answers that relate only to more rationalised and cognitive theories of practice. It leaves under-examined the collective tacit knowledge or practical reasoning that make certain practices more or less likely. Interviews framed in terms of reasons for a particular kind of behaviour already, by the fact of inviting someone to be interviewed about it, frame it as thinkable, but as Bourdieu warns (Bourdieu 1977: 19), inviting insiders' accounts of their behavioural choices sets up an inevitably theorised subjective account of practice, rendering invisible the conditions of possibility for cycling or stopping running. It is these practical kinds of knowledge – less easily rendered up as statements in interviews – that may provide more clues to why actions change or don't change.

Acknowledgements

Judith Green would like to thank colleagues on the cycling study (in particularly Rebecca Steinbach, Jessica Datta and Gemma Phillips, who generated the data drawn on here) and the participants who talked in detail about their transport practices. This study was funded by the National Health Service Camden and Transport for London's Smarter Travel Unit. Sarah Nettleton would like to thank those runners who participated in the study and James Gunn for transcribing the interviews.

References

Aldred, R. and Jungnickel, K. (2012) Constructing mobile places between 'leisure' and 'transport': a case study of two group cycle rides, *Sociology*, 46, 3, 523–39.

Bourdieu, P. (1977) *Outline of a Theory of Practice*. Cambridge: Cambridge Univerity Press.

Collins, H. (2010) *Tacit & Explicit Knowledge*. Chicago: Univerisity of Chicago Press.

De Nazelle, A., Nieuwenhuijsen, M.J., Antó, J.M., *et al.* (2011) Improving health through policies that promote active travel: a review of evidence to support integrated health impact assessment, *Environment International*, 37, 4, 766–77.

Department of Health (2004) *At Least Five a Week: Evidence on the Impact of Physical Activity and Its Relationship to Health*. London: Department of Health.

Department of Health (2011) *Start Active, Stay Active: a Report on Physical Activity from the Four Home Countries' Chief Medical Officers*. London: Department of Health.

Gard, M. (2010) Truth, belief and the cultural politics of obesity scholarship and public health policy, *Critical Public Health*, 21, 1, 37–48.

Green, J., Steinbach, R. and Datta, J. (2012) The travelling citizen: emergent discourses of moral mobility in a study of cycling in London, *Sociology*, 46, 2, 272–89.

Guell, C., Panter, J., Jones, N. and Ogilvie, D. (2012) Towards a differentiated understanding of active travel behaviour: using social theory to explore everyday commuting, *Social Science & Medicine*, 75, 1, 233–9.

Hillsdon, M., Cavill, N., Nanchahal, K., Diamond, A., *et al.* (2001) National level promotion of physical activity: results from England's ACTIVE for Life campaign, *Journal of Epidemiology and Community Health*, 55, 10, 755–61.

Horton, D. (2007) Fear of cycling. In Horton, D., Rosen, P. and Cox, P. (eds) *Cycling in Society*. Aldershot: Ashgate.

Killoran, A., Doyle, N., Waller, S., Wohlgemuth, C., *et al.* (2006) *Transport Interventions Promoting Safe Cycling and Walking: Evidence Briefing*. London: NICE.

Nettleton, S. (2013) Cementing relations in a social field: fell running in the English Lake District and the acquisition of existential capital, *Cultural Sociology*, 7, 2, 196–210.

National Institute for Health and Clinical Excellence (NICE) (2006) *Four Commonly Used Methods to Increase Physical Activity: Brief Interventions in Primary Care, Exercise Referral Schemes, Pedometers and Community-Based Exercise Programmes for Walking and Cycling*. London: NICE.

Ogilvie, D., Egan, M., Hamilton, V. and Petticrew, M. (2004) Promoting walking and cycling as an alternative to using cars: systematic review, *BMJ*, 329, 7469, 763–6.

Pate, R.R., Pratt, M., Blair, R., Haskell, W.L., *et al.* (1995) Physical activity and public health: a recommendation from the Centers for Disease Control and Prevention and the American College of Sports Medicine, *Journal of the American Medical Association*, 273, 5, 402–7.

Polanyi, M. (1966) *The Tacit Dimension*. London: Routledge & Kegan Paul.

Shilling, C. and Mellor, P. (2011) Retheorising Emile Durkheim on society and religion: embodiment, intoxication and collective life, *Sociological Review*, 59, 1, 17–41.

Steinbach, R., Green, J., Datta, J. and Edwards, P. (2011) Cycling and the city: a case study of how gendered, ethnic and class identities can shape healthy transport choices, *Social Science & Medicine*, 72, 7, 1123–30.

Steinbach, R., Green, J. and Edwards, P. (2012) Look who's walking: social and environmental correlates of children's walking in London, *Health and Place*, 18, 4, 917–27.

Wacquant, L. (2004) *Body & Soul: Notebooks of an Apprentice Boxer*. Oxford: Oxford University Press.

9

Providers' constructions of pregnant and early parenting women who use substances

Cecilia Benoit, Camille Stengel, Lenora Marcellus, Helga Hallgrimsdottir, John Anderson, Karen MacKinnon, Rachel Phillips, Pilar Zazueta and Sinead Charbonneau

Introduction

Use of substances by women who are pregnant or new parents is often conceptualised within an individualised framework. It is commonplace to employ the language of substance abuse when referring to pregnant women who use drugs and other substances and who are targeted for intervention (Campbell and Alexander 2006, Claus *et al.* 2007, Lefebvre *et al.* 2010). While it seems to be a minor problem, this choice of language suggests that pregnant women who use substances are breaching their ethical responsibilities to themselves and the foetus: by 'choosing to abuse' substances and allowing themselves to become addicted they have become 'pregnant addicts' (Young 1994). Rutman *et al.* (2000) state that this moralising language tends to 'imply some amount of judgement toward the woman and encourage an avenue of thinking that separates her from the context of her life' (p. v).

The belief that individuals are chiefly responsible for their health behaviour fundamentally shapes theories of health, disease and addiction to alcohol and other substances (Room 1983, Reinarman 2005, Schneider 1978). This notion also informs harm reduction approaches that aim to empower individuals with the tools and services to change substance use patterns, learn to consume substances in a safer manner, and engage in other forms of behaviour to reduce drug-related harm (Lenton and Single 1998).

Results from research studies have shown that drinking alcohol and using other drugs during pregnancy and early parenthood cuts across social divisions; yet the societal disapproval and accompanying stigma of substance use tends to be disproportionately attached to women of disadvantaged backgrounds (Campbell and Ettorre 2011, Lester *et al.* 2004). Researchers used urine samples to test the substance use of pregnant women in a Florida county and found that although the rates of substance use were fairly equal between private and public clinics and between Black and White women, Black women were ten times more likely than White women to be reported to health authorities based on their practitioners' risk assessments, and poor women were also reported at a much higher frequency than wealthy women (Chasnoff *et al.* 1990). Other studies have documented unequal testing for

From Health Behaviours to Health Practices: Critical Perspectives, First Edition. Edited by Simon Cohn. Chapters © 2014 The Authors. Book Compilation © 2014 Foundation for the Sociology of Health & Illness / Blackwell Publishing Ltd.

substance use comparing White populations with ethnic minorities (Kerker *et al.* 2006, Lloyd 2010). Finally, although prescription drug use and misuse during pregnancy is on the rise in many countries, the more punitive focus from health and social services authorities continues to be on illicit substance use (such as marijuana, cocaine, heroin and crystal methamphetamine), again often bringing attention to women from more disadvantaged backgrounds (Campbell and Ettorre 2011).

Pregnant and early parenting women who are likely to be identified as problem substance users also experience various forms of social inequity and marginalisation that often precede substance use, including inadequate material resources, unstable or deficient housing and low education (Bailey *et al.* 2012, Greaves and Poole 2008, Schempf and Strobino 2008). In the USA many women in this situation also lack health insurance (Roberts and Pies 2011). These factors have been identified as necessary considerations for contextualising drug use during the reproductive period, but also as evidence of the way that surveillance of maternal substance use intersects with class and racial discrimination (Salmon 2011). Furthermore, the stigma associated with maternal substance use engenders a host of social, material and psychological marginalisations that have adverse consequences for both the mother and her child, including their avoidance of services even when they are available for fear of being harshly judged (Poole and Isaac 2001).

While the recent growth of targeted programmes aim to minimise the risk of health and social problems for disadvantaged mothers, many of these programmes and associated policies are oriented towards identifying individual risk and tend to employ social surveillance in the form of risk assessments of infants by the state, rather than focusing on the empowerment and inclusion of women of disadvantaged backgrounds who lack access to key social determinants of health (Murphy 2000, Zadoroznyj 2006).

Unlike these individualised treatment programmes, community-based programmes are inclusive, participant-centred, harm reduction interventions that focus on addressing both the social and health dimensions of substance use during pregnancy and early parenthood. Since the 1990s a handful of such harm reduction integrated programmes have emerged across Canada, including Breaking the Cycle and New Choices in Ontario, the Maxxine Wright Place Project in the Fraser Valley region of British Columbia (BC) and Sheway in Vancouver, BC. HerWay Home (HWH), an abbreviation for 'housing first, empowerment, respect, women, acceptance, your choice, health, opportunity, mother and equality', is situated in Victoria, BC, and builds on these earlier successful initiatives. The programme was officially launched in 2013 and is designed to be a cross-sectorial, community-based, culturally safe service site for women, infants and families who are experiencing barriers to health care due to intersecting marginalisation. The HWH core programme services include basic needs support (for example, nutrition and child-minding), primary health and perinatal services, counselling for substance use, trauma and mental health issues and support in accessing and maintaining housing. HWH is the result of efforts by an interdisciplinary and cross-sector network of local health and social care professionals, outreach agencies, members of charitable organisations and government agencies, and an advisory group of women who identify as representatives of the HWH service population. The HWH initiative is informed by a harm reduction philosophy and a social determinants of health framework that together recognise the importance of providing services to help reduce the harm associated with substance use while providing access to crucial resources such as safe and secure housing, income assistance, social support, food security and educational and employment opportunities.

There is a growing body of academic literature that critically examines recent public health interventions, such as HWH, that are aimed at implementing harm reduction and health promotion techniques in service delivery. This literature situates public health discourse within the context of neoliberalisation, welfare state reform and the social origins of health inequities, highlighting the ways in which new public health discourses advance individual solutions to problems alongside social understandings of health, with adverse and contradictory consequences for disadvantaged groups (Campbell and Ettorre 2011, Cockerham 2005, Greaves and Poole 2008, Link and Phelan 2006, Navarro 2009, Zadoroznyj 2006). Drawing on this literature, we examine qualitative data from representatives of the HWH network of health and social care providers and programme funders. We focus, in particular, on these providers' conceptualisations of problematic substance by women during pregnancy and early parenting. First, we briefly describe our study and methodology.

Sample and methods

The data presented in this chapter were gathered as part of a mixed-method study entitled Interventions to Promote Health and Health Equity for Pregnant and Early Parenting Women Facing Substance Use and Other Challenges, which was funded by the Canadian Institute of Health Research and received ethical review from the Human Research Ethics Board at the University of Victoria.

The study aimed to shed light on: (i) the factors that promote open communication and the full participation of all team members of the HWH so that continuity of primary maternity care is established and sustained over time and the clients are treated with respect and dignity by providers; and (ii) the factors that enhance client access to other health and social services that are key in harm reduction and health promotion strategies for women affected by substance use during pregnancy and early parenting. Semi-structured interviews were initially conducted with the core team of health and social care providers connected with the HWH and key local community and provincial governmental stakeholders, and the study was eventually expanded to include interviews with a more diverse sample of providers who had a role in serving pregnant women and persons affected by substance use, but with a more limited knowledge of HWH. Our qualitative results, presented below, are based on interviews conducted with 56 persons. More specifically, the analysis focuses on providers' responses to the question: 'How do you define problematic substance use among pregnant and early parenting women?'

Findings

Our findings reveal the most popular conceptions of problematic maternal substance use identified in the data. It was not uncommon for participants to draw on more than one of the broad conceptualisations noted below when seeking to explain problematic substance use. It was not apparent that differences in the emphases that providers placed on certain perceptual frameworks could be linked to their professional background. One exception might be that providers who worked in outreach and other community-based services for street-based populations were more likely draw on the language of harm reduction in their explanations. Many participants who espoused a harm reduction point of view were reluctant to embrace it fully: a response with both semiotic and discursive features that characterise the ethical complexity of foetal and maternal rights for advocates of individualistic harm reduction models.

The difficulty of defining the problem

While many of the participants work in the context of pregnancy, parenting and substance use in their everyday action as service providers, very few had a ready definition of problematic substance use and, indeed, struggled momentarily with the question. This moment of discomfort in identifying suitable language is likely to be a reflection of the social, legal and moral ambiguity within which maternal substance use behaviour occurs. Thus, the issue of problematic substance use among pregnant and early parenting women was not readily articulable, as illustrated in this participant's response: '[Silence] Oh that's really interesting, I never sort of thought about actually defining it'. Similarly, another participant responded with the answer: 'That's so funny; I've never really sort of considered that, that question'. One participant noted that she does not need to define the concept for her practice:

> [I]t's not something I've really thought about defining. I mean, take away problematic and I'm comfortable with ... just working with people who use substances. I don't know whether I'd define problematic substance use in my practice. (Rebecca[1])

Two participants stated explicitly that their professional definitions are different from their personal definitions:

> [J]ust, whatever my personal thoughts or fears are ... I know that in my role in my job, it's not up to me to be deciding like what's right or wrong for them. (Sarah)

> [L]ike, I had a different idea for myself when I was pregnant ... so I guess it kind of varies, like professionally, that's my professional answer. (Emily)

In the case of the latter respondent, she was clearly struggling with her own experience of pregnancy and her professional view of substance use among pregnant clients. Drawing distinctions between and discrete boundaries around the ideologies employed in private and public realms is difficult. However, we report these examples here because they are symptomatic of a more widespread tension among participants to articulate a moral–ethical hierarchy that guides their definitions of problematic maternal substance use and their related practices as service providers. The attempt to separate personal from professional practices is indicative of the degree to which maternal substance use can be considered in moral terms over other acts of substance use. Since the views of some of the providers we spoke to reflected popular notions of maternal purity and the sanctity of the foetus, an artificial elision between personal and professional practices occurs, allowing providers to maintain their private ethic and image of appropriate maternal behaviour while still striving to provide care in a non-judgemental way. Whether this division could actually be maintained in practice is unclear, but the need to identify these distinctions indicates that some provider's perceptions are deeply entrenched in moral judgements.

The most common perceptual frameworks that participants drew upon to define problematic substance use focused on terms such as safety, risk and ability to care and the notion that the individual woman is the arbiter of what constitutes problematic substance use in her own life. Some participants acknowledged and foregrounded the ways in which perceptions of problematic substance use are generated in the broader representational hierarchy wherein bodies bound to certain spaces and classes are read and labelled as problematic.

Safety, risk and ability to care

Just over half the participants focused on problematic substance use as a loss of the ability to care. The ability to care was referenced in relation to keeping oneself safe, securing material resources and, most importantly, the responsibility of the woman to optimise the health of her foetus and infant. Quotes from three different participants are provided as examples:

> [I]t might not be so problematic [for a woman]. She might be coping. But it might be problematic for her child: either the physical growth of her baby during pregnancy or her ability to parent that child. (Monica)

> [I]f they can say 'I'm gonna go and party, and mom's looking after the baby'... if it's not consuming their life and that's, that's what they do and they go out to the bar and have some drinks I think that's fine within, you know, reason, but ... if the, you know, baby is in the crib and friends come over and, they party or they're, you know, abusing drugs then how can they safely parent their child? (Christine)

> You could be middle to upper class and be a regular heroin user but you can afford to pay for a nanny, so therefore someone's taking care of your children. But then, you can argue that the connection between parent and child is harmed. So, for me, the focus would be on the children. (Marlon)

The final two passages also portray the way that maternal responsibility can be offset by the availability of another woman to care; problematic substance use is thus, in part, defined by a lack of substitute maternal care.

While some respondents highlighted women's safety as a dimension of problematic substance use, many of these instances linked women's safety and wellness to foetal health and the care for children, thus positioning women's health as a means to the end of the health of the infant or child. As one participant put it: 'when ... substances are interfering with her ability to have a level of stability, and safety for her and either ... for her most importantly, and then for her children'. Another participant similarly commented on the perceived potential of a conflict between women's bodily autonomy and foetal and infant health:

> And it's a balancing act, right? We want to be very woman-focused, and I absolutely approach my work from that mind frame, but there's still a baby involved ... I'm very pro-choice but ... when she said 'I'm choosing to keep this pregnancy', then it's a baby. It's no longer a foetus. She's made the decision already that it's a baby. (Kate)

While it is certainly true that engaging in practice or discourse about maternal substance use (or, for that matter, the actual practice of mothering) is a balancing act of rights, responsibilities and needs, this participant's narrative posits a morally construed conflict between the mother and the foetus that is not justified by the Canadian legal context (Poole and Isaac 2001). By using the term 'baby', this participant is making an ontological leap with significant normative implications. In deconstructing this participant's discourse, the intention is not to sublimate the experience of providing care for pregnant women who are likely themselves to relate to their foetuses as babies. Faced with this normalising practice on a day-to-day basis, practitioners' dialectical relation to the pregnant woman and her foetus affects language that is contextually important (to validate pregnant women's experiences) but may also have unintended social consequences.

In sum, one can extrapolate from the data concerning safety, risk and ability to care that one operational definition of problematic substance use is any departure from the vigilance women are expected to exhibit, first over their pregnant bodies as vessels for foetal health, and second in relation to their primary responsibility to protect children (Bordo 2003).

Participants had little to say about either the pharmacological actions of substances or a more medicalised notion of addiction as a disease (Reinarman 2005). This is not to suggest that biomedical knowledge of the effects of substance use on foetuses and women would necessarily lend itself to a more incontrovertible conceptualisation of problematic substance use, but it is interesting that framing problematic substance use in pharmacological terms or as a biomedical disease with identifiable physical health outcomes and symptoms was often entirely absent from, or only vaguely referenced, in professional accounts of substance use. The following quote from one of the participants indicates how the pharmacological effects of drugs were given meaning via notions of maternal responsibility:

> I don't make that distinction that if it's prescribed it's OK. So I'm looking at all different drug use. And, if it comes to the point where it's a, if it's higher than what could be safely used in breastfeeding … then that's problematic. If it's impairing the mom's ability to parent the baby, then that's problematic.

Some participants expressed confusion about, or specifically noted the absence of, a body of evidence that might inform a more biomedical definition of problematic substance use among pregnant and early parenting women:

> So especially if they're continuing to drink, you know, that we know that that causes, you know significant issues. For a lot of other substances, I think that the research is kind of limited about, you know, how much it affects babies. And so I try not to get super-judgmental about stuff, and really work from a harm reduction perspective, of like, 'How much can you reduce your pot smoking?' (Olivia)

> I think that the latest research is indicating that any alcohol or substance exposure during pregnancy can result in a problem. I mean, there are women who drink throughout their whole pregnancy and their children are not affected. Other women, before they knew they were pregnant, they drank socially, and their children are affected, so who really knows? (Tara)

These findings echo other sociological research that addiction as a disease remains an elusive concept. Despite the search for a specific genetic basis to addiction no physiological cause for substance use has been found, resulting in a range of suggested causal mechanisms, which has been referred to as an 'embarrassment of riches' (Reinarman 2005). It is possible that the lack of reference to biomedical effects or a disease concept among participants is because maternal substance use is regarded as so deviant that even the disease concept, which is often taken up in other discourses of addiction, is not as readily utilised in the case of maternal substance use. Another possibility is that a disease concept of problematic substance use as addiction does not often come up because, in the case of pregnant women, what is problematic about substance use has little to do with notions of addiction.

Not surprisingly, given the way substance use is associated with a reduced ability to care and wide-ranging possibilities regarding its effect on foetal and infant health, abstinence was, with only a few exceptions, regarded as the only normative substance use pattern among pregnant women. As this participant explains:

> The way I would see that is a pregnant woman using a substance, whether it's alcohol or tobacco or any other drug that would have adverse impact on her foetus or herself. (Joanne)

A few respondents made specific references to how social class intersected with substance use. One participant framed the socioeconomic readability of problematic substance use within a harm reduction perspective:

> A safe consumption site which can just be as simple as being housed, 'coz most of us have the opportunity to go and use what we like … But I do it at home so nobody, it's not in front of everybody. (Emily)

However, given that any substance use by women during pregnancy and early parenting is generally regarded as problematic, harm reduction is ultimately viewed as a less desirable practice than promoting abstinence, as the following excerpts indicate:

> Of course, the recommendation is that women abstain from alcohol use, they abstain from any street drug use, they abstain from smoking during, during pregnancy … but we also have clients where they've been using crack cocaine but they actually get themselves off that and they just are smoking during the pregnancy, and when you look at that in terms of harm reduction, do I consider that problematic? Well, gosh; it would be great if she wasn't smoking, but its way better than her using throughout the pregnancy. (Sarah)

> Using at all is problematic and, and we would be having that conversation with them around their use and how they feel about, decreasing their use or stopping their use, and how they think they can get there. (June)

In sum, drawing on rhetorical framings that focused on ability to care and risk and safety, substance use is regarded as a problem because it interferes with women's natural and essential responsibility to not only protect but to optimise the health of the foetus and infant child. While women's own safety and wellbeing is viewed as being connected to this principle task, it is subordinated under a more pressing focus on the protection of the foetus and infant child. An alternative popular framing of maternal substance use focused on women's right to define the concept for themselves.

Woman as arbiter of the problematic

When asserting that women must define problematic substance use for themselves, participants tended to deploy a couple of supporting arguments. First, some participants noted that only by allowing women to define what is problematic behaviour would they be likely to feel less judged and more likely to access health and social services such as those proposed in the HWH programme. As one participant said:

> I define problematic substance use [as] how each woman would define problematic substance use in their life. So my goal in having a conversation with a woman who's using is to talk about how that's going, and if that's causing any problems in her life or what the problems are in her life, and if there's any linkages to the drug use. (Lauren)

A second, similar logic was that women are not receptive to support or changes in substance use behaviour until they come to a realisation that it is a problem:

> It may be that her [health service professional] has said, 'If you engage in this use, it's going to have a negative effect on your baby, which, you know, will have a negative

effect on you in your life' ... I feel like a holding of a kind of tension in that because there is such a desire to protect unborn children and to have, you know, to force women into programming, to force them to stop using substances and it's just not as simple as that. (Jennifer)

This participant suggests that the focus on women defining problematic substance use for themselves is a strategic service strategy rather than a definition of problematic substance use. Respondents who held this view may not substantially differ from their colleagues in terms of their notions of the harm of substance use among pregnant and early parenting women; however, they assert that the imposition of these views is unlikely to result in successful service encounters.

Discussion and conclusion

In writing this chapter, we were interested in how service providers directly or indirectly involved with a new harm reduction integrated intervention – HWH – define problematic substance because these definitions are likely to be influential in shaping the policies and practices of healthcare provision. The research literature indicates that problematic substance use as a kind of health behaviour is poorly understood, sometimes being viewed as deviance and disease, and most often viewed as both (Aboud and Singla 2012, Reinarman 2005, Schneider 1978). There is also intense debate on how to properly conceptualise the origins of health behaviour and the conditions and manner of agency exercised as individuals perform in different social contexts (Cockerham *et al.* 1997, Link and Phelan 2006, Navarro 2009). This is complicated further when we consider the case of pregnancy because the pregnant body is a site where ideological wars are engaged and competing rights claims are generated (Marcellus 2004, Wright and Walker 2007).

In addition to being interested in how theoretical models of maternal substance use as health behaviour are applied by services providers, this study was practically oriented, as several of the authors are involved in researching HWH and are therefore interested in a knowledge exchange that will improve service delivery. Many of the participants who took part in the interview process have contributed to the development of HWH and endorse the model that health behaviour is socially determined, as well as the need to improve healthcare delivery to pregnant and parenting women affected by substance use.

Yet most participants regarded any substance use during the reproductive period as fundamentally problematic. This framing of problematic substance use is accomplished via a gendered responsibilisation of women as foetal incubators and primary caregivers of infants. Substance use is regarded as essentially harmful, particularly in the context of the reproductive female body, despite the absence of a well-developed body of scientific evidence to support this claim (Young 1994). Furthermore, while acknowledging the role of social inequities in the production of health behaviour and health outcomes, the providers we interviewed relied largely on an individualising and moralising notion of what is problematic about substance use rather than focusing, for example, on the range of socio-structural factors that contextualise substance use (Graham 2004), the fact that substance use is both a common and widely culturally endorsed activity (Room 1983) and at the individual level, an interactional accomplishment (Becker 1967).

Similarly, although matters such as the influence of social class were invoked to portray the ways in which some subgroups of women were subjected to greater surveillance and had fewer resources to draw upon to mitigate the perceived harms of substance use, there was no substantive argument put forward by participants to suggest that the harm associated with substance use was in fact a by-product of larger systems of economic disadvantage. A possible implication of this cursory analysis of class, then, is that substance use is perceived as a risk for lower class women, while leaving unexamined the assumption that substance use is a deviant, rather than normative, activity within the context of pregnancy and parenting. The framings of substance use offered by participants do little to intervene in the social condemnation and 'stigma life sentence' associated with addiction (Lloyd 2010: 46). Indeed, it might be argued that the more ostensibly women-centred framing of problematic substance use emphasised by some of the participants, while being a potentially practical service delivery strategy, has the unintended consequence of downplaying both the role of socio-structural factors on dispositions to perceive and act and the societal responsibility to provide health and social care.

These findings are not surprising when you consider that health service providers are caught between a number of competing relevant discourses informed by neoliberalisation, the Canadian public health abstinence policy for pregnant and parenting women, the harm reduction movement, the medicalisation and criminalisation of substance use, and the deeply moral constructions of the pregnant body and motherhood, especially in Indigenous women (Kline 1993, Salmon 2011). Even government documents acknowledge that the language of substance use consists of complex and high-level discourses that often have little practical meaning at the point of care delivery. Dialectics that prioritise foetal or maternal health not only permeate popular public perceptions but also Canadian public policy on reproductive health and reproductive rights. In fact, the right of the child to protection is inscribed in legislation and the providers who took part in this study were both keenly aware of the power of this legislation to define problematic substance use and their ethical and professional duties in enacting such definitions. This recognition rests uneasy with their knowledge that many marginalised women affected by substance use avoid seeking services due to fears regarding that their child might be taken by the state (Niccols *et al.* 2010, Suchman *et al.* 2006). Flavin and Paltrow (2010) express this concern by highlighting the inherent unfairness of a system that expects disadvantaged women to provide their foetuses with health care and safety that they themselves are not able to access.

Not only did participants' conceptualisations of problematic substance use reflect the structure imposed by policy and legislation, but they are also probably conditioned by the allocation of resources in the health and social service sector where neoliberalisation processes have resulted in the simultaneous retrenchment of universal services and increasing surveillance of at-risk populations as well as accountability models that use the criterion of cost effectiveness of care and place the responsibility on individuals for their health and wellbeing. Service providers must forge definitions of substance use in the context of their ability to practise and the daily interactions they have with service recipients. Given their often limited role in identifying and ameliorating identified risks and the limited resources made available to address the socio-structural origins of health (that is, poverty and access to education), service providers have little opportunity to enact and sustain alternative explanations of problematic substance use.

In conclusion, our qualitative evidence supports our general conclusion above – that is, that providers' constructions of maternal substance use are largely focused on individualised notions of health agency. Their constructions are a reflection of the weighty moral forces and competing public health messages they negotiate in attempts to enact an empowering model of care in the face of dominant cultural ideals of the good mother, the hybridisation of substance use as both deviance and disease and the overall retrenchment of funding for health and social services in Canada.

These findings suggest that any health intervention programme that is grounded in moral frameworks regarding mothering and prioritises foetal and infant rights will not bode well for the delivery of an empowering and non-judgemental model of care; rather, women's rights to health will remain subordinated and they will continue to be seen as a potential threat to their child and society. As echoed through this special issue, there is an urgent need to move away from a dominant focus on health behaviour and instead capture in research the way people carry out and make sense of health-related practices.

Acknowledgements

This research was supported by a Canadian Institutes of Health grant, Interventions to promote health and healthy equity for pregnant and early parenting women facing substance use and other challenges, co-principal investigators, Dr Cecilia Benoit, Centre for Addictions Research of BC & Dept of Sociology, University of Victoria, Canada and Dr. Lenora Marcellus, School of Nursing, University of Victoria, Canada. We wish to acknowledge the editorial assistance of Ms. Marie Marlo-Barski. Above all, we wish thank the women and men who participated in interviews. Without their input, this work would not have been possible.

Note

1   Pseudonyms are used to protect the identity of the participants.

References

Aboud, F.E. and Singla, D.R. (2012) Challenges to changing health behaviours in developing countries: a critical overview, *Social Science & Medicine*, 75, 4, 589–94.
Bailey, B., McCook, J., Hodge, A. and McGrady, L. (2012) Infant birth outcomes among substance using women: why quitting smoking during pregnancy is just as important as quitting illicit drug use, *Maternal and Child Health Journal*, 16, 2, 414–22.
Becker, H.S. (1967) History, culture and subjective experience: an exploration of the social bases of drug-induced experiences, *Journal of Health and Social Behavior*, 8, 3, 163–76.
Bordo, S. (2003) *Unbearable Weight: Feminism, Western Culture, and the Body*. Berkeley: University of California Press.
Campbell, C. and Alexander, J. (2006) Availability of services for women in outpatient substance abuse treatment: 1995–2000, *Journal of Behavioral Health Services and Research*, 33, 1, 1–19.
Campbell, N.D. and Ettorre, E. (2011) *Gendering Addiction: the Politics of Drug Treatment in a Neurochemical World*. Basingstoke and New York: Palgrave Macmillan.
Chasnoff, M.D., Landress, H.J. and Berrett, M. (1990) The prevalence of illicit-drug or alcohol use during pregnancy and discrepancies in mandatory reporting in Pinellas County, *Florida, New England Journal of Medicine*, 322, 1202–06.
Claus, R.E., Orwin, R.G., Kissin, W., Krupski, A., *et al.* (2007) Does gender-specific substance abuse treatment for women promote continuity of care?, *Journal of Substance Abuse Treatment*, 32, 1, 27–39.
Cockerham, W.C. (2005) Health lifestyle theory and the convergence of agency and structure, *Journal of Health and Social Behavior*, 46, 1, 51–67.
Cockerham, W.C., Rütten, A. and Abel, T. (1997) Conceptualizing contemporary health lifestyles, *Sociological Quarterly*, 38, 2, 321–42.
Flavin, J. and Paltrow, L. (2010) Pushing pregnant drug-using women: defying law, medicine, and common sense, *Journal of Addictive Diseases*, 29, 2, 231–44.

Graham, H. (2004) Social determinants and their unequal distribution: clarifying policy understandings, *Milbank Quarterly*, 82, 1, 101–24.

Greaves, L. and Poole, N. (2008) Bringing sex and gender into women's substance use treatment programs, *Substance Use & Misuse*, 43, 1271–3.

Kerker, B.D., Leventhal, J.M., Schlesinger, M. and Horwitz, S.M. (2006) Racial and ethnic disparities in medical history taking: detecting substance use among low-income pregnant women, *Ethnicity and Disease*, 16, 1, 28–34.

Kline, M. (1993) Complicating the ideology of motherhood: child welfare law and First Nation women, *Queen's Law Journal*, 18, 306.

Lefebvre, L., Midmer, D., Boyd, J.A., Ordean, A., *et al.* (2010) Participant perception of an integrated program for substance abuse in pregnancy, *Journal of Obstetric, Gynecologic, & Neonatal Nursing*, 39, 1, 46–52.

Lenton, S. and Single, E. (1998) The definition of harm reduction, *Drug and Alcohol Review*, 17, 2, 213–20.

Lester, B.M., Andreozzi, L. and Appiah, L. (2004) Substance use during pregnancy: time for policy to catch up with research, *Harm Reduction Journal*, 1, 5.

Link, B. and Phelan, J. (2006) Stigma and its public health implications, *The Lancet*, 367, 9509, 528–9.

Lloyd, C. (2010) *Sinning and Sinned Against: the Stigmatisation of Problem Drug Users*. Crowborough: UK Drug Policy Commission.

Marcellus, L. (2004) Feminist ethics must inform practice: interventions with perinatal substance users, *Health Care for Women International*, 25, 8, 730–42.

Murphy, E. (2000) Risk, responsibility, and rhetoric in infant feeding, *Journal of Contemporary Ethnography*, 29, 3, 291–35.

Navarro, V. (2009) What we mean by social determinants of health, *International Journal Health Services*, 39, 3, 423–41.

Niccols, A., Milligan, K., Sword, W., Thabane, L., *et al.* (2010) Maternal mental health and integrated programs for mothers with substance abuse issues, *Psychology of Addictive Behaviors*, 24, 3, 466–74.

Poole, N. and Isaac, B. (2001) *Apprehensions: Barriers to Treatment for Substance-Using Mothers*. Vancouver: British Columbia Centre of Excellence for Women's Health.

Reinarman, C. (2005) Addiction as accomplishment: the discursive construction of disease, *Addiction Research & Theory*, 13, 4, 307–20.

Roberts, S. and Pies, C. (2011) Complex calculations: how drug use during pregnancy becomes a barrier to prenatal care, *Maternal and Child Health Journal*, 15, 3, 333–41.

Room, R. (1983) Sociology and the disease concept of alcoholism. In Cappell, H. (ed.) *Research Advances in Alcohol and Drug Problems*. New York: Plenum Press.

Rutman, D., Callahan, M., Lundquist, A., Jackson, S., *et al.* (2000) *Substance Use and Pregnancy: Conceiving Women in the Policy Making Process*. Ottawa: Status of Women Canada.

Salmon, A. (2011) Aboriginal mothering, FASD prevention and the contestations of neoliberal citizenship, *Critical Public Health*, 21, 2, 165–78.

Schempf, A. and Strobino, D. (2008) Illicit drug use and adverse birth outcomes: is it drugs or context?, *Journal of Urban Health*, 85, 3, 858–73.

Schneider, J.W. (1978) Deviant drinking as disease: alcoholism as a social accomplishment, *Social Problems*, 25, 4, 361–72.

Suchman, N.E., McMahon, T.J., Zhang, H., Mayes, L.C., *et al.* (2006) Substance-abusing mothers and disruptions in child custody: an attachment perspective, *Journal of Substance Abuse Treatment*, 30, 3, 197–204.

Wright, A. and Walker, J. (2007) Management of women who use drugs during pregnancy, *Seminars in Fetal and Neonatal Medicine*, 12, 2, 114–18.

Young, I.M. (1994) Punishment, treatment, empowerment: three approaches to policy for pregnant addicts, *Feminist Studies*, 20, 1, 33–57.

Zadoroznyj, M. (2006) Surveillance, support and risk in the postnatal period, *Health Sociology Review*, 15, 4, 353–63.

10

Staying 'in the zone' but not passing the 'point of no return': embodiment, gender and drinking in mid-life

Antonia C. Lyons, Carol Emslie and Kate Hunt

Introduction

Alcohol consumption and excessive drinking have received considerable research and public health attention. Much of this work has conceptualised alcohol consumption as an individual behaviour resulting from rational choice, although public health approaches based on such assumptions are relatively ineffective (Babor *et al.* 2010). Some researchers have explored drinking behaviour in its social context, employing in-depth qualitative methodologies to theorise drinking as a practice located in people's social worlds (for example, Griffin *et al.* 2009, Lyons and Willott 2008). This research has conceptualised heavy (binge) drinking behaviour as calculated hedonism, a controlled loss of control (Measham 2006) and a way of signalling taste and identity preferences (for example, McCreanor *et al.* 2005). Yet it has focused almost exclusively on young people and paid little attention to drinking practices in terms of embodiment. Here we explore how men and women in mid-life represent their alcohol consumption as an embodied social practice. Embodiment is central to drinking practices as it allows the consideration of emotions, feelings and gender, highlights the complexities of drinking behaviour and emphasises the limitations of individual-level approaches to health practices.

Individually focused health promotion efforts to reduce alcohol consumption fail to capture the meanings and the context of drinking. Interventions frequently focus on increasing people's knowledge of a particular behaviour (for example, a recommended number of standard alcohol units) and assume that people will automatically amend their drinking in line with recommendations. This social cognition approach has been heavily criticised for its lack of success in predicting or changing behaviour (Mielewczyk and Willig 2007), being simplistic (Richmond 1998) and conceptually problematic (Ogden 2003), portraying individuals as primarily rational beings whose behaviour is devoid of social context or social meaning (Backett and Davison 1995) and failing to take affective factors into account (Mielewczyk and Willig 2007).

While physiological and behavioural responses to alcohol intake are most easily understood as phenomena occurring within an individual body, we argue that how these are experienced and interpreted is inevitably social, cultural and gendered. Choosing to drink alcohol, and decisions about continuing to drink, take place within our experience of both having and being a gendered physical body. Most young adults strive to keep some control

From Health Behaviours to Health Practices: Critical Perspectives, First Edition. Edited by Simon Cohn. Chapters © 2014 The Authors. Book Compilation © 2014 Foundation for the Sociology of Health & Illness / Blackwell Publishing Ltd.

over achieving and maintaining a desired state of intoxication, carefully choosing what, when and where to drink, who to drink with and when to stop or slow drinking (Measham 2006). These decisions and their meanings are intertwined with cultural practices of gender (for example, Griffin *et al.* 2013, Willott and Lyons 2012). Yet we know little about the processes through which such controlled intoxication is achieved and maintained, what people's gendered embodied experiences are and how they influence such decisions. We know even less about older men's and women's embodied experiences of drinking or of exceeding acceptable levels of intoxication and their decisions to cease drinking alcohol during a specific drinking episode. There are material limits to consuming alcohol within a drinking session due to the consequences of alcohol on physical bodies (for example, slurring, passing out and vomiting). Exploring these material limits, and how they are understood by men and women from different backgrounds and life stages, is crucial to understanding drinking practices. Furthermore, conceptualising drinking as an embodied practice allows fuller consideration of emotions and feelings such as pleasure, which is corporeal and subjective, felt and experienced within the body (Duff 2008). Health-promotion approaches aiming to reduce consumption tend to privilege cognitive and perceptual factors over these pleasurable, corporeal experiences (Duff 2008).

Scholars have argued for a consideration of gendered embodiment in both alcohol research (for example, Thurnell-Read 2011) and critical perspectives on health promotion and public health (Robertson and Williams 2010). Drinking is a gendered activity, with men drinking more often and more heavily than women internationally (Rahav *et al.* 2006), and traditionally expected to drink (primarily beer) excessively and in public (Lemle and Mishkind 1989). We enact varied gender identities by taking part in behaviour that has cultural meanings that are associated with versions of masculinity and femininity (Hunt *et al.* 2013, Lyons 2009); here gender is an ongoing bodily performance (Butler 1993). Young men and women engage in particular drinking practices to perform and maintain desired gender identities (de Visser and McDonnell 2012, Lyons and Willott 2008). Men use public drinking to demonstrate their relationship to hegemonic masculinity (Peralta 2007, Willott and Lyons 2012), a set of idealised social practices and norms that legitimise the interests of the powerful and the dominant position of men over women (Connell 1995). Simultaneously, young women limit or control their drinking, being aware that breaching traditional feminine boundaries may lead to their being seen as bad, promiscuous or masculine (Griffin *et al.* 2013, Peralta 2007). Older women talk about their drinking in ways that resist and deflect the stigma often associated with excessive drinking in women (Rolfe *et al.* 2009), illustrating how moral discourses around drinking are highly gendered (Day *et al.* 2004). Men and women drink heavily for pleasure and fun but this plays out in different ways for masculinities, femininities and gender relations for young (Lyons 2009) and older adults (Emslie *et al.* 2012, 2013).

While informative for linking drinking practices with gender identities, this work rarely considers the body. Yet the corporeal body is crucially important, as it is in and through our bodies that we negotiate daily life and experience the world. Young women's drinking practices in rural England have been shown to be embodied performances negotiated in relation to rural space and society (Leyshon 2008). Thurnell-Read's (2011) research with men drinking on a stag tour in Eastern Europe found they displayed an unconstrained embodiment (in contrast to traditional bounded and controlled embodied masculinity), which involved pleasurable bodily transgressions, the display of leaky bodies (through vomiting and urination) and illness and fatigue. He argues that 'the unruly drunkenness of collective drinking rituals has become, for many men, the location of their most notable or, at least, most vivid engagement with their own bodies' (p. 987) which functions to reassert male friendships and bonds.

Our research was designed to address the call for a 'richer and fuller understanding of the relationship between embodiment, emotions and alcohol, drinking and drinking practices' (Leyshon 2008: 285) and provide further knowledge of men's and women's drinking in mid-life. Below we utilise empirical data to argue that alcohol consumption needs to be understood as an embodied social practice that occurs at the complex intersection of the physiological effects of alcohol, embodied gendered identities, emotions and feeling states, and external materialities including places, people and spaces.

Study background, design and method

The DrAM (Drinking Attitudes in Mid-life) study aimed to explore experiences and understandings of alcohol consumption in mid-life adults (see also Emslie *et al.* 2012, 2013). We defined mid-life as ranging from 30–50 years to distinguish our participants from the younger adults who are frequently the focus of alcohol research. The study was informed by a social constructionist epistemology, which views the world as involving multiple systems of understanding that occur through social and cultural experiences, which in turn are largely influenced by the active and constructive nature of language (Burr 2003). This raises some difficulties for studying embodiment, as social constructionism has no adequate notion of embodied subjectivity (Cromby 2004) and lived bodily experience is not always reducible to language. We drew on Cromby's (2004) notion of embodied subjectivity to develop an integrated critical realist constructionism that takes both materiality and embodiment into account. Here the physical, material body and its corporeal processes are recognised but it is acknowledged that their meanings are socially constructed, subject to change culturally and historically. As Robertson and Williams (2010: 59) argue, 'the representational and the material aspects of bodies are not readily separable'; our understandings of bodies and being in the world are wrapped up in discourse. Thus, we sought to explore embodied experience by asking people explicitly to recall their lived embodied sensations, feelings and states when they consumed alcohol. As we were also interested in the inherently social nature of drinking and how these subjective experiences were interwoven with the social, we conducted discussion groups with people who were friends or work colleagues and who drank together occasionally. We chose to conduct same-sex and mixed-sex groups to provide greater diversity in the contexts of the discussions, and to explore similarities and differences in gendered, embodied experiences across different groups.

Our recruitment strategies involved approaching potential participants on the street and in bars, e-mailing people, inviting them to forward study information to friends and colleagues, contacting community groups and workplaces and advertising on community websites. People interested in taking part were asked to invite up to five friends or colleagues in the desired age range who regularly drank alcohol to join them in a group discussion with a researcher. The participants gave their written, informed consent to be audiotaped and completed a drinking grid estimating their alcohol consumption in the previous week. Discussions were facilitated by CE using a semistructured interview schedule covering topics such as changes in drinking over time, occasions and feelings when participants had drunk more than they intended, attempts to reduce drinking and distinctions between men's and women's drinking. The participants were given a £20 voucher towards compensating them for their time and costs incurred. Group discussions lasted between 60–95 minutes, were transcribed verbatim and checked against the recordings for accuracy. Pseudonyms were used and any identifying features were changed or removed. Detailed field notes were written after each focus group and shared with the research team.

In all, 15 group discussions were conducted in Glasgow between 2009 and 2011 following approval from Glasgow University's Faculty of Law, Business and Social Sciences Ethics Committee. Here we present data from 14 groups (six mixed sex, three all-male and five allfemale), excluding a group of non-drinkers (FG7) recruited to provide a different perspective on the cultural context of alcohol. Details of the groups are provided in Table 1. The 56 participants (22 men and 34 women) were all white, aged mostly in their thirties and forties and came from diverse socioeconomic backgrounds. A total of 30 participants lived with a partner and 25 had at least one child under 18 years of age living with them on a day-to-day basis. The participants reported having consumed a range of units of alcohol in the previous week (where each unit represents 8 grams of pure alcohol). Two participants had not consumed alcohol, while 16 men and 16 women had consumed in excess of the

Table 1 *Details of focus groups and participants (N = 56)[1]*

Group type	Participants	Ages	Deprivation category[2]	Alcohol units past week	No. drinking at 'hazardous' level[3]
FG1 Council workers	2 M, 2 F	44–49	intermediate	9–15	1 F
FG2 Male pub friends	4 M	44–50	mixed	49–90	4 M
FG3 Lecturers	2 M, 2 F	34–49	mixed	21–33	2 M, 2 F
FG4 Female friends	4 F	44–48	affluent/ intermediate	14–60	3 F
FG5 Sales workers	1 M, 4 F	40–50	mixed	9–36	1 M, 3 F
FG6 Community group (deprived area)	4 M, 3 F	41–mid 50s?[4]	deprived	0–92	1 M
FG8 Office workers	4 F	36–47	affluent/ intermediate	0–27	2 F
FG9 Community group (affluent area)	3 F	35–45	affluent	3–15	1 F
FG10 Heterosexual couples	2 M, 2 F	32–35	affluent/ intermediate	14–28	1 M, 1 F
FG11 Best friends and girlfriend	2 M, 1 F	31–33	mixed	25–65	2 M, 1 F
FG12 Gym group mums	4 F	30–31	deprived	3–20	1 F
FG13 Unemployed friends	2 M	28–31	affluent/ intermediate	29–38	2 M
FG14 Old school friends	3 M	30–32	deprived	27–48	3 M
FG15 Toddler group mums	5 F	30–41	affluent/ intermediate	1–19	1 F

[1]This dataset excludes group 7, a group of non-drinkers recruited for an alternative perspective on the cultural context of alcohol.
[2]Carstairs scores calculated for residential postcodes: affluent = DEPCAT 1 and 2, intermediate = DEPCAT 3–5, deprived = DEPCAT 6 and 7, mixed = respondents from each of these three categories present in one group.
[3]'Hazardous' drinking: more than 21 units/week for men, 14 units/week for women.
[4]Two participants in FG6 did not give their age.
F, female; M, male.

threshold for hazardous drinking (over 21 units of alcohol for men and 14 units for women) according to UK National Health Service (2011) guidelines.

Thematic analysis (Braun and Clarke 2006) allowed us to identify, analyse and report patterns in the data, and thus provide rich, detailed and complex accounts informed by our theoretical frameworks. The transcripts were read a number of times by all authors. One researcher (AL) identified initial patterns in the data, which were then coded for more detailed scrutiny. This process generated 12 general themes and sub-themes (for example, feelings, emotions, feeling-body states, physiology, contextual factors, reasons to drink/stop drinking, social experiences, ageing and health-promotion messages). Another author (CE) independently coded the transcripts, focusing on gender and gender roles. There was a significant overlap in the themes identified, particularly around reasons given for drinking, feelings and emotions and physiological responses to alcohol. Next AL reformulated these initial themes into higher order conceptual groupings, focusing primarily on bodies, including embodied pleasures, constraints and experiences. These themes were reworked repeatedly through an ongoing discussion with all researchers to ensure they were grounded in the data and oriented to gender.

Findings

The participants varied widely in how much alcohol they consumed, and how often, where and what they drank. Most distinguished between their drinking practices when they were younger, which were associated with the physical effect of alcohol on the body and getting drunk, and their current, wiser, drinking practices which they framed as being more about enjoyment, and taste (see Emslie, Hunt, and Lyons 2012). Yet the participants also recounted stories of recent drunken or heavy drinking episodes and social pressures to drink. Despite this diversity of drinking practices there were striking commonalities in the data around the pleasurable sensations that alcohol and drinking practices provided, the point at which participants just knew it was time to curtail or cease drinking, the factors that influenced their reducing consumption and their awareness of public health information. Below we highlight these key similarities in relation to gendered material bodies.

Embodied pleasures of drinking practices and alcohol consumption:
older bodies and the material world
The participants all described their enjoyment of alcohol. This was most commonly associated with feelings of relaxing, winding down, stopping activity and distinguishing between everyday practices and rest time. It was discussed as making 'you feel nice and calm' (Cath FG4), as taking away 'the aches and pains from the day's work' (Craig FG1), and providing that 'nice sense of relaxation' (Anne FG12). Alcohol consumption also marked a space away from domesticity and childcare for many women; for example Anne (FG12) framed drinking as 'a declaration of adulthood' and Madeleine (FG15) as 'the end of Mummy day'.

Below Michael explains how the immediate embodied sensation of drinking a chilled glass of wine at the end of the day evokes a strong, positive emotional response:

Michael: Wine's a good comforter – you know? If you've had a hard day at work or something. I used to work quite, I won't say stressful but it was relatively stressful at one time, you know? And you used to come in and get a glass of wine just tae [to], you know?
Grace: Oh yes, yes, I've had that.

Michael: The cold hit at the back of the throat and you think, 'Oh, that's my best pal'. [laughter] (FG5)

Hugh provided a vivid illustration of the embodied enjoyment of anticipating going to the pub and drinking with his mates, and constructed drinking in traditional embodied masculinity terms, involving working hard, then having the reward of drinking at the pub:

Hugh: You know, the thing is that, going to the pub feels to me like how I used to feel when I was 10 and I wanted to go out to play. It's that feeling of, 'Right, I can cope with school, I can cope with doing all the boring stuff, blah de blah de blah', but you're just *bursting* to get out with your mates ... You know most of the time, you know you've got at least a 35-hour working week, maybe more, you know. And, week in, week out, month in, month out. And you have to have the discipline to get through all that, whatever it is you're doing, *grind* most of the time ... it is like a reward. (FG2)

Some women also discussed alcohol enabling an escape from the grind of mundane work, but in the different context of unpaid domestic work or combining domestic and paid work, reinforcing traditional notions of femininity involving the domestic realm:

Hannah: We always have wine with our meal because, you know, I like to set the table and sit down and, you know, 'coz it's the only chance you get to sit down and have a, you know, an hour sort of niceness, then, before you've got to load the dishwasher, do the ironing, you know, and so on and so forth. (FG8)

In contrast, some participants said they did not drink alcohol to relax or escape, but to binge drink and get drunk, which Ruth described as 'a release valve':

Ruth: It's not really about relaxation for me, as such –
Lynn: Yeah, I'm the same –
Ruth: It's, like, about sociable, party –
Lynn: I think, yeah, I think – I drink to get drunk. I think, unless I'm with people who aren't like that, and I would have a glass of wine not thinking – no, but I think I do, I do think I'm definitely a binge drinker ... I don't think I could ever just be a moderate drinker. It's – you binge. You don't do it again for 3 months. You binge. And it's just like that, you know.
Ruth: It's like a kind of, like, release valve, like a kind of pressure valve, letting off steam. (FG12)

Here Ruth and Lynn describe a particular embodied engagement with their social world, where feelings of pressure built over time were released through binge drinking. The pressure valve metaphor implies catastrophe if release is not achieved, representing drinking as both necessary and important and intimately tied to experiential, embodied contexts.

Drinking alcohol marked a transitory time and space that altered participants' subjective embodied experience to differentiate it from normal, everyday embodied experience (see Jayne *et al.* 2010, Leyshon 2008). This was gendered due to the differences in everyday social roles (such as childcare, paid and unpaid work and housework). Generally, for men, drinking alcohol provided embodied pleasure as a reward for working hard, while for women it enabled an embodied sense of enjoyment, winding down and escape from busy lives involving multiple roles.

Mid-life bodies: constraints to drinking

Both the materiality of ageing bodies (thought to process alcohol less well than youthful bodies, leading to unpleasant hangovers) and the social contexts of being in mid-life (such as the responsibilities of paid work and childcare) were perceived to limit excessive drinking. Participants found it difficult to fully disentangle the effects of ageing from social constraints, as Vicky described in relation to her body not 'handling it as much now':

> Vicky: The headaches last for longer and they're probably a bit more intense. You find, as well, that you can't lie in bed all day the day after – you've got things to do that you didn't have to do before – so you're kind of dragging yourself around. You're just punished for it a lot more. I think that really is a physicality of just getting older. So that means that you're less likely to binge. (FG6)

Ageing bodies and social responsibilities were the primary reasons given for reducing alcohol consumption. Decisions to moderate alcohol consumption were also influenced (to a lesser extent) by driving the following day and weight concerns (see Emslie, Hunt, and Lyons 2012). Two men and two women mentioned weight considerations when deciding whether and what to drink, with Fi (FG10) commenting that if she wanted to lose weight 'I'll consciously think, right, I'm not gonnae [going to] drink or I'm gonnae drink a spirit instead of a wine' and Anne (FG12) saying 'I've just begun to think I would much rather have that many calories in a chocolate rather than in beer form!'

Many participants discussed gender differences in size, physiology and hormones in relation to tolerance to alcohol and the different health-promotion advice given to men and women about drinking. Audrey's account illustrates her embodied experience of her changing tolerance to the physiological effects of alcohol, which she linked to hormonal changes:

> Audrey: It is like a small poison. I mean, that sounds ridiculous, but if it hits me at the wrong time of day and, probably the wrong time of the month as well, and maybe even when I've got other things on my mind – all these things combined, then it tastes like it is something that my body is *rejecting* … It's physical. It's hugely physical. (FG8)

The participants were aware of public health alcohol advice and recommendations regarding units, which have been central to public health and prevention approaches. However while this knowledge increased their thinking about their health outcomes, it did not alter their drinking practices. Some were quite cynical about health promotion advice on alcohol and units, which was viewed as shifting sands (Stella FG15), arbitrary (Madeleine FG15) and a bit abstract (Elizabeth FG9). Thus, when limiting their consumption participants did not count units (see also Jayne *et al.* 2012), but instead monitored their changing embodied states.

Embodied knowing: staying in the zone but not passing the point of no return

The feelings attached to social drinking practices were frequently concerned with going with the flow and enjoying the good atmosphere and mood derived from alcohol, company and environment, as Matt explains:

Matt: It's spontaneous now, if I ever sort of get carried away, and drink a lot, it's because it's been spontaneous, you're in good company, you're having a good night, you're really enjoying it, you're enjoying the company, you're enjoying the chat, whatever, and you just keep going. (FG10)

These positive feelings were described consistently as loss of inhibitions, exaggerated responses to everything, becoming 'an enhanced person – 10 per cent more charismatic, 10 per cent more exciting, 10 per cent more funny' (Callum FG13). Both men and women described this state of enjoyment as being in the zone or that perfect level:

Bill: I'd love to drink *all* night but not get drunk. Get to that level of – that perfect level, you know, and stay there … in the zone, that's what it is.
Facilitator: Yeah. So is the zone, is that kind of feeling it a little bit then? Is that –
Bill: [Overtalking] Uh huh, that's when you've managed to untie your tongue enough and your brain seems to be working faster, and everything you say is really fascinating to other people [laughs] – and that happens to me all the time! But it's for about 10 minutes or something [laughter]. And thereafter it's all downhill. But there is that wee point where you think, I'm really enjoying myself. [Others agree]. And then there's the point where you get – the next day you're probably thinking, 'And that's when I should have stopped'.
Eleanor: I know.
Facilitator: And is that alcohol or is that people, or is it both?
Bill: I think it's just both. It's the reduction of inhibitions so that you're feeling more confident and cheerful perhaps. It's the social context as well. (FG3)

Here the desirable feeling arises from the interplay between the physiological effects of alcohol and the social context. A key part of achieving this perfect level was sharing this with people who were ideally getting in the zone or on the same wavelength (Eric FG10). The social bonding over this calibrated consumption could mean that being the only sober person was 'horrible', 'just terrible' and socially isolating.

This desired embodied state was also influenced by participants' moods, frame of mind, environment, time of day, the stage of women's hormonal cycle, what alcohol was being consumed and how much food had been eaten. Alongside achieving this enjoyable state, the participants talked about reaching a tipping point or a point of no return (Mandy FG10, Callum FG13), when they realised they had consumed too much alcohol and were feeling less pleasant sensations. Women were much more likely to describe acting on this knowing sensation by stopping drinking:

Mandy: You just start to get a sensation that, maybe, I really don't know, maybe things start to slow down a tiny bit, or maybe you start to realise your own behaviour is, like, maybe you're, you know, you spill something, or you, like, make a mistake when you're speaking, like you say the wrong word, or something like that, and you think, 'That's not normal for me'; I'm at this, you know, I've sort of gone beyond the stage of, you know, what I'm happy with. But it's quite, it's very hard to articulate the actual physical sensation of it, I think. (FG10)
Tara: I feel like I've developed an internal kind of gate, which I know I don't want to go through – and I don't really know what it is, I just *know* there's been

quite a lot of nights out where I've just gotten to the point where I'm like, 'If I have one more drink, I'm really not going to be happy. It's just gonna push past that point, and I just know that I don't want anymore', and I'll just stop ... And it must be, through many years of experience of me [laughs] going past that point – and I think it's hard to verbalise the feeling that it is. I mean, it's not necessarily that I feel sick or I feel dizzy – although, they would be obviously strong signs. It's, there might be a point of being full – of just being full and, I don't know, maybe happy. I don't know, I'm just like, 'No, that's it. That's enough'. It's definitely subconscious, I think. (FG11)

Tara's embodied feeling of knowing when to stop consuming alcohol (her internal gate) developed through experience and thus now operated at a 'subconscious' level, implying that bodily experiences become so well-rehearsed that they no longer require conscious intervention or scrutiny. Some women also linked getting to the point that they have had too much with 'thinking about the next day. Your time's too precious' (Isobel FG8). While the women were willing to engage with questions around how they knew when they had drunk enough, many men noted that they just know. For example, Paul (FG6) talked about how 'Something tells me I've had enough ... My brain, I'm just trained, I just know when I've had enough' Graham (FG2) described it as 'just an internal thing you just know', while Ewan (FG2) stated that 'instinct is experience coalesced'.

The corporeal feelings of going past one's limit were described in various physical and embodied ways (and appeared easier for participants to articulate than describing approaching that limit). For example, participants talked about not being able to communicate, stumbling, slurring, having double vision, an upset stomach, numb gums; feeling nauseous, queasy, fuzzy, blurry, tired; keeling to the side, bumping into people and becoming too loud. They also described it as when 'the liquid won't go down their throat' anymore, feeling bloated, and getting to a point where they no longer liked the taste of alcohol. In three groups, participants discussed blackouts (FG5, FG13, FG14); for Finn (FG13), it was 'passing out in the club, done that once' while for Rach (FG5) blackouts occurred 'all the time':

Rach: I get blackouts wae [with] wine all the time – get blackouts, just don't remember. [laughs] ... So now I don't drink wine when I go out. I very, very rarely, don't I? Very, very rarely.
Grace: No, you're on the vodka maybe more ...
Facilitator: So you can know where you are a bit more?
Rach: Aye, because I know that once I go on that wine, I just don't remember. And I do, literally, take blackouts. I just don't remember – get up in the morning and all my lights is on, my telly's on, the fire's on. (FG5)

Gavin and Mark discussed drinking to a point that they were not able to remember what happened and Mark described having 'that blackout at the end of the night', implying these were a relatively regular (and normative) experience:

Gavin: See my problem is I don't know, I just wake up the next day and go, 'Right, well, I don't remember, from this point on, so I must've but' – so that's essentially my problem. But then yeah.
Mark: You can probably tell we know each other quite well, but we've discussed this before, it generally tends to be more when we're drinking whisky that you have

that blackout at the end of the night. [Others agree] How did I get home, sort of thing. (FG14)

Both male and female participants discussed vomiting after excessive alcohol consumption, as illustrated by Susan below. In the next extract Callum explains how he would preplan what he ate before a 'fairly big night out' in anticipation of being sick from excessive drinking:

Susan: I can have a bottle of wine and I really, I'm OK, I've obviously been
             drinking but I'm OK. If I have a bottle and a *glass* then something happens,
Cath: It's that glass that did it! Not the bottle, it's the glass.
Susan: I turn my head to the side and it's such a queasy feeling that I am actually,
             I'm sick, so I know that that's me, I'm absolutely finished. [Others agree]
             And it does make me feel really nauseous or else I *am* physically sick and I
             can't have any more. That's that. (FG4)

Callum: Subconsciously as well, I would *always*, if I knew I was going out for a
             fairly big night out, have soup. This sounds really, really grim, like it sounds
             terrible, but what I'm thinking is, 'What if I get so drunk that I'm sick, or
             even sick in my sleep. If I'm being sick liquid, I'll survive'. [Laughter]. But I
             think if I have a big meal, I'm far more likely to be sick, and also if I'm sick
             and it's just soup at least it's liquid coming out, if it's horrible big, you
             know, meat or whatever, then it's going to be fatal. And you shouldn't be
             thinking like that, but [overtalk] that's always in there. (FG13)

Lynn and Ruth (FG12) discussed making themselves vomit so they could keep drinking during a night out. Ruth was reluctant to discuss this topic, while Lynn appealed to their friend Anne not to 'judge' them, illustrating their awareness of the gendered morality that is attached to drinking (Day, Gough, and McFadden 2004), particularly behaviour linked to excessive consumption.

Changing physical stance and/or moving away from the immediate social situation (for example, going to the toilet or standing up) was frequently the first moment when participants realised that they had passed that limit. These social and physical perturbations act as sobering moments; they provide time out for a more objective assessment of physical state. Jeff (FG6) commented that 'it doesn't really hit me till I get out in the air', while Jody (FG5) noted 'I just feel perfectly fine and then I'll go to stand up, or go to go into the kitchen or something'. Group 12 described these moments as follows:

Erin: Yeah, it's the going to the toilet thing, and realising that it's [alcohol] having an
           effect. 'Coz I think – it's more like you're either talking or you're just like, busy,
           and then you're – going to the toilet's the first time you actually get to think
           how the night's going and then, 'how many drinks have I had'. [Group
           laughter].
Ruth: I hadn't actually thought about it like that but it probably is.
Erin: It's the first time you're kind of like – the lights are different and you're like oh!
Lynn: The music isn't in your ears (FG12)

Thus the embodied, subjective experience of intoxication involves physical sensations in the body, but their interpretation depends upon the context, environment, space and place in which people are located. Alcohol facilitates togetherness and sociability, and drinking with others in the same space enables shared embodied experiences with everyone aiming for an ideal level of intoxication. Knowing when to stop and heeding the physical signs that are hard to articulate was linked to age, gender and experience. Women were more willing to state that particular physical sensations led them to stop drinking, quite suddenly at times. Men may present themselves as drinking heavily without a great deal of consideration, given that this behaviour is itself part of hegemonic masculinity. In contrast, women may take more notice of bodily signs and sensations. Femininity has traditionally been linked to an awareness of health and the body, thus women may be more conscious of physical changes while drinking, perhaps finding it easier to describe feelings of intoxication and bodily sensations than men. Further, women may monitor such changes and cease drinking when they occur because hegemonic femininity requires women to remain in control (ensuring respectability). However for both women and men, their own experiential and embodied knowledge was more important in regulating consumption during a drinking episode than health promotion advice.

Conclusions

This research demonstrates that drinking is an embodied social practice that is both gendered and related to age and life stage. For these adults in mid-life, drinking with others was about marking out temporary spaces from everyday life in which they could alter their way of being in the world. This was frequently gendered; a shift from domestic work and childcare (often in addition to paid work) for women, and from paid work for men. Furthermore, by mid-life, participants were able to draw on a history of drinking over at least a decade or two that enabled them to position themselves as 'experienced' drinkers who knew their own physical bodies, how to achieve a desired level of intoxication and how to sustain this level by knowing when they had passed the point of no return and needed to stop drinking. Embodied feelings or sensations of intoxication, and decisions about when to stop or moderate their drinking, were articulated in more detail by women than men.

These findings foreground the relational and contextual nature of drinking practices and reinforce the need to critically interrogate the concept of alcohol consumption as a straightforward health behaviour. Most health behaviour theories exist at an individual level and neglect the contextual realities and broad influences that shape behaviour (Crosby and Noar 2010). Our results demonstrate that health promotion information is competing with, and undermined by, embodied knowledge accumulated through years of experience of drinking. The enjoyable, embodied and affective nature of drinking practices experienced by men and women at mid-life are in stark contrast to current political, policy and popular concerns regarding alcohol (Jayne, Valentine, and Holloway 2010). As Griffin et al. (2009) have argued, excessive alcohol consumption is positioned in governmental discourses as irresponsible, risky and dangerous and as 'away from the rationality, self-control and moderation that is at the heart of neo-liberal subjectivity' (p. 460). The adults in our study described end-of-day controlled drinking as a rational activity within the context of their busy lives and, for women, their multiple roles. They also employed notions of experience and embodied knowing while drinking to resist being positioned as irresponsible or risky drinkers.

If individualised health behaviour messages are ineffective for men and women in mid-life, what is required to alter potentially harmful drinking practices? Our findings highlight drinking as a collective activity involving the achievement of shared desirable embodied states and the importance of not going past the point of this enjoyable embodied intoxication. Health promotion approaches may usefully draw on these notions of embodied pleasure while drinking and embodied knowing of excessive drinking. Physical perturbations (for example, standing up or going to the toilet) can act as sobering moments providing a space to (re)assess one's physical state and decide to stop or slow down drinking, and may be key points for intervention strategies to focus on. Future research might usefully focus on alterations in environmental contexts and the cues that may facilitate this process.

The lived meaning of embodied drinking practices cannot be divorced from gender. Women's drinking was more strongly associated with their emotional and relational lives and men's with their external work lives, highlighting gendered styles of engagement with alcohol (Ettorre 2004). As gendered bodies consume alcohol for pleasure and enjoyment, they appear to be monitored and controlled more closely by women than men. In regulating consumption, 'bodies are bound up in society's values of discipline and order, essential to wellbeing' (Ettorre 2004: 331); bodies are the site for performing masculinity and femininity, as well as the site for regulation (Gill *et al.* 2005). Drinking for pleasure may be a resistance to gender roles, caretaking or passive femininity (Ettorre 2004). Simultaneously, alcohol was a way for both men and women to cope with the different demands and responsibilities of their daily lives. It is notable that the alcohol industry has succeeded in aligning drinking with reward and relaxation for daily coping among men and women at mid-life, as well as with celebrations and special occasions.

Our exploratory findings need to be considered cautiously. We employed friendship discussion groups to investigate both subjective embodied experience and co-constructed accounts of socialising and drinking together. This may have encouraged discussion of embodied experiences and heightened the level of similarity of the topics and ideas discussed but it may also have limited the disclosure of more personal, private or sensitive material on individual embodied experience. Future research could beneficially explore the use of individual interviews or ethnographic approaches to gain further insights.

Embodied, gendered experiences are central to drinking practices and are important in conceptualising health behaviour as beyond the individual. We cannot fully comprehend drinking and alcohol consumption practices without the consideration of bodies and their social and cultural location in terms of age, gender and life stage. Health promotion needs to move beyond this neglect of the body and engage with drinking as a gendered, embodied activity. Bodies are intertwined with self and culture and inextricably link the material and the discursive (Gill, Henwood, and McLean 2005). Our research suggests that the drinking, mid-life body is one that culturally symbolises relaxation, enjoyment, control, pleasure and wellbeing, at least until a point where the physical processing of alcohol in the (ageing) body asserts a changed relationship. Any attempt to change drinking behaviour will need to take such cultural significance and lived past and present experience into account.

Acknowledgements

We would like to thank our colleagues Catherine Ferrell, Elaine Hindle, Kate Campbell, Nicola Smart, Julie Watson and Janice Reid for help in recruiting people for the study. Thanks to Sally Macintyre and the reviewers for useful comments. We are very grateful to all the respondents for talking freely about their drinking. The study was funded by the UK Medical Research Council (5TK50). Kate Hunt is currently funded by the Medical Research Council (GU:25605200: 68094), as was Carol Emslie when these data were collected.

References

Babor, T., Caetano, R., Casswell, S., Edwards, G., *et al.* (2010) *Alcohol: No Ordinary Commodity – Research and Public Policy*. Oxford: Oxford University Press.

Backett, K. and Davison, C. (1995) Lifecourse and lifestyle: the social and cultural location of health behaviours, *Social Science & Medicine*, 40, 5, 629–38.

Braun, V. and Clarke, V. (2006) Using thematic analysis in psychology, *Qualitative. Research in Psychology*, 3, 2, 77–101.

Burr, V. (2003) *Social Constructionism*, 2nd edn. London: Routledge.

Butler, J. (1993) *Bodies that Matter: On the Discursive Limits of 'Sex'*. London: Routledge.

Connell, R.W. (1995) *Masculinities*. Cambridge: Polity.

Cromby, J. (2004) Between constructionism and neuroscience: The societal co-constitution of embodied subjectivity, *Theory and Psychology*, 14, 6, 797–821.

Crosby, R. and Noar, S.M. (2010) Theory development in health promotion: are we there yet?, *Journal of Behavioural Medicine*, 33, 4, 259–63.

Day, K., Gough, B. and McFadden, M. (2004) Warning! Alcohol can seriously damage your feminine health, *Feminist Media Studies*, 4, 2, 165–83.

de Visser, R.O. and McDonnell, E.J. (2012) 'That's OK. He's a guy': a mixed-methods study of gender double-standards for alcohol use, *Psychology and Health*, 27, 5, 618–39.

Duff, C. (2008) The pleasure in context, *International Journal of Drug Policy*, 19, 5, 384–92.

Emslie, C., Hunt, K. and Lyons, A.C. (2012) Older and wiser? Men's and women's accounts of drinking in early midlife, *Sociology of Health & Illness*, 34, 4, 481–96.

Emslie, C., Hunt, K. and Lyons, A.C. (2013) The role of alcohol in forging and maintaining friendships amongst Scottish men in midlife, *Health Psychology*, 32, 1, 33–41.

Ettorre, E. (2004) Revisioning women and drug use: gender sensitivity, embodiment and reducing harm, *International Journal of Drug Policy*, 15, 5–6, 327–35.

Gill, R., Henwood, K. and McLean, C. (2005) Body projects and the regulation of normative masculinity, *Body and Society*, 11, 1, 37–62.

Griffin, C., Bengry-Howell, A., Hackley, C., Mistral, W., *et al.* (2009) 'Every time I do it I absolutely annihilate myself': loss of (self)-consciousness and loss of memory in young people's drinking narratives, *Sociology of Health & Illness*, 43, 3, 457–76.

Griffin, C., Szmigin, I., Bengry-Howell, A., Hackley, C., *et al.* (2013) Inhabiting the contradictions: hypersexual femininity and the culture of intoxication among young women in the UK, *Feminism and Psychology*, 23, 2, 184–206.

Hunt, K. M.C., Gray, C, Mutrie, N and Wyke, S. (2013) 'You've got to walk before you run'. Positive evaluations of a walking programme as part of a gender sensitised weight management programme delivered to men through professional football clubs, *Health Psychology*, 32, 1, 57–65.

Jayne, M., Valentine, G. and Holloway, S.L. (2010) Emotional, embodied and affective geographies of alcohol, drinking and drunkenness, *Transactions of the Institute of British Geographers*, 35, 4, 540–54.

Jayne, M., Valentine, G. and Holloway, S.L. (2012) What use are units? critical geographies of alcohol policy, *Antipode*, 44, 3, 828–46.

Lemle, R. and Mishkind, M.E. (1989) Alcohol and masculinity, *Journal of Substance Abuse Treatment*, 6, 4, 213–22.

Leyshon, M. (2008) 'We're stuck in the corner': young women, embodiment and drinking in the countryside, *Drugs: Education, Prevention and Policy*, 15, 3, 267–89.

Lyons, A.C. (2009) Masculinities, femininities, behaviour and health, *Social and Personality Psychology Compass*, 3, 4, 394–412.

Lyons, A.C. and Willott, S.A. (2008) Alcohol consumption, gender identities and women's changing social positions, *Sex Roles*, 59, 9–10, 694–712.

McCreanor, T., Greenaway, A., Moewaka Barnes, H., Borell, S., *et al.* (2005) Youth identity formation and contemporary alcohol marketing, *Critical Public Health*, 15, 3, 251–62.

Measham, F. (2006) The new policy mix: alcohol, harm minimisation, and determined drunkenness in contemporary society, *International Journal of Drug Policy*, 17, 4, 258–68.

Mielewczyk, F. and Willig, C. (2007) Old clothes and an older look: the case for a radical makeover in health behaviour research, *Theory and Psychology*, 17, 6, 811–37.

National Health Service (2011) Alcohol misuse: definition. Available at http://www.nhs.uk/Conditions/Alcohol-misuse/Pages/Definition.aspx (accessed 8 February 2013).

Ogden, J. (2003) Some problems with social cognition models: a pragmatic and conceptual analysis, *Health Psychology*, 22, 4, 424–8.

Peralta, R.L. (2007) College alcohol use and the embodiment of hegemonic masculinity among European American men, *Sex Roles*, 56, 11–12, 741–56.

Rahav, G., Wilsnack, R., Bloomfield, K., Gmel, G., *et al.* (2006) The influence of societal level factors on men's and women's alcohol consumption and alcohol problems, *Alcohol and Alcoholism*, 41, 1, 147–55.

Richmond, K. (1998) Health promotion dilemmas. In Gerrmov, J. (ed.) *Second Opinion: an Introduction to Health Sociology*. Melbourne: Oxford University Press.

Robertson, S. and Williams, R. (2010) Men, public health and health promotion: towards a critically structural and embodied understanding. In Gough, B. and Robertson, S. (eds) *Men, Masculinities and Health: Critical Perspectives*. Palgrave Macmillan: Basingstoke.

Rolfe, A., Orford, J. and Dalton, S. (2009) Women, alcohol and femininity a discourse analysis of women heavy drinkers' accounts, *Journal of Health Psychology*, 14, 2, 326–35.

Thurnell-Read, T. (2011) Off the leash and out of control: masculinities and embodiment in Eastern European stag tourism, *Sociology*, 45, 6, 977–91.

Willott, S. and Lyons, A.C. (2012) Consuming male identities: masculinities, gender relations and alcohol consumption in Aotearoa New Zealand, *Journal of Community and Applied Social Psychology*, 22, 4, 330–45.

11

Complexities and contingencies conceptualised: towards a model of reproductive navigation
Erica van der Sijpt

Introduction

Over the past few decades there has been growing international attention to reproductive health behaviour in different cultural settings. A major catalyst for this trend has been the 1994 International Conference on Population and Development in Cairo, where previous demographic attempts to manage population growth were denounced and a reproductive health approach was proposed instead. Not numbers, but individuals and their behaviour became the focus of attention. The new global aim was to achieve a situation in which all people would have 'the capability to reproduce and the freedom to decide if, when and how often to do so' (*Program of Action*, paragraph 7.2). This approach – and the numerous fertility-related studies, policies, and interventions that it has inspired – situates reproductive behaviour in a framework of individual rights and decision-making, to be enhanced through education and empowerment. Although local variations and dynamics in fertility behaviour are supposed to be taken into account, the overall discursive framework is universalist in nature, and heavily inspired by a western celebration of human rights, autonomous action and rational choice.

As a result, the current global debates and local interventions in this health domain are often pervaded by some misconceptions about reproductive practices on the ground. The idea that individuals should be free to act in accordance with their reproductive intentions and that, in doing so, they will attain their desired fertility outcomes, first of all portrays fertility intentions as unambiguous and a priori defined. However, as many qualitative studies have already shown, reproductive desires are often contested, multiple and changing over the course of an inherently uncertain gestational process and over the entire reproductive life-course (Bledsoe 2002, Cornwall 2007b, Earle 2004, Earle and Letherby 2002, 2007).

Secondly, this idea suggests that fertility outcomes can and should be rationally calculated, whether in terms of an envisaged ideal family size at the outset of a woman's fertility career or through assessments of the desire for another child at each pregnancy (Bulatao and Fawcett 1983). Yet this rather economic projection is highly problematic in the field of sexuality and reproduction; sexual activities are often spontaneous and reproductive outcomes unanticipated or uncertain. The physical fertility events people experience can be completely disconnected from their initial intentions; reproductive agency and manipulation are always limited in one way or another.

From Health Behaviours to Health Practices: Critical Perspectives, First Edition. Edited by Simon Cohn. Chapters © 2014 The Authors. Book Compilation © 2014 Foundation for the Sociology of Health & Illness / Blackwell Publishing Ltd.

This also brings us to a critique of the predominant focus on men and women as individual agents who (have the right to) make free and informed decisions on the number of children they want. Such an individualist approach excludes an explicit acknowledgment of the social complexity in which reproductive practices are embedded. It overlooks the other social relations and their power dynamics that are often implicated in reproductive decision-making (see also Brand 2001, Ortner 2006, Watkins 1993). The growing theoretical recognition that structural constraints and agency are mutually implicated rather than two distinct versions of reality (Bourdieu 1977, Giddens 1986) seems to be of only limited relevance to the discursive and interventionist establishment that takes the above conception of reproductive health behaviour as a starting point.

In this chapter I provide sociocultural evidence for a different conceptualization of reproductive health behaviour. On the basis of long-term anthropological fieldwork in the East Province of Cameroon I analyse the social complexities and contingencies of local fertility-related decisions. Two case-studies from the field will enhance an in-depth understanding of the minutiae of reproductive decision-making. Their focus on very different fertility events allows for unravelling more general patterns of what I call reproductive navigation – that is, the ways in which people give direction to their reproductive trajectories. The aim is to move away from predefined assumptions of reproductive health behaviour and to formulate a grounded theory of reproductive navigation instead.

In this I draw upon the theoretical work on social navigation by Henrik Vigh (2006). Focusing on terrains of war in Guinea-Bissau, Vigh argues that social navigation 'is primarily a question of evaluating the movement of the social environment, one's own possibilities for moving through it, and its effects on ones [sic] planned and actual movement' (2006: 13). In this view, individual behaviour is no longer conceptualised as the fulfillment of prior intentions and fixed calculations in a social vacuum. Vigh's understanding of social navigation stresses the constant interplay between a person's actions and complex social forces, both of which are in continuous motion. It captures the creativity, contingency and uncertainty of decision-making within constantly changing structural contexts – something that others have conceptualised as judicious opportunism (Johnson-Hanks 2005), subjunctivity (Whyte 2002) or tactical pragmatism (de Certeau 1984, Cornwall 2007a, 2007b).

Investigating women's reproductive health practices as reproductive navigation thus allows me to situate fertility-related decisions within their specific contexts. Not only does such an approach highlight the creativity with which women in real life manage their fertility careers; it will also help me to theroise the interrelationship between reproductive decisions and particular structural configurations and, thus, to move away from universalist and individualist assumptions about reproductive health behaviour.

Methodology

The empirical data provided in this chapter were obtained during an elaborate anthropological research project unfolding over 15 months between 2004 and 2009 in a village in east Cameroon. In this study I investigated Gbigbil women's experiences with, and decisions on, different forms of interrupted fertility such as miscarriages, stillbirths, induced abortions, infertility or child death. To gain insight into women's perceptions and practices during such critical reproductive events I was in close contact with 25 purposefully selected informants who had experienced at least one instance of interrupted fertility in their lives. This group included women from all ages, with different educational histories, economic backgrounds, marital statuses and reproductive ambitions.

The longitudinal character of the research project allowed me to follow my informants over time and to observe and discuss the many developments in their reproductive trajectories. I investigated their reproductive experiences both retrospectively and concurrently. I tried to capture the situational dynamics of important past happenings through multiple and extended life history interviews with these women as well as with some key individuals in their lives. Through participant observation, I took part in the real-time reproductive events my informants experienced during my fieldwork. The valuable knowledge thus obtained was complemented with insights gathered through 12 focus group discussions and numerous thematic interviews with other women and men in the village. Group discussions that focused explicitly on reproductive health decision-making were often initiated with vignettes or hypothetical case studies, upon which informants were asked to reflect together. Further, I conducted a household survey in order to map the marital and reproductive histories of all 290 village women.

The analytical insights that I present in this chapter with regard to the specific cases of Laura and Mama Rosie were developed in the context of all the above described activities and interactions. Although I use the two case studies as illustrations of the central argument of this chapter, my conclusions about patterns of reproductive navigation are based upon the study of many other cases as well, in which similar processes as the ones described in this chapter seemed to be at play.

Both during and after fieldwork, ethical reflections and considerations were dealt with as proposed by research ethics committees. Because of the highly confidential and often secret information that my informants would share with me, I always asked them for their explicit consent when interviewing them and recording our interactions. All names appearing in the case studies are pseudonyms and personal details that could lead to the identification of my informants have been omitted from the descriptions.

Reproductive contexts and contingencies

In the east Cameroonian village in which this research took place, daily activities in general and gender relationships in particular are profoundly shaped by marital and kinship configurations. Ideally, marriage is considered to be a family affair rather than an arrangement between individual partners. A marital union should traditionally be concluded through a set of bride-price exchanges between both partners' families, whereupon the woman moves to the compound of her new husband and his kin. With bride-price payments to the family of the woman continuing, every child born in this marriage is supposed to belong to the father and his relatives. In cases where a woman would leave her husband and return to her own family her children should stay with their patrikin.

However, as payment of (parts of) the bride-price is often postponed or completely disregarded, this ideal situation rarely manifests itself in practice. The economic crisis that has plagued Cameroon since the late 1980s makes it increasingly difficult for families to engage in such matrimonial exchanges (Abega 2007, Johnson-Hanks 2006, Meekers and Calvès 1997). Only 31 per cent of the 174 women who considered themselves to be married declared that the complete bride-price had been paid. Many marriages – particularly those of young people – are not more than informal arrangements in which a man and a woman live, eat and sleep together. Both partners take time to explore each other's traits: women want to be ensured of a man's good character and (financial) responsibility before settling down in his family, whereas men await a proof of a woman's fertility before a more formal engagement. These informal unions, in which bride-price payments have not yet been made, are easily dissolved and replaced by another one. In this context, municipal or religious unions are rare. With polygyny being widespread in the region, men especially seem to be hesitant to preclude the option of taking another wife in the future–much to the women's lamentation, who indicate that relations between co-wives are often characterised by jealousy and conflict.

Within this flexible marriage setting, bearing children is not always the primary aim of either partner nor does it necessarily lead to the consolidation of a union. For women, to conceive can be an important strategy to convince their partners of their worth and of the need to initiate negotiations between families. But, at the same time, many young women indicate that their boyfriends often miraculously disappear when they discover a pregnancy, while married women complain that their childbearing does not benefit their own families in any way – thus denouncing the absence of any bride-price payments made by their husbands and in-laws. Furthermore, women themselves may, for several reasons, refuse to get pregnant or to carry their pregnancies to term; of all pregnancy interruptions that were recorded during the survey, 11 per cent had been consciously provoked (van der Sijpt 2011).[1]

As reproductive goals and gains are often uncertain, to whom the children belong has become a complicated and contested matter: sometimes, men (and their families) are eager to acknowledge their children so as to enlarge their patrilineage. At other times they abandon their pregnant partner, whose child will then automatically belong to the maternal family or to another lover willing to recognise the child as his own. Irrespective of a man's alleged intentions, a woman's relatives are also prone to claim the children of their daughter as long as they have not received any bride-price payments. Little is left, then, of the patrilineal ideal in which children automatically belong to and grow up within their paternal family. Indeed, of the 287 women surveyed, 34 per cent stated that, contrary to the prevailing norms, their child (ren) resided in their maternal rather than their paternal families. Kinship connections are, like conjugal relations, characterised by flexibility and fluid interactions between norms and practices. It is within these dynamics of plural sexual relationships, fragile conjugal arrangements, continuous kinship demands and divergent personal aspirations that we should understand people's reproductive practices.

The stories of a young woman attempting to abort several pregnancies and of a village mama experiencing secondary infertility will provide empirical insights into the dynamics of such reproductive practices. As the two cases could be considered two extremes on a reproductive continuum, they will also form a starting point to generate some general insights about reproductive navigation and the ways in which different dynamics affect its outcome.

Laura

Laura is 21 years old and is following a sewing training course in the provincial capital when she accidentally conceives a pregnancy with Omar, a Muslim from the north of Cameroon. Fearing that this pregnancy might interfere with her education, Laura uses all the abortifacients her classmates advise her to swallow or insert: nivaquine pills, salt water, Nescafé; nothing helps. That month she leaves the city to spend the summer holidays with her parents. After sending a letter to Omar announcing her pregnancy and abortion plans, she continues to take abortifacients upon her arrival in the village. Her practices are, however, soon detected by her mother, who, upon hearing the news of a potential pregnancy with Omar, agrees with her daughter's attempts at abortion. 'My mother is afraid of the reaction of my father, she doesn't like Omar at all, and she wants me to finish school first', Laura states. Yet no blood loss is achieved; instead Laura starts to feel ill. In the village dispensary where her mother takes her, the doctor immediately reprimands her and gives her injections to prevent the termination of her pregnancy.

From this moment onwards, Laura's mother starts insisting that Laura should keep the pregnancy and give the child to her. Since she herself has only one daughter and two sons and has experienced three additional reproductive losses, she will consider this first grandchild as an extra child for herself. This proposal makes Laura furious; trying to prevent her mother from taking her child, she returns to the city and tells Omar that she is still pregnant. Omar, however, has other ambitions and refuses to assume any responsibility. After bearing her son Stéphane, Laura therefore returns to the village where her mother is eager to take care of her grandchild. After a few years of constant familial conflicts about who Stéphane belongs to, Laura decides to leave the boy behind with her mother and move to a nearby city. She starts to concentrate on schooling again, which she finances with petty trade activities and the money she receives from temporary boyfriends.

In her relationship with one of those boyfriends, Jean, Laura conceives again. While Jean seems willing to recognise his paternity Laura is reluctant to bear another child at this point:

> I thought, 'I still love Stéphane's father. If he will come back to take me into marriage, what will he say if he sees me with another pregnancy?' And what is more, Jean told me he would take my child, but not me. So why would I keep this pregnancy? Two children, without a marriage? No. I had made this decision in my life that I would only bear children with one man.

With the help of a doctor in the hospital, Laura has an abortion. She informs only her cousin about the event.

One year later, while working in a tailor's shop, Laura is told by her boss that she has a sister-in-law who wants her as a wife for her son. While initially taking this as no more than a flattering joke, Laura soon enough finds herself forced to converse with this son, named Philippe. Philippe takes Laura home and, finding out that she is in her fertile period, forces her to have sex with him. Laura is afraid and furious at the same time:

> When he penetrated me, I told him that he had raped me now. He said, 'Take it as you want. But from today onwards, since I climbed upon you, know that you are my wife. And voilà my baby that you carry in your belly'. I told him that I would take some pills [to abort] as soon as I would arrive home. He refused. He locked me up in his house for several days so that I couldn't do that.

Philippe, an unmarried father of seven children, and his mother, desperate for a daughter-in-law, do everything they can to keep the pregnant Laura (and eventually also her son Stéphane) with them. Their constant supervision, as well as their hasty announcement of the pregnancy to Laura's family not only prevent Laura from aborting but also push her into marriage with Philippe, much to the delight of Laura's mother. She tells her daughter that a second child should be borne within a marital framework, that Laura should abandon all her informal sexual affairs, and that the willingness of Philippe and his mother to commit financially is rare to find these days. Laura resigns herself to the situation. But then she starts suffering from very early pregnancy symptoms and her new husband suspects that she was pregnant before she went to live with him. He suggests she should terminate the pregnancy:

> I told him, 'How can I abort now? I won't. I also want another child. Do you want me to stick to Stéphane only? What will I do when he returns to his father? No, even if

you don't want the pregnancy, I will keep it. I will go and find my mother in the village. We will take care of the child.

Laura bears a daughter and stays in the marriage.

Soon after this birth, Philippe moves to another city and does not make contact for a year before he invites Laura and his daughter to join him. Here, it turns out that Philippe has been engaged in a relationship with an old, rich woman – a situation that Laura vehemently opposes. The violence with which Philippe responds to her opposition makes Laura want to flee. While her mother first advises her daughter over the phone just to 'endure the suffering' she ends up supporting Laura's refusal to marry Philippe; after all, he has also neglected his obligations towards his parents-in-law in the last year. Her initial encouragement of the marriage turns into a refusal of any formal engagement and a support for Laura's contraceptive plans – thus keeping the option of separation open.

Yet, contraception comes too late; in order to prevent Laura's departure, Philippe forcefully makes her pregnant again. Laura desperately wishes to terminate the pregnancy but fails again after administering various local abortifacients. Mother and daughter therefore agree that Laura should attempt to flee to the village, where I – the anthropologist who is aware of the situation – could bring her to a well-known abortion specialist. And so it happens; Laura escapes and the abortion is performed. When I leave the field right after the intervention and ask Laura about her plans for the future, she tells me that she will soon start with contraceptive pills and take time to see what the future will bring.

Mama Rosie

Born as the third child of the second of her father's three wives, Mama Rosie grows up in an enormous extended family. Being one of the few girls in the entire household, she is well cared for. She is sent first to primary school and then to a training centre for Catholic women. It is only here, at the age of 17, that Mama Rosie starts to menstruate. Freed from her worries about the absence of a normal menstrual cycle, she initiates sexual relationships. The love affair that develops between her and Etienne, the son of the village catechist, makes him initiate bride-price payments, whereupon she moves into his house. After some time, however, Etienne's mother opposes the relationship because it takes Mama Rosie too long to conceive with her son, and she proposes that he marries an albino woman who had already given birth elsewhere. This proposal is met with resistance. Etienne flees the village by joining the army while Mama Rosie's family members come to take their daughter back home. Nevertheless, the two lovers continue to write and occasionally meet in secret.

During Etienne's absences, Mama Rosie engages in sexual relationships with two teachers, Bernard and David, at the same time. She conceives with Bernard at the age of 21 and rejoices in the fact that, 4 years after the onset of menstruation, she has finally become pregnant. Bernard, however, leaves the village for a position elsewhere soon after Mama Rosie discovers her missed period. Etienne also puts an end to their secret relationship as soon as he detects the pregnancy and he marries another woman. With the biological father gone and with Etienne engaged in a new marriage, Mama Rosie decides to tell her other lover David that he is the father. David is willing to commit financially and arrives with baby presents after the birth of Mama Rosie's son. His marriage proposal is, nonetheless, declined by Mama Rosie. 'I didn't want to marry anymore, because my first husband had deceived me and the father of my child had deceived me as well'.

However, 3 years later Papa Gerie convinces her to come and marry him in his village. As a descendant of a rather influential family, he is known to and recommended by Mama Rosie's aunt, who married a man in the same village. Having one son and one daughter from a deceased wife, as well as two daughters with a wife 'who showed small weaknesses in her habits', Papa Gerie is searching for a new wife 'who would be able to cook for me'. After Papa Gerie agrees to take care of her son and to transfer gifts to her family, Mama Rosie decides to visit him. Her arrival is met by the enormous resistance of her co-wife Mama Cathérine. Mama Cathérine, strongly supported by her mother-in-law, who originates from the same natal village and who has arranged her marriage with Papa Gerie, accuses Mama Rosie of using indigenous remedies to take away her husband's love and her own position as a first wife. Many quarrels and fights ensue.

After 4 years of marriage, at the age of 29, Mama Rosie stops menstruating:

> I didn't feel any pain in my belly. But you should have seen my breasts! One would say that I was pregnant. Mama Cathérine started to fear that if I would bear a child for her husband, she would lose her place. She started to talk everywhere. But the pregnancy didn't show itself. People mocked me and my co-wife's family accused me of inventing a pregnancy. Others suspected me of having aborted the pregnancy.

A long health-seeking itinerary follows, in which Mama Rosie tries to identify the cause of her amenorrhoea. When repeated hospital visits and treatments do not have the hoped-for effect, Mama Rosie decides to visit some local healers:

> They said that Mama Cathérine blocked my menstruation. That she has taken my underwear stained with menstruation blood and attached it somewhere through witchcraft, so that I would not deliver anymore. That she is afraid that her husband wouldn't pay attention to her anymore once I would bear children.

Comforted by her husband's reassurance that he will not refuse her because of her childlessness, and by the existence of a son from a previous relationship, Mama Rosie stops searching for a cure.

Yet it does not take long before Papa Gerie decides to marry a third wife. Mama Rosie opposes this marriage so forcefully that she is sent back to her own family. After a few years, however, Papa Gerie invites her to come back. Encouraged by her many brothers, who are eager to see their infertile sister married, Mama Rosie decides to 'regain my place in marriage and never leave again'. And indeed, as the third wife departs for good and Mama Cathérine – who just delivered her fifth child – seems to play a marginal role in the household, Mama Rosie manages to re-establish herself, even up to the point that Papa Gerie marries her officially. Marital security seems guaranteed.

Her influence starts to reach also beyond the household: she assumes several responsibilities in the village and in the local clinic. Even if she remained childless in this marriage, many village children get named after her and numerous adults come to seek the advice of this 'mother of everybody', as Mama Rosie likes to call herself:

> I know I have this power that my family-in-law gave me. The women who first arrived as wives in this family have a lot of power because they are the oldest. They are able to give me respect, dignity and power if they want. That's what they did. They appointed me as a president of the women's association. They gave me the power that makes everyone listen to me when I speak. And there is my brother-in-law Albert [who, due

to his administrative function, is very respected in the village]. He appointed me as the governor of his *quartier* [neighborhood]. Albert always said that I have good habits. I am the one who helps to raise the children. I am hospitable to the visitors. I prepare a lot of food. So I am a wife of the family. And it is the work that you do in front of the people and your husband that makes a marriage and that makes you a woman. Even if you don't bear children.

Mama Rosie's position does not remain completely uncontested, though. Due to her infertile status and her sudden rise in power, witchcraft accusations are omnipresent. The sudden death of her 30-year-old son in 2007 exacerbates this insecurity:

Formerly, I knew that if somebody insulted me, my child would come and defend me. But now, even if somebody wants to hit me, who will respond for me in the place of my son?

More is at stake than physical defence, however. Without her son Mama Rosie's rights to inheritance are minimal. As Mama Cathérine has one son, she is likely to inherit all the goods of her husband's family, while Mama Rosie will, even with a marriage certificate, possibly encounter problems upon her husband's death. Villagers whisper that Mama Rosie will surely be sent back to her family empty handed. The 56-year-old Mama Rosie may symbolically be one of the biggest mamas in the village now but whether she will continue to be so in the future remains to be seen.

Reproductive behaviour socially situated

The above two cases present the stories of two women who encountered completely different reproductive events in their lives. While Laura dealt with four unexpected pregnancies, Mama Rosie's desired and belated pregnancy was followed by secondary infertility and the death of her only child. What is striking in both stories is that the options these women encountered and the choices they made over their reproduction were often not in line with their initial intentions or ambitions. Their reproductive pathways were often based on improvisation. These unique stories should therefore be understood in their own terms and dynamics; both women directed their reproductive lives in idiosyncratic ways. Yet my aim is to also trace some meaningful patterns out of those particularities. How is reproductive improvisation channelled and circumscribed in this particular context? What common factors affect the reproductive options and choices – no matter how divergent – of these and other women in east Cameroon?

By contextualizing the reproductive events that featured in the lives of Laura and Mama Rosie I have attempted to show that reproductive decisions – in all their possible variations and improvisations – are far from being deliberate, free choices. The options women have at crucial reproductive moments are always socially circumscribed. Indeed, the reproductive acts of Laura, Mama Rosie and many other Gbigbil women seemed inherently related to several social configurations that are predominant in east Cameroon. These forms of sociality are neither mutually exclusive nor always equally relevant. Yet, taken together, they form a repertoire of significant interrelationships underlying the reproductive navigation of east Cameroonian women.

Firstly, a woman's reproductive options and decisions are affected by her position within a wider body of kinship relations. It matters whether she is her mother's first or last daughter; whether she was born in or outside marriage; whether she grew up in her own patrilineage or among her maternal uncles and whether she has few or many siblings. Women who share the former characteristics – first daughters or ones with few sisters who are born and raised within their own patrilineage – are more likely to have their relatives involved in their reproductive affairs. One only needs to recall the stories of Laura, who was the first and only daughter of her parents, and Mama Rosie, who grew up among many siblings, to see the difference. With their premarital reproduction considered an extension of their parents' reproduction and that of their patrilineage, women like Laura are more likely to be pressured to bear children before marriage and to give these children to their own mothers or fathers. The marital lives of such women are also more easily influenced by the interests and wishes of family members. As first or single daughters are highly valued for the bride-price they are expected to bring to the family, their relatives often pressure them to enter into and endure marriage, and to bear children to encourage their husband and in-laws to fulfil their financial obligations. In the absence of bride-price payments, their relatives will more easily enter into conjugal disputes and accept their daughters coming home to 'rest'. They may even advise them to abort pregnancies or force them to leave the marriage altogether, as Laura's mother did.

Secondly, the position of a woman's kin group within the village determines which reproductive options are feasible. In the current atmosphere of political and economic nepotism in Cameroon, daughters from extended families in which important individuals enjoy informal political power or formal employment are better positioned to profit from the social and financial capital that they have established. These women may be less inclined to cling to motherhood and wifehood and be supported by their family members and other villagers in this deviation from local norms of femininity. They may also enjoy greater access to financial support to pursue alternative ambitions. In some cases, the position of the patrilineage of one's partner may be of similar influence. The fact that the childless Mama Rosie was respected within and beyond the household, for instance, was largely attributable to the influential status of Papa Gerie's lineage in general and to certain benevolent in-laws in particular.

Thirdly, a woman's reproductive navigation depends on the particularities of the sexual or marital relationship with the (potential) father of the child to be born. It is not so much the volatility or stability of the relationship that matters, as both informal and formal unions are highly fragile. Instead, it is the partner's (perceived) ambitions and reactions to a pregnancy that inform a woman's options and actions. Especially when her partner acknowledges paternity and is willing to commit financially after her pregnancy has proven her fertility and worth as a (potential) wife, motherhood and marriage can become immediate priorities. When reciprocity and signs of commitment are absent, however, a woman may prefer to terminate her pregnancy. Indeed, the presence or absence of (parts of) the bride-price is often a decisive factor in reproductive decision-making. Laura, for instance, radically altered her plans regarding her pregnancy with Philippe once some initial bride-price transactions had been made and the marriage seemed secure.

Fourthly, a woman's reproductive navigation is influenced by the proximity of unrelated others with stakes in the children born in a particular relationship. The co-presence of in-laws in virilocal marriages can lead to their increased control and encouragement of reproduction as they are generally eager to see their patriliny expand. In such circumstances a woman's reproductive decisions will be influenced by the wishes and demands of her husband's kin. The existence of co-wives may also affect a woman's reproductive navigation since these female competitors are often experienced as a threat to continued reproduction – as was seen in the interaction between Mama Rosie and Mama Cathérine. Fertility events occurring in a context of direct female competition are generally surrounded by more contestation and explicit (re) consideration of one's reproductive decisions.

Finally, reproductive options and decisions are informed by a woman's personal reproductive trajectory and the social status she derives from it. The absence of children and of the status of mother may allow young women like Laura to focus on ambitions unrelated to maternity such as education, employment, small-scale trading or relations with affluent sexual partners. Although pregnancies do not necessarily imply motherhood or marriage at the beginning of one's reproductive career – thus keeping alternative options open for young women like Laura – social pressure to find a suitable husband and to take care of one's children increases with the number of childbirths one has. Thus, over time, marriage and motherhood are likely to increase their saliency as aspirations directing women's reproductive navigation. If those goals remain unattained for too long, however, marital and maternal options can become foreclosed. Women with a long history of unsuccessful fertility, for instance, may be abandoned in marital or sexual relationships in which they could at least try to become pregnant. They more easily turn their focus to virtues unrelated to motherhood, as seen in Mama Rosie's emphasis on her good character and organizational skills rather than the absence of children in her life.

What does all this mean for our understanding of women's reproductive navigation in eastern Cameroon? And how do those insights relate to the assumptions about reproductive health behaviour that underlie the current global reproductive health framework? These questions are addressed in the last section of this chapter.

Towards a framework of reproductive navigation

The social configurations described above affect women's reproductive navigation as they all define the availability of options in reproductive conjunctures. As such, they constitute the possibilities or constraints to the realization of women's ambitions. Reproductive decision-making is thus a socially contingent affair, embedded in different forms of sociality and power relationships. Since the influence of relevant others – parents, siblings, partners, in-laws, co-wives, other villagers – depends in turn on their own life contingencies, their previous pathways and their current stakes, one could further argue that decisions are inter-contingent (Becker 1994). In other words, life stories intersect; women's reproductive navigation is never independent from the navigations of those around her. The outcomes of reproductive happenings are not the predictable result of individual deliberation and design but the contingent result of the involvement of social others and of the ways in which women constantly reconfigure their choices in relation to these others.

While this is arguably the case for all forms of navigation in daily life, reproductive navigation becomes complicated by the fact that women also rely upon, and make use of, their bodies while navigating. The discussion above has shown that in Cameroon, as probably elsewhere, nothing is more social than reproduction; but nothing is more physical either.[2] Bodily experiences of fertility are not to be discarded in the study of reproductive navigation. For bodies sometimes appear to have a will of their own, as the two case studies in this chapter have illustrated. Laura attempted to abort her first and last pregnancies but failed as her body refused to release the foetus. Mama Rosie, while young and desperate for children, was suddenly confronted with an infertile body that made any future reproductive success highly unlikely. Such physical surprises affect the fertility-related options open to women. Reproductive decision-making is therefore possible or constrained not only because others act but also because bodies act.

Such an acknowledgment asks for a comprehensive understanding of reproductive navigation; one that adds the primacy and praxis of the body to the individual–social dialectic discussed above. The body does not only enable or constrain women's navigation but it needs to be navigated itself as well; it both directs and demands navigation. Since acting bodies are unpredictable women have to constantly manage the broad range of options, outcomes and obstacles their bodies present to them. They are confronted with a material world in which anything can happen – the incoherent logics of the body varying between women and over time. This bodily navigation – individual and intimate in nature – is always dialectically related to social navigation as women try to align their unpredictable bodies with their social projects. Women manipulate physicalities to successfully navigate socialities. Current theorisations of social navigation – or of similar dynamics captured in a different concept (Cornwall 2007a, 2007b, Johnson-Hanks 2005, Vigh 2006, Whyte 1997) – seem to be oblivious to these body basics underlying social practice. Yet it is only when we acknowledge this interplay of the social, the individual and the body that we can come to fully understand reproductive decision-making in people's daily lives.

This understanding of reproductive navigation is useful for the analysis of fertility dynamics beyond the local context in which these insights were developed. We may assume that socialities and physicalities are always implicated in reproductive issues around the world, even if they take different forms and shapes in different localities. The conceptualisation of reproductive decision-making proposed here thus allows for cross-contextual application while remaining sensitive to local variation.

Further, this chapter questions many of the implicit assumptions about reproductive behaviour informing current international reproductive health programmes and policies. The stance that women should a priori be able to control their fertility and fertility outcomes becomes untenable once we acknowledge that personal reproductive intentions are always inherently related to largely unpredictable socialities and physicalities. Contrary to the stability that family planning campaigns attribute to women's fertility desires, this chapter has shown that reproductive ambitions change with the hopes and horizons that emanate from women's individual and social bodies. It has also highlighted how certain situations are initially not chosen but eventually accepted; how some choices are not made or impossible to make despite one's aspirations; how certain options are explored but abandoned again and how some decisions forcibly ensue from the unexpected actions of women's bodies from interactions with other social actors. The directions women take on their reproductive pathways are less a matter of control than the result of a contingent interplay of connectedness, creativity and corporeality.

Acknowledgements

The research project in which the presented insights were generated has been funded by the Amsterdam Institute for Social Science Research in The Netherlands. The author would like to thank Dr Josien de Klerk, as well as the anonymous referees, for their comments on earlier drafts of this chapter.

Notes

1   Real abortion numbers are probably much higher. As induced abortions are illegal in Cameroon many voluntary pregnancy terminations were most likely not mentioned at all or reported as spontaneous pregnancy losses in my survey.

2   In line with the arguments of Becker (1995), Lock (1993), and Lambert and McDonald (2009) it can be claimed that the physical is always social. My aim here is not to explore the intersections between social and bodily experiences but to draw attention to the fact that bodies, next to socialities, influence reproductive decision-making in ways that have been largely overlooked.

References

Abega, S.C. (2007) *Les violences sexuelles et l'état au Cameroun*. Paris: Karthala.

Becker, A.E. (1995) *Body, Self, and Society: the View from Fiji*. Philadelphia: University of Pennsylvania Press.

Becker, H.S. (1994) 'Foi por Acaso': conceptualizing coincidence. *Sociological Quarterly*, 35, 2, 183–94.

Bledsoe, C. (2002) *Contingent Lives: Fertility, Time, and Aging in West Africa*. Chicago: University of Chicago Press.

Bourdieu, P. (1977) *Outline of a Theory of Practice*. Cambridge: Cambridge University Press.

Brand, S.M.A.A. (2001) *Mediating Means and Fate: a Socio-political Analysis of Fertility and Demographic Change in Bamako, Mali*. Boston: Brill.

Bulatao, R.A. and Fawcett, J.T. (1983) *Influences on Childbearing Intentions Across the Fertility Career: Demographic and Socioeconomic Factors and the Value of Children*. Honolulu: East-West Center.

Cornwall, A. (2007a) Of choice, chance and contingency: 'career strategies' and tactics for survival among Yoruba women traders, *Social Anthropology*, 15, 1, 27–46.

Cornwall, A. (2007b) Taking chances, making choices: the tactical dimensions of 'reproductive strategies' in Southwestern Nigeria, *Medical Anthropology*, 26, 3, 229–54.

de Certeau, M. (1984) *The Practice of Everyday Life*. Berkeley: University of California Press.

Earle, S. (2004) 'Planned' and 'unplanned' pregnancy: deconstructing experiences of conception, *Human Fertility*, 17, 1, 39–42.

Earle, S. and Letherby, G. (2002) Whose choice is it anyway? Decision making, control and conception, *Human Fertility*, 5, 2, 39–41.

Earle, S. and Letherby, G. (2007) Conceiving time? women who do or do not conceive, *Sociology of Health & Illness*, 29, 2, 233–50.

Giddens, A. (1986) Action, subjectivity, and the constitution of meaning, *Social Research*, 53, 3, 529–45.

International Conference on Population and Development (1994) *Program of Action*. New York: UN.

Johnson-Hanks, J. (2005) When the future decides: uncertainty and intentional action in contemporary Cameroon, *Current Anthropology*, 46, 3, 363–86.

Lambert, H. and McDonald, M. (2009) *Social Bodies*. New York: Berghahn.

Lock, M. (1993) Cultivating the body: anthropology and epistemologies of bodily practice and knowledge, *Annual Review of Anthropology*, 22, 133–55.

Meekers, D. and Calvès, A.E. (1997) 'Main' girlfriends, girlfriends, marriage, and money: the social context of HIV risk behaviour in sub-Saharan Africa. *Health Transition Review*, 7, 361–75.

Ortner, S.B. (2006) *Anthropology and Social Theory: Culture, Power, and the Acting Subject*. Durham: Duke University Press.

Van der Sijpt, E. (2011) 'The vagina does not talk': conception concealed or deliberately disclosed in Cameroon, *Culture, Health, and Sexuality*, 14, 1, S81–94.

Vigh, H. (2006) *Navigating Terrains of War. Youth and Soldiering in Guinea-Bissau*. New York: Berghahn.

Watkins, S.C. (1993) If all we knew about women was what we read in demography, what would we know? *Demography*, 30, 4, 551–77.

Whyte, S.R. (1997) *Questioning Misfortune: the Pragmatics of Uncertainty in Eastern Uganda*. Cambridge: Cambridge University Press.

Whyte, S.R. (2002) Subjectivity and subjunctivity: hoping for health in eastern Uganda. In Werbner, R. (ed.) *Postcolonial Subjectivities in Africa*, 171–190. London: Zed.

12

Sustained multiplicity in everyday cholesterol reduction: repertoires and practices in talk about 'healthy living'
Catherine M. Will and Kate Weiner

Introduction

It is commonplace in the sociology of food that people's eating habits reflect an attempt to balance different concerns or priorities – for example, pleasure and sociality as well as health. Yet the idea of a healthy diet continues to be a central plank of public health policy, including recent campaigns around helping the public make healthier choices (Department of Health n.d.). The assumptions underlying such policy have been critiqued by Mol (2008), who – like the editors of this volume – draws attention away from decisions to practices.

In this chapter we return to these discussions using data from two studies concerned with the practices of cholesterol reduction: one study with users of functional foods such as spreads or yoghurt with cholesterol-lowering properties, and a second with people offered statins for cardiovascular risk reduction. We use these data to illustrate the repertoires that feature in talk about both eating and exercising but also to draw attention to the varied ways of accounting for multiplicity in discussing health in relation to lifestyle. We argue that talk about finding a balance in accounts of healthy living might be seen as one attempt at reconciliation between different repertoires in both talk and practice, but that there are other attempts at reconciliation and, importantly, a readiness to live with apparent incoherence.

Where is health in everyday living?

Sociologists have long pointed to the limited salience of health in the everyday (Calnan and Williams 1991), especially for people with no embodied sense of illness. Explicit concern about health must jostle with a desire for personal pleasure and for shared enjoyment or sociality in shaping people's diets (Caplan 1997, Murcott 1998),[1] as well, of course, as being restricted by the numerous structural or environmental factors emphasised by sociologists seeking to reduce the focus in public health on the individual (Graham 1993, 2007, Keane 1997).

Both pleasure and sociality have their theorists. Coveney and Bunton (2003) describe four forms of pleasure that they consider relevant for public health: carnal, disciplined, ascetic and ecstatic pleasure. Eating is most clearly linked for them with carnal pleasure, but

From Health Behaviours to Health Practices: Critical Perspectives, First Edition. Edited by Simon Cohn. Chapters © 2014 The Authors. Book Compilation © 2014 Foundation for the Sociology of Health & Illness / Blackwell Publishing Ltd.

Coveney (2000) notes that current public health discourse promotes disciplined pleasure and that in lay discourse food associated with pleasure may also bring anxiety and guilt. This ambivalence can be explained by Crawford's suggestion (2006) that an ethic of discipline is in constant tension with a contemporary ethic of consumption, where pleasure is acceptable, even required. Jallinoja *et al.* (2012) suggest that the concept of negotiated pleasures allows us to capture the idea of some compromise, illustrating this with reference to discussions of moderate indulgence among their focus group participants, as well as attempts to substitute healthy for more unhealthy treats.

Sociality is even more central to the concerns of sociology and investigations of eating as social interaction go back to the work of Simmel. A number of influential collections have explored different dimensions of this theme, bringing together social anthropologists, psychologists and sociologists (for example, Caplan 1997, Murcott 1998). There is a broad body of work on people's concepts of the proper meal as something shared, often between family members. Yet Fischler (2011) has suggested that commensality is given different weight in different cultural contexts. For example, he argues that eating has been individualised and medicalised in the USA and to some extent in the UK but that there continues to be much greater focus on commensality in other European countries, where eating well is much more closely related to the context of eating than nutritional content.

When discussing how these different concerns are reconciled, the literature has reported on the use of metaphors of balance in interviews, suggesting that these refer both to attempts to keep different parts of life in some kind of proportion and claims about the virtues of a varied diet, which includes the occasional treat (Backett 1992, Panjari *et al.* 2006) as well as an appropriate range of food groups (Calnan 1990). The balance metaphor appears closely related to others used by sociologists that have greater calculative implications, with the suggestion that people engage in trading off (Backett 1992, Henson *et al.* 1998, Keane 1997) or seek a golden mean (Fischler 1986). Such accounts fit with broader commitment in sociology of health and illness to give dignity to lay beliefs or reasoning. However, we have argued elsewhere that they risk describing behaviour as the result of conscious decisions and thus present an overly rational view of the actor (Weiner 2011, Will and Weiner 2013). In addressing this problem, Mol (2008) usefully suggests that the metaphor of balance should be 'the balance of the high wire' not the accounting sheet. Crawford's (1984) discussion of the recursive pattern of control and release (discipline and pleasure) has a similar effect.

Reconciling different concerns in practice

Focusing analytic attention on practices offers one way to limit assumptions about calculation behind action. Theories of practice emphasise the interest of habitual behaviour, which is often unreflective (Williams 1995). They offer a way to investigate activities that combine embodied and mental activities, artefacts, understandings and normative and affective elements (Reckwitz 2002, Warde 2005). This trend has been clear in the sociology of consumption where Gronow and Warde (2001) have emphasised the importance of routine, ordinary and inconspicuous consumption, and in the sociology of food drawing on this theory. For example:

It is not possible to know what 'healthy food' might consist in without analysing how 'doing health food consumption' is carried out in relevant interaction and in the intersectings of several different practices. (Halkier and Jensen 2011: 106)

This theoretical commitment throws up methodological challenges both in data collection and analysis. Though ethnographic work is possible it is time-consuming and thus expensive to capture behaviour that is spread across mundane interactions day after day. Most work is still based on interviews or focus groups but, to the extent that these represent unusual opportunities for summarising everyday life and contain social pressures to appear responsible, they may elicit unduly rational ordered accounts (Callon and Rabeharisoa 2004). This may vary according to different social groups: for example Lawton *et al.* (2007) argue that White British respondents were particularly likely to engage in self-conscious narrations of individual agency around diabetes. We argue that Mol's ethnographic focus on objects and practices that are 'thick, fleshy and warm' (Mol 2002: 31) is particularly helpful in side-stepping these issues, even in interviews. In her recent work Mol (2008) seeks to foreground practicalities, materialities and events – paying attention to both habitual and object-centred action. Furthermore she insists on keeping an open mind about when and how actors seek to prioritise or create hierarchies between different practices or attempt other forms of calibration (Mol 2002). Thus, in this study we used interviews to elicit talk about practices rather than priorities, entering the field through questions about particular objects – functional foods and statins – that are marketed as lowering cholesterol.

Our respondents had typically had at least one high cholesterol reading but did not inhabit a sick identity (cf. Farrimond *et al.* 2010) and rarely defined themselves in terms of a risk of heart disease. Our focus in this chapter is when and how the conceptual contents of health behaviour might be both articulated and enacted by people doing health outside the clinic. We observed that the notion of healthy eating or activity was hard for our respondents to hold stable when accounting for many interwoven daily practices. Where the sociology of health behaviour talks of people seeking a balance between different priorities, we found sustained multiplicity (Mol 2002). Though interviews elicited talk about moderation and compromises between different concerns, they could also be held apart in the interviews, and perhaps in practice. Before discussing these issues in more detail, we first outline our methodology.

Methodology

The chapter draws on data from two projects with people who identified as having bought or used different products for heart health between 2008 and 2011. The first was a study of users of functional foods such as spreads, drinks and yoghurt containing phytosterols for cholesterol reduction. The second recruited people who had purchased or been offered statins for cardiovascular risk reduction. The projects were conceived and designed collaboratively by the authors as comparative cases and carried out consecutively.

Recruitment and data collection were deliberately community-based and kept apart from clinical encounters and organisations because of the concern to avoid influencing talk about health and compliance (see also Henwood *et al.* 2011). Users of phytosterol products and prescription statins were recruited through advertisements in our own universities and the newsletters of elders' forums and councils in East Sussex, greater Manchester and Newcastle upon Tyne. Users of statins purchased over-the-counter (in pharmacies) were recruited at a national level, using an advert appearing with a Google search for 'Heart pro' or 'Zocor' (brand names for the licensed product). A total of 45 people claiming to eat or buy functional foods, or have done so in the past, were interviewed in the first study and 44 people who had bought or been prescribed statins in the second study. In each case we selected respondents among potential participants for maximum diversity in age, gender and socioeconomic background. The respondents' ages ranged from 24–90 years, including all eight groups in the National Statistics socioeconomic classification. In this chapter respondents are identified in two groups according to project – Phyt indicates phytosterol users; Stat indicates statin users. However, there was considerable overlap between groups in that many phytosterol users also took statins and statin users talked about functional foods.

An ethical review was carried out at the authors' institutions before data collection started. The interviews lasted between 30 and 80 minutes and were recorded and transcribed verbatim. The topic guide was broadly similar for both projects, though tailored to the different products and employed flexibly. Importantly, the interviews were object-centred: all participants were asked about how they came to purchase different heart health products, and about their use (or in some cases rejection) of statins and other medications, supplements or foods, as well as about conversations with primary care practitioners, pharmacists and others about the products. As a result, though some of our data was explicitly about decision-making, we generated much more talk about the practicalities of daily living, including food preparation, snacking and shopping.[2]

Iterative thematic analysis was carried out for both datasets following the outline proposed by Hammersley and Atkinson (1995). This involved making listening and analytic notes, identifying recurrent phrases or talk on particular topics and paying particular attention to aspects that initially appear puzzling or surprising. For the first dataset this was carried out by Author 2 working alone. Themes from this analysis were considered in relation to the second dataset and some amendments were made, along with significant additions. However, there was clear potential to compare the two studies, as anticipated, especially on data on common themes relating to diet, exercise, smoking, weight and weight loss and other concerns, which incorporated talk about family and work responsibilities and ill health, aside from cardiovascular risk, along with more conceptual themes like moderation.

In reporting this data we have chosen to talk of multiple repertoires for describing eating and exercising. Though described in the literature variously as diverse priorities (Murcott 1998), logics (Mol 2008) or rules of thumb (Green *et al.* 2003), we feel that repertoire reduces the suggestion of calculation. Coming from science and technology studies, we are familiar with the concept of repertoires from the work of Gilbert and Mulkay (1984), who borrow it from Potter and other discourse analysts. For these authors:

> Interpretative repertoires are recurrently used systems of terms used for characterizing and evaluating actions, events and other phenomena. A repertoire ... is constituted through a limited range of terms used in particular stylistic and grammatical constructions. (Potter and Wetherell 1987: 149)

In their account of scientists' talk and writing, Gilbert and Mulkay identify two repertoires, the empiricist and contingent, and what they call reconciliation devices that allow people to move between the two repertoires in a short time, for example, in interview, both signalling and managing an apparent contradiction. We suggest that the theme of balance – described above with reference to the previous literature – is one such reconciliation device: or, to use Mol's (2002) terms, a form of calibration between different objects and practices. In the rest of this chapter we briefly illustrate different repertoires (especially health, pleasure and sociality) for readers not familiar with food literature and draw attention to the importance of a fourth pragmatic repertoire, which combined talk about convenience, thrift and the mundane practices of food provision, storage and preparation. However, our main focus is on how and when these repertoires are reconciled or calibrated, that is, related across interviews and in daily life. In this sense, we have read interviews as both narrative presentations of the self and accounts of practices (as both topic and resource [Hammersley and Atkinson 1995]), seeking analytical clarity about these different components.

Findings

The limited purchase of health

Unsurprisingly perhaps, our respondents were quick to tell us about their concern with health, employing a diverse vocabulary to describe efforts to eat more healthily in terms of a low fat, low carbohydrate or low salt diet, as well as the general, vaguer term. However our questions about what they actually did (what they ate the day before the interview, when and how they were active) highlighted the limits of this concern in shaping daily life. For example, Stat 15 (woman, 61 years old, retired), started the interview by telling us that 'mostly I think I eat fairly healthily' and 'I try to have a balanced diet' – but her narrative of the day's food up until the interview included a pecan turnover and lunch of leftovers fried with bacon justified with reference to thriftiness ('it's better to use stuff up rather than waste it').

In other interviews, talk about practice might quite unselfconsciously replace a focus on health with talk about other goods such as the variety, freshness or homemade quality of food consumed:

> Stat1:   Er, I try to eat as healthily as I can … So I have quite a few salads and that. I stay, oh I stay away from cheese a bit and eggs and stuff like that … But no, I try to just eat an ordinary healthy diet if I can … I like steak, I must admit. I just vary my diet as best I can … I like fruit and vegetables and things like that …
>
> I: OK, er, let's just play a what did you eat yesterday game.
>
> Stat1:   Right er, I'm terribly when I'm at work … We had bacon and sausage on toast for the breakfast … And then normally I very rarely eat through the day … I just have a few cups of coffee, then last time night went home and we had chicken, salad and chips.
>
> I: Right, something that you cooked at home?
>
> Stat1:   Well my wife did yeah [laughs].
>
> I: Yeah, yes, OK, but not, not chips from the chippa[3]?
>
> Stat1:   No, no, no, made in the house.
>
> I: Made in the house, OK. In a pan, on the top or oven chips?
>
> Stat1:   Deep fat fryer.
>   (Man, 58-year-old deputy building superintendent)

This interview illustrated the importance of digging beyond claims to eat healthily to explore consumption across different locations and times. For this man healthy eating had no place at work. In the home his wife had jurisdiction over food preparation. In other interviews foods like porridge and soup might be celebrated for their domestic preparation as much as for nutritional advantages, such as oats being thought to lower cholesterol, or soup as a low-fat lunch option. One older woman told us early on that 'being healthy is very important' (Stat14, woman, 77-year-old retired superannuation officer) and described some changes made to her diet, including making soup for lunch. Yet again, such changes appeared more limited as the interview progressed. A long-term smoker, she described few opportunities for activity: 'I can't walk by myself and there's nobody to walk with'. She had recently started buying butter again after a period of using margarine for the pleasure of tasting butter on crackers. We recount these examples not to present our respondents as dissimulating but, rather, to illustrate that people moved relatively easily between the repertoires of health, pleasure and practicality in a single interview.

Moral work in mixing narratives of health and indulgence

Almost all the interviews contained hints of the moral work (Radley and Billig 1996) carried out by our respondents. Above, this was apparent in attempts to justify and minimise deviations from healthy living rules. But it was also true for people who appeared to be highly motivated by health concerns. Discussions of dietary denial might be tempered with accounts of other forms of indulgence:

Stat21:   So if I have any vices I probably drink too much, in fact I know I drink too much, that's my major vice. But I hardly eat any meat whatsoever … I will eat a little bit of chicken occasionally and maybe a bit of fish every now and again, but I have a very low fat diet. I don't eat any cheese, any yoghurts. I tend to avoid all the obvious things. I don't eat any cakes or biscuits, anything like that. (Man, 53-year-old engineer)

Here the appearance of healthy living is counteracted by a desire to avoid being seen to be so involved in health that you have no vices. Discussing pleasure taken in ostensibly healthy food like yoghurt or porridge, or in exercise, also seemed to protect interviewees from appearing over concerned with their health:

I: So how did the swimming start, have you always done it?
Stat1:   Always, oh yeah, I've always loved to go for a swim yeah. I mean we don't do hundreds of lengths … we split it up because we go in the sauna for a bit, come out maybe do five lengths, come back in again, come back; like that.
I: So I kind of get a sense of people swim for all sorts of reasons. Is it for enjoyment or is it partly for health or is it for fitness or can you remember why
Stat1:   Sheer enjoyment I think.
         (Man, 58-year-old deputy building superintendent)

In an inversion of this approach, respondents, especially women, talked about not eating discredited foods such as full fat dairy products, burgers, sausages, sweets or crisps because of taste rather than health for lack of enjoyment. If exercise was not linked to enjoyment then it might be presented as a matter of ordinary everyday activity and routines:

Stat4:   And I get more than enough leg work in the course of a day er I don't, I don't go walking and ??, I walk to the precinct or walk round the cricket ground or go for a walk in the park but you know, er, I don't go hiking or anything like that. I don't go to the gym. (Man, 54-year-old building superintendent)

Here the speaker distanced himself from conscious attempts to be fit, signified by references to the gym. Where people did talk of gym going they appeared to make strong interactional efforts to avoid being seen as a health freak (Backett 1992):

Stat34:   I wouldn't say I was terribly fit but I've been to the gym this morning
I: OK
Stat34:   But I'm not terribly fit so I don't go for huge long runs and that sort of
          thing. (Man, 66-year-old retired building society manager)

In summary, then, talk about health and pleasure could be mixed and, indeed, the interviews revealed efforts to bring the different repertoires into some relation, either by discussing the pleasures that accompanied broader dietary restrictions or exercise or working to deny any contradiction between health and pleasure-seeking by aligning them. These narratives had the effect of portraying respondents as ordinary, and that ordinariness as limiting or mitigating the extent to which their behaviour reflected health concerns.

Temporal distributions of pleasure
A similar problem of reconciling discussions of health with talk about pleasure was evident in stories about the temporal distribution of different eating habits. Here rather than balance over a day or week (Backett 1992) Crawford's (1984) notion of control and release appeared a better fit with narratives of weeks or months of denial after a cholesterol test result, followed by a relaxation of dietary rules as this anxiety faded:

Phyt1:   I love Lurpak [butter], I love cheese, I love chocolate, um, but I decided to
          be 100% on a diet and switched to Benecol [spread] and the probiotic drink
          in the morning. I cut out totally all saturated fats. I don't eat red meat
          anyway. Out with the cheese, chocolate, the ice cream and all my pleasures
          and I stuck to a diet high in vegetables and fruit and crisp breads and rice
          breads and chicken and I did it by the book … and then I think because
          I'm human I went back to, um, I'm not fat, but I eat butter and I like ice
          cream and I eat at night and the chocolate. (Woman, 56-year-old
          administrator)

In this and similar quotes there was a self-conscious attempt to justify eating for pleasure as well as for health in the present. Other temporal frames were apparent: seasonal eating and enjoying more fatty food at weekends.

I: So you, you have an afters, a pudding or a sweet?
Stat13:   Yes, I must say in winter we probably do … I probably just have a piece of
          fruit, a banana, well I do like custard you know if its winter … I now
          certainly enjoy a weekend breakfast with some eggs, a couple of eggs on
          toast.
          (Man, 58-year-old science manager)

As previously described in the literature, it was very common to describe treats at the weekend if people had a traditional working week (Murcott 2000). In such talk a possible contradiction between health and pleasure is consciously alluded to and attempts are made to justify actual eating with reference to the infrequency of the unhealthy options or the ability to relax rules on certain days. Thus though the discursive repertoires of health and pleasure were rather carefully combined in interviews, we were told stories of quite strong separations of healthy eating and indulgence in practice, across months and years as well as days and weeks.

Eating as a social practice

Efforts to combine the repertoires of pleasure and health might involve giving priority to one over the other or a description of moves between them as human, ordinary and moderate. Narratives about eating and sociality were expected to follow a similar pattern: privileging eating together over health (or not) or invoking temporality to describe particular meals as a special event or treat (for example, Warde 1997). Yet again, the moral aspects of eating were important in interviews, for as Green *et al.* (2003) point out, it is important not to be fussy about food in company. Thus one man who had previously narrated instituting a fair number of healthy dietary changes quite unselfconsciously described having bacon sandwiches followed by chocolate biscuits with his mother the evening before the interview. More explicitly:

> Stat40:   If you go somewhere for a meal, and they've made, you know, I mean I
>   wasn't going to have desserts that have got cream and things like that, and
>   you just feel a bit rotten that you know they've gone to a lot of trouble
>   and you're not going to eat it. (Woman, 74-year-old retired social worker)

Though eating out was a common moment of release (Crawford 1984), especially for middle-class respondents, it was narrated less as a treat than as a social duty. Yet most of the practices described in the interviews were about everyday eating and related to households. Here we might have expected people to eat similar meals to their partners, whether that meant participating in a dietary change or sharing less healthy options (Henson *et al.* 1998). Accounts of compromises in the household were strongly gendered. Women are still often delegated or take on the role of providing or preparing food to meet the tastes or needs of household members (Beagan *et al.* 2008, Caplan, 1997, Henson *et al.* 1998, Murcott 1983). This may mean they temper their health-related consumption. So, for example, one woman said she had recently swapped from low-fat margarine to Anchor butter for the sake of her young children and another woman explained that she bought plant sterol margarines for herself but would use a different spread when cooking for the whole family:

> Phyt9:   If I have toast or I have to butter bread or something, then I will use it for
>   myself and I'm the only one who uses it … when I do cooking it's for
>   everyone so I would just use something low fat for everyone. (Woman in her
>   forties, professional gardener)

Other interviewees, mostly men, talked of accepting vitamins, supplements or plant sterol foods bought by partners specifically on their behalf, yet such gifts might not be accepted, leading to complicated practices of eating different things at a single mealtime:

> I: And did that [wife's attempts to lose weight] mean that your diet changed
>   because you eat the same as your wife?
> Stat9:   Probably yeah, sometimes though, er, she'd give me my mine separate. For
>   instance, if I was having chips she wouldn't have chips, she'd have a jacket
>   potato or whatever. And she'd say 'Why don't you have a potato and I'd say
>   'What chips do we have? You know just being' …
> I: Yeah, OK, are there other things that you do or things that you buy or that
>   you eat that are specifically connected to keeping a healthy heart?
> Stat9:   Er, yeah, she gets that margarine what's, for instance the margarine with –
>   what is it – less polyunsaturates or something, that is supposed to be better for

your heart. Now she buys the bread with seeds in it all the time, we
have that.

(Man, 63-year-old deputy building superintendent)

Here it is notable that the wife is reported to have encouraged the interviewee to have the
lower fat food (baked potato) but would ultimately provide her husband with his preferred
food (chips). Furthermore, a question concerning what things the interviewee might do for
a healthy heart elicits a response about products that his wife buys, the details of which he
is not completely aware. As in both Stat18 and Stat9, men commonly emphasised their
delegation of much work with food and thus of the pursuit of health. For example, respondents might not remember the name of a particular food or suggest a degree of uncertainty
about the nature of the supposed benefits.

As found by other authors, accounts of eating practices in our data were thus full of
references to the social context of meals and particularly the household. However these
relationships shaped diet in quite different ways for different respondents or food items. In
one version of the sociality repertoire, social obligations meant that people ate things to
please partners or others, which might be unhealthy or high-fat foods, or a more healthy
food or supplement. This applied to both men and women. In a second version, people
talked of food being bought or prepared specifically for the sake of partners or others, for
example plant sterols or vitamins. The people doing the purchasing or preparing were often,
though not always, women. Thirdly, the accounts of some interviewees, mostly men, worked
to distance themselves from provisioning and preparation. It is clearly very difficult to talk
of health behaviour in relation to these men regarding practices, the rationale for which they
are only vaguely aware of.

The importance of practical considerations

These and other examples of talk about the practicalities of diet and exercise were of particular interest to us. Some aspects of this such as convenience and thrift have been mentioned in previous work (for example, Green *et al.* 2003); however in our object-focused
interviews this also included a lot of talk about using up fresh or perishable products and
responding to other physical characteristics of particular items – which could be thought
of as a pragmatic repertoire. In one case, a woman who lives alone explains that she eats
plant sterol margarines when she has sandwiches, which is sporadically, depending on
whether she has bought bread. Another talked of the need to finish an open packet of bacon:

I: And how often might you have sandwiches?
Phyt17:   Well it varies whether I buy bread … if I get a loaf and I'm going to have
            to consume it within 4 days then I might have a bread patch so I might have
            sandwiches two or three times during the loaf period and then once I've got
            rid of the loaf I won't buy a loaf immediately after that because it's going to
            be hanging about getting mouldy. (Woman, 65-year-old retired health
            promotion professional)
Stat12:   I've had bacon this week because I've got a pack of bacon … and I'm
            broke because it's nearly payday. (Woman, 58-year-old university
            administrator)

In other interviews people avoided buying unhealthy foods so that they were not in the house
and could not be consumed. Talk in this vein did not present the respondent as self-denying
or in control but rather as taking simple practical steps to reduce temptation.

In the pragmatic repertoire, the temporal patterning of eating practices was related to different routines at weekends, rather than the concept of the treat. Weekends could see both less and more healthy practices. For example one man had more of the cholesterol-lowering spread at the weekends because he typically had 'a few more slices of toast when I've got a bit more time' (Phyt38). References were also made to the availability of particular foods and different activities as distractions:

I: I was interested in you saying about your eating habits, how you graze, is that different at the weekends or when you're on holiday?

Phyt1: I probably eat less at the weekend because I am in an office with other people who eat all the time, and crisps and biscuits and cakes and there's always stuff in the kitchen at work and of course you get up earlier, so probably at the weekends and in the summer I'm outside a lot, I'm in the garden a lot, so I only eat when I think about it. (Woman, 56-year-old administrator)

In this quote the distribution of more and less healthy consumption was as much spatial as temporal: about avoiding an office full of snacks in the week and spending time in the garden at weekends. Within the pragmatic repertoire, we noted an absence of references to health and pleasure and their relations to such practicalities. In contrast to the constant interaction between repertoires of health and pleasure, this repertoire stood alone.

Discussion and conclusions

Talk about cholesterol reduction was interwoven with talk about all the environmental, social and practical factors that shaped both eating and exercise. Our interviews may have elicited a kind of summary of people's overall behaviour. Yet for most there was no clear hierarchy between these factors. Behaviour was rarely described as purely health-motivated but neither was it governed by pleasure, sociality or pragmatic considerations alone. Yet despite several decades of health promotion messages (Crawford 1984, 2006), health was perhaps a more occasional and peripheral topic than others, especially as time had elapsed since the clinical consultation that had usually first raised the problem of cholesterol. While respondents tended to rehearse, at least to some extent, narratives of healthy eating, it was not apparently necessary to present as wholly or even partly health-focused. Most identified only limited instances of dietary change and created some distance in their talk from the health-focused consumer imagined in health policy.

Though we had relatively few instances of the actual concept of balance, talk about moderation and mixing repertoires allowed people to present themselves as avoiding the risk of taking themselves and their health too seriously: not being faddish continued to appear to be important alongside claims to health-seeking behaviour. This chimed with the instincts that Backett (1992) identified in her respondents to deny any kind of fanaticism and locate themselves at a mid-point on a spectrum of behaviour. In other cases, a potential contradiction was invoked only to be denied in a kind of layering of the benefits in which health and pleasure were aligned: healthy food was also pleasurable food, unhealthy food was disliked, exercise was pursued for enjoyment. At the level of discourse, this has also been observed briefly by Backett (1992), who talked about people's desire to describe receiving gratification from healthy behaviour, for example, enjoyment in running, and recently by Halkier and Jensen (2011) who noted that some of their Danish Pakistani respondents talked about the greater convenience and economies of oven-cooking compared with frying.

Building on this work in a more theoretical vein, we suggest that the concept of moderation and the discursive alignment of health and pleasure act as reconciliation devices that facilitate moves between repertoires (after Gilbert and Mulkay 1984). Talk of reluctantly prioritising the social occasion over a desire for healthy eating had the same effect. Such devices both highlight interactional difficulties in talking about apparently contradictory concerns and allow people to move between different kinds of talk relatively smoothly while acknowledging the health moralities (Backett 1992) that influence talk about food.

In our data a further pragmatic repertoire, encompassing talk about food provisioning, storage and cooking and about the physical realities of exercise, provided another means of managing the moral components of the issues. This repertoire did not appear to require a self-conscious reconciliation with health concerns. Instead, it appeared as a valuable means of presenting oneself as ordinary – an alternative moral position (Eborall and Will 2011).

This observation allows us to make some further more tentative suggestions about the use of the different repertoires of lifestyle or health behaviour. It appeared in our data that the repertoires of health, pleasure and, to some extent, sociality, interacted in people's narratives and required reconciliation, whereas the pragmatic repertoire did not appear to elicit the same efforts at justification against a competing desire to pursue health: one might say it was relatively inert. We therefore propose that there may be some repertoires that can be mixed together and some that remain separate, and that this concept of interactive and inert repertoires may prove useful in other research.

So much for discourse. What, if anything, can be said about the practices of eating and exercise that were narrated in these interviews? While we noted there were interactional difficulties in talk with us, we are not convinced that people have the same problems in reconciling the different repertoires in practice. Green et al. (2003) have argued that different rules of thumb act as rhetorical devices in focus group talk about dietary practice, but leave it unclear how this might translate into what they call decision-making. As noted in our introduction we started from a desire to avoid any assumptions about calculative behaviour by avoiding the language of the trade-off or decision. It is true that some participants narrated their efforts at some form of calibration (Mol 2002) between different objectives, for example, priority-setting; however, we have observed that others went out of their way to deny they made a significant calculation in their everyday eating in particular. Instead, our interviews illustrated the significance of temporal, spatial and social distribution (another central concept in Mol's account) in allowing people to pursue different priorities, logics or repertoires through everyday practices.

In analysing the detailed accounts of foods and meals consumed or activities undertaken, we noted several different forms of distribution between more or less health-motivated activities. For example, moderation might be learned over quite long periods as well as enacted across a single week in the familiar talk about weekend treats (Murcott 2000, Short 2003). Healthy and unhealthy eating or activities might be associated with particular spaces like offices and the parental home as well as the restaurants identified by Warde and Martens (1998). Often then, like Mol (2002), we saw little emphasis on coherence in the practices described. Rather than calculated trade-offs, we found instead sustained multiplicity, as people tried out different foods or routines, incorporated products into everyday life and made messy compromises in the space of the household and beyond.

Acknowledgements

The work on which this chapter was based was funded by a small grant from the ESRC to both authors on DIY Heart Health (RES-00–2203324) and a Leverhulme Early Career

Fellowship (award no. 40344) held by Kate Weiner. We are grateful to them, to all who've discussed our findings at our conference presentations, and to the people who shared their thinking about everyday cholesterol reduction with us over the course of both projects.

Notes

1   As well as other behaviour like smoking (Gabe and Thorogood 1986, Graham 1984).
2   We also gathered information about much longer time periods than was covered in some similar studies (for example, Farrimond *et al.* 2010), which have interviewed people at specific times after clinical encounters.
3   Chippa is a colloquial term for takeaway chip shop.

References

Backett, K. (1992) Taboos and excesses: lay health moralities in middle class families, *Sociology of Health & Illness*, 14, 2, 255–74.

Beagan, B., Chapman, G., D'Sylva, A. and Basset, R. (2008) 'It's just easier for me to do it': rationalizing the family division of foodwork, *Sociology*, 42, 4, 653–71.

Callon, M. and Rabeharisoa, V. (2004) Gino's lesson on humanity: genetics, mutual entanglements and the sociologist's role, *Economy and Society*, 33, 1, 1–27.

Calnan, M. (1990) Food and health: a comparison of beliefs and practices in middle-class and working-class households. In Cunningham-Burley, S. and McKeganey, N. (eds) *Readings in Medical Sociology*. London: Tavistock and Routledge.

Calnan, M. and Williams, S. (1991) Style of life and the salience of health: an exploratory study of health related practices in households from differing socio-economic circumstances, *Sociology of Health & Illness*, 13, 4, 506–29.

Caplan, P. (1997) Approaches to the study of food, health and identity. In Caplan, P. (ed.) *Food, Health and Identity*. London: Routledge.

Coveney, J. (2000) *Food. Morals and Meaning. The Pleasure and Anxiety of Eating*. London: Routledge.

Coveney, J. and Bunton, R. (2003) In pursuit of the study of pleasure: implications for health research and practice, *Health*, 7, 2, 161–79.

Crawford, R. (1984) A cultural account of 'health': control, release, and the social body. In McKinlay, J.B. (ed.) *Issues in the Political Economy of Health Care*. London: Tavistock.

Crawford, R. (2006) Health as a meaningful social practice, *Health*, 10, 3, 401–20.

Department of Health (n.d.) *Public health*. Available at https://www.gov.uk/government/topics/public-health (accessed 4 September 2013).

Eborall, H. and Will, C. (2011) Prevention is better than cure, but preventive medication as a risk to ordinariness?, *Health, Risk and Society*, 13, 7–8, 653–68.

Farrimond, H., Saukko, P.M., Qureshi, N. and Evans, P.H. (2010) Making sense of being at 'high risk' of coronary heart disease within primary prevention, *Psychology & Health*, 25, 3, 289–304.

Fischler, C. (1986) Learned versus 'spontaneous' dietetics: French mothers' views of what children should eat, *Social Science Information*, 25, 4, 945–65.

Fischler, C. (2011) Commensality, society and culture, *Social Science Information*, 50, 3–4, 528–48.

Gabe, J. and Thorogood, N. (1986) Prescribed drug use and the management of everyday life: the experiences of black and white working class women, *Sociological Review*, 34, 4, 737–72.

Gilbert and Mulkay (1984) *Opening Pandora's Box. A Sociological Analysis of Scientists' Discourse*. New York: Cambridge University Press.

Graham, H. (1984) *Women, Health and the Family*. Brighton: Harvester.

Graham, H. (1993) *When Life's a Drag. Women, Smoking and Disadvantage*. London: HMSO.

Graham, H. (2007) *Unequal Lives: Health and Socio Economic Inequalities*. Buckingham: Open University Press.

Green, J.M., Draper, A.K. and Dowler, E.A. (2003) Short cuts to safety: risk and 'rules of thumb' in accounts of food choice, *Health, Risk and Society.*, 5, 1, 33–52.

Gronow, J. and Warde, A. (eds) (2001) *Ordinary Consumption*. London: Routledge.

Halkier, B. and Jensen, I. (2011) Doing 'healthier' food in everyday life? A qualitative study of how Pakistani Danes handle nutritional communication, *Critical Public Health*, 21, 4, 471–83.

Hammersley, M. and Atkinson, P. (1995) *Ethnography: Principles in Practice*. London: Routledge.

Henson, S., Gregory, S., Hamilton, M. and Walker, A. (1998) Food choice and diet change within the family setting. In Murcott, A. (ed.) *The Nation's Diet: The Social Science of Food Choice*. London: Longman.

Henwood, F., Harris, R. and Spoel, P. (2011) Informing health? Negotiating the logics of choice and care in everyday practices of 'healthy living', *Social Science & Medicine*, 72, 12, 2026–32.

Jallinoja, P., Pajari, P. and Absetz, P. (2012) Negotiated pleasures in health-seeking lifestyles of participants of a health promoting intervention, *Health*, 14, 2, 115–30.

Keane, A. (1997) Too hard to swallow? The palatability of health eating advice. In Caplan, P. (ed.) *Food, Health and Identity*. London: Routledge.

Lawton, J., Ahmad, N., Peel, E. and Hallowell, N. (2007) Contextualising accounts of illness: notions of responsibility and blame in white and South Asian respondents' accounts of diabetes causation, *Sociology of Health & Illness*, 26, 6, 891–906.

Mol, A. (2002) *The Body Multiple. Ontology in Medical Practice*. Durham and London: Duke University Press.

Mol, A. (2008) *The Logic of Care: Health and the Problem of Patient Choice*. London: Routledge.

Murcott, A. (1983), 'It's a pleasure to cook for him'. Food, mealtimes and gender in some South Wales households. In Gamarnikov, I. E. *et al.* (eds) *The Public and the Private: Social Patterns of Gender Relations*. London: Heinemann.

Murcott, A. (1998) Food choice, the social sciences and 'The Nation's Diet' research programme. In Murcott, A. (ed.) *The Nation's Diet: the Social Science of Food Choice*. London: Longman.

Murcott, A. (2000) Understanding life-styles and food use: contributions from the social sciences, *British Medical Bulletin*, 56, 1, 121–32.

Pajari, P., Jallinoja, P. and Absetz, P. (2006) Negotiating over self-control and activity: an analysis of balancing in the repertoires of Finnish healthy lifestyle, *Social Science of Medicine*, 62, 10, 2601–11.

Potter, J. and Wetherell, M. (1987) *Discourse and Social Psychology: Beyond Attitudes and Behaviour.* London: Sage.

Radley, A. and Billig, M. (1996) Accounts of health and illness: dilemmas and representations, *Sociology of Health & Illness*, 18, 2, 220–40.

Reckwitz, A. (2002) Towards a theory of social practices: a development in culturalist theorizing, *European Journal of Social Theory*, 5, 2, 243–63.

Short, F. (2003) Domestic cooking practices and skills: findings from an English study, *Food Service Technology*, 3, 3–4, 177–85.

Warde, A. (1997) *Consumption, Food and Taste: Culinary Antinomies and Commodity Culture*. London: Sage.

Warde, A. (2005) Consumption and theories of practice, *Journal of Consumer Culture*, 5, 2, 131–53.

Warde, A. and Martens, L. (1998) A sociological theory of food choice: the case of eating out. In Murcott, A. (ed.) *The Nation's Diet. The Social Science of Food Choice*. London: Longman.

Weiner, K. (2011) The subject of functional foods: accounts of consuming foods containing phytosterols, *Sociological Research Online*, 16, 2, 7. Available at http://www.socresonline.org.uk/16/2/7.html (accessed 24 September 2013).

Will, C. and Weiner, K. (2013) Do-it-yourself heart health? 'Lay' practices and products for disease prevention, *Health Sociology Review*, 22, 1, 8–18.

Williams, S. (1995) Theorising class, health and lifestyles: can Bourdieu help us?, *Sociology of Health & Illness*, 17, 5, 577–604.

Williams, S.J. (2003) *Medicine and the Body*. London: Sage.

13

Enjoy your food: on losing weight and taking pleasure
Else Vogel and Annemarie Mol

In an interview shortly after she had managed to lose 15 kilos, Isa, a 25-year-old Dutch woman, told us that she had achieved this feat with a low carbohydrate diet and a range of additional strategies:

> I now drink water. It's a great trick. If I get hungry I drink a large bowl of coffee and then I am full again ... I have cut a fat index out of a magazine and hung it up in my food cupboard. It says how many calories a snack contains and how many minutes you must walk to lose those calories.[1]

Strategies like these are widely used by people who want to lose weight. They relate to food as energy and help people to absorb less energy than they burn. But despite the ingenious character of the tricks, it is not easy to shift one's energy balance. A year after the interview Isa had regained her original weight, plus a bit more. This happens to many people who diet. All too easily the conclusion is drawn that those concerned are not strong-willed enough to give up the gratification that eating and drinking offer. That they live in an obesogenic environment does not help. Jointly, or such is the argument, weakness of will and the abundance of readily available calories cause an increase in overweight and obesity. In response to this problem public health advocates seek to address the obesogenic environment. However, it appears to be difficult to achieve a world with fewer adverts, fewer fatty foods outlets, smaller servings of soft drinks and better access to healthy food. Working towards these goals clashes with the market organisation of food production and consumption and with the interests of the food industry. What remains is the possibility of addressing consumers and urging them to make healthy food choices. Hence, the public is provided with information about food (its calories; its carbohydrate content; its fatty acids and so on) and warned that overweight and obesity cause health problems (diabetes, vascular disease, osteoarthritis and so on). Such campaigns target what public health research calls health behaviour. They admonish us to behave, that is, to take control over what we eat and abstain from excessive food pleasures.

It is not just nutrition scientists, government officials, healthcare professionals and diet gurus who sing this song. In the social sciences the tension between health and pleasure tends to be taken for granted as well. There are social scientists who explore how people negotiate their concern with health and their desire for pleasure in their daily lives. Some wonder how people's ability to exercise control might be strengthened (Coveney and Bunton

---

From Health Behaviours to Health Practices: Critical Perspectives, First Edition. Edited by Simon Cohn. Chapters © 2014 The Authors. Book Compilation © 2014 Foundation for the Sociology of Health & Illness / Blackwell Publishing Ltd.

2003, Jallinoja *et al.* 2010, Rozin 1999, Williams 1997, Wilson 2005). Others argue that siding with health is disciplining or normalising and go on to suggest that, instead, we would do well to give free rein to our desires (Smith 2008). While these views are in opposition to one another, a similar scheme is at work in both: rationality and control are disentangled from, and contrasted with, desire and excess.

It was against this background that we started our ethnographic inquiries into care practices in The Netherlands for people who want to (or, as they often put it themselves, have to) lose weight. One of the present authors, AM, while wondering about possible escapes from the 'control versus excess' paradigm, was being interviewed by an online journal for dieticians. She used the occasion to ask for volunteers willing to participate in a further inquiry into weight loss in practice. Starting out from these volunteers, and then adding others through the snowball method, the other author, EV, was able to conduct twenty formal interviews (with dieticians, weight consultants, coaches, doctors, nutritionists, psychologists, physiotherapists, fitness trainers and a surgeon). In addition we did ethnographic observations. AM with a general practitioner, a dietician and a coach; EV with two different dieticians, two movement support groups, a weight loss training group and various professionals in an obesity clinic. In addition EV participated in a mindfulness training as a trainee. It turned out that in practice things are more complex than we had been led to expect. Firstly, we found that the control versus pleasure paradigm comes in strikingly different variants. Secondly, some professionals appear to work with it in interestingly creative and innovative ways.[2] And thirdly, we came across professionals who did not fit into the control versus pleasure paradigm at all. The present chapter is based on the work of the latter group. Drawing their inspiration from a variety of resources, these professionals are experimentally developing practical alternatives to the control versus pleasure paradigm. Intrigued, we sought them out. They readily gave us access to their work, pleased that someone wanted to learn about it. Their clients agreed to our presence as well, either because they were generally in favour of openness or because they hoped that this would help others to get the kind of care that they were receiving themselves.

The practices analysed here do not seek to strengthen people's will-power. Instead they try to cultivate their capacity for pleasure. The ideal at their horizon is not self-control, but self-care. Self-care is not easy. In this chapter we draw out a few techniques for fostering it. They involve feeling pleasure and pain, sensing one's needs and crafting situations and meals that give joy. The goals of self-care are varied. They include not just health and weight loss but also joy, pleasure, satisfaction, ease and calm. As we analyse what is at stake in the practices that we studied we do not claim that they lead to paradise. They have blind spots, hit up against perplexing resistances and generate new and difficult dilemmas. But while the logic of control has been reiterated over and over again, the intricacies of self-care have so far received less attention. They deserve to be brought out into the open, discussed, amended and tinkered with. We hope that our articulations will strengthen and sharpen the theoretical creativity of our informants and help their insights to travel beyond their daily practices. As we address what public health calls health behaviour we argue that this term is not simply a label pinned to something going on out there. Instead, it indexes the paradigm in which control contrasts with pleasure. Self-care is better served with other words.

Productive practices

As the alternative practices we present here go against the received wisdom that weight loss crucially depends on taking control over one's appetites, the first task that our informants set themselves is to spell out the fact that such control may not be all that helpful and may even be counterproductive. This is the idea: if people succeed in controlling their food intake the result is not simply that they come to absorb less energy than they burn. Their bodies are affected in other ways as well. They get hungry.

> Annette is a coach and her practice is called *Liever slank*. This Dutch phrase translates as preferably slim, but also as slim in a way that is kinder. On a fine evening in autumn 12 people have gathered to learn more about this. They exchange experiences. At one point, Kees (as we call him here) says: 'If I am hungry, I immediately feel like yes, I am going to stay hungry for an hour, because then I will lose weight'. His hunger gives Kees a sense of achievement. Tanja adds: 'If I don't eat, I feel I'm on the right track.' The drawback, however, is that such happiness doesn't last. Annette uses a moment of silence to ask: 'But is this really a good idea, to suffer so heroically? For you won't be able to sustain this. Eventually you will eat, because your body wants it. And then you will feel bad. Angry with yourself. Or guilty.'

The tables are turned. If the hunger that follows from heroic attempts to control one's body undermines one's ability to stay in control, it may well be that the gluttony that conventional wisdom takes to precede dieting, rather follows from it. This is one of the reasons that successes tend to be short lived: dieting practices produce what they seek to counter. In addition, they also produce bad feelings:

> Another participant at the meeting, Tessa, says: 'Then I eat something and I think, oh, that's another 200 calories. Too bad.' Everybody nods. Annette nods, too. And then she counters: 'How can you enjoy what you eat once you start thinking 'that's another 200 calories'? While you feel bad, too bad, you do not taste'.

While Tessa-in-control counts calories, Tessa out-of-control consumes them. The 'too bad' indicates that she lives this as a failure. But where does this failing originate? The control paradigm suggests that the origin lies in Tessa's uncontrolled desire to eat. Annette, by contrast, suggests that the very attempt to take control is to blame because it drags a person into a vicious circle.[3] As control kills pleasure it precludes satisfaction. And as long as a person is not satisfied, she will want to eat.

What emerges here is that there is no such thing as the body. Instead, there are two ways of configuring bodies, two versions of the body and these are in tension. In the first, external control (provided by a set of rules or a mind) is needed to stop a body from absorbing more energy than it burns. In the second, bodies are taken to have an internal feedback system that keeps them in balance. Pleasure is a crucial part of this feedback system because it signals 'enough'. Thus, when there is no pleasure – as a consequence of guilt, or haste or a list of other intervening factors – the feedback system does not get its crucial feedback. Hence no balance:

> Annette takes it that people who want to lose weight would do well to enjoy their food. She talks about her own experience. At one point she had put on weight and started to complain about it. A colleague advised her to not start dieting but to try to take more pleasure from her food. And indeed, as she began to shift her attention to what she ate, things started to change. Instead of finishing a box of chocolates in one sitting, she would indulge in one or two pieces. She began to take more effort with her cooking. She sat down whenever she ate and concentrated on it. After her story, Annette challenges her clients who have just admitted to all kinds of binge eating

incidents. She says: 'When you really take pleasure in eating, you can't eat an entire pack of cookies. You only ever do that when you gobble them up thoughtlessly'.

Like the body, the subject also comes in different versions. In the logic of control, the subject is a cognitive centre making decisions. It receives advice about what to eat (a diet plan) or it gathers information (for instance, about calories) that will allow it to make its own plans. In addition, it must somehow muster the motivation to act on these plans. In the self-care logic that informs Annette's way of working, the subject starts out by feeling. It feels hunger, guilt, a sense of failure. It feels like being slim or in need of comfort. It may feel a sense of achievement or of calm and satisfaction. These two subjects have different relations to their body. For the first subject the body is an object of knowledge and control. For the second the body is a locus. It is one of the sites where feelings reside and emerge. In this site so-called emotional feelings such as fear or joy encounter (hit up against or get confused with) so-called physical feelings, such as hunger or cold. Disentangling these feelings is not easy. Even feeling itself appears difficult to do.

Feeling pleasure

The practices we studied share the idea that feeling, even feeling pleasure, does not come naturally. As long as people are busy counting calories, running around or reproaching themselves, they are unlikely to feel the gratifications that eating and drinking potentially provide. Feeling depends on being attentive. You better attend, is the idea, to what you taste.

> The conference is on healthy eating; there are lectures and workshops. Guido gives one of the workshops and starts by handing out crisps and nuts. 'You might want to taste both, first one, then the other. Then, make a few notes. What did you expect and what do you experience? Is there a difference? And what happens to the flavour as you are eating, does it build up or fade away? Once you've swallowed, what do you feel then? For now don't talk, please, first concentrate'. A bit later everybody's notes are compared and they appear to be strikingly similar. The crisps are covered with salt. They mainly taste of salt and, though they are not particularly good, they induce a craving for more, perhaps due to the initial intense sensation provided by the salt. The nuts are completely different. They have been roasted but they are not salted. Their flavour increases as you chew, there is substance to them, they feel nutritious. A small handful is good; nobody wants more.

Here Guido tries to convey the fact that sensing what one eats depends not just on eating but on stopping short, turning inwards and protecting one's sensations from being overrun by the talk of others. What emerges is that if she is not attentive a person might be inclined to eat more and more crisps, not because they are particularly enjoyable but rather because they are not. This comes as a surprise to most participants and that is the point of the exercise. The moral is that you may hope to feel what is truly satisfying by tuning in on your food.[4] However, satisfaction depends on more than good food and attention alone. It may be tied up with endless other intricacies of life.

> Maria is a dietician working in what she calls a holist way. In her consulting room Helen, one of her clients, says that things are improving. In last few weeks she no longer overate every day. However, things still 'go wrong' three nights out of seven.

Then she gets takeout food, for example, from the Chinese restaurant on the corner. She knows that home-cooked food would make her feel better and taste better, but there it is. Maria asks about cooking. If that is the problem, it might help to cook two or three meals in energetic moments and put the spare ones in the freezer. Helen says no. 'When I'm tired I am not just lazy, but also crave for salty and fat stuff. For junk food. Even after dinner I dive into the fridge for cheese or salami'. Maria nods. 'It's very good that you are at least able to notice this. That's quite a big step already. So, now, let's see. It is when you are tired that you eat more than you would like to. Is there something you are trying to keep at a distance? Something you do not want to feel?' Helen pauses to think. Then, slowly, she nods.

Since she started visiting Maria, Helen has gradually learned to recognise that feeling tired may go together with feeling the need for salty, fatty foods. Now the next step is to learn that the comfort that food provides may help to keep other feelings at bay, nasty feelings that are more difficult to face than tiredness. Maria does not explore what the feelings are that Helen might be pushing aside. She takes this to be a task for a psychologist. However, she does insist that learning to feel threatening emotions may be a crucial step towards losing some weight. Another client, Stella, has picked this up and is learning to give her unwelcome feelings a name.

Stella talks about a day at work. She was hungry and once she had eaten the food she had brought from home, she ate a few of the sandwiches that had been laid out for a lunch meeting. Even then her hunger did not go away. Her surprise about this made her stop and think. And only then did she realise that it was not exactly hunger that she felt, but rather frustration. 'And then it didn't take me long to realise why I was frustrated. And that was okay, it had to do with a situation at work that was, well, frustrating. So I allowed myself that feeling. And the urge to keep on eating disappeared'.

Maria's work is based on the experience that if eating is done out of frustration, to keep threatening feeling away, food pleasure has no chance. If, by contrast, an emotion such as frustration is simply allowed to exist it does not have to be driven away by eating. All this means that in treatment practices different kinds of feelings, emotions and bodily sensations need to be attended to together. This idea also informs the psychomotor therapy given to people with obesity as part of their follow-up treatment after bariatric surgery.

Mariette, the therapist, hands out balloons and asks all six members of the treatment group plus the ethnographer to stand up and place a balloon on the seat of their chair. 'Push on it, go ahead, as much as you dare, go!' There is some giggling, but not a lot. After some pushing time Mariette wants to know what we feel. She writes the answers on a whiteboard. Petra is 'afraid the balloon will burst'. 'Where do you feel this fear?' 'Well, just fear,' Petra says, shivering a little. 'But where do you feel it *in your body?*' 'Ehm … well, in my chest, my heart rate'. Rinse suggests: 'In your breathing?' More sensations appear on the whiteboard: 'get hot', 'belly pain', 'have to pee'. Anja proclaims: 'I do not feel anything. What should I feel?' 'You may have to push harder,' says Mariette. Anja tries. She pushes the balloon into the chair as hard as she can. '*I* feel something just by looking at you!' Petra sighs. Anja shakes her head and looks around. Is this a defiant look or is she excusing herself? 'No, still nothing.' BANG! The balloon bursts. A little startled, Anja admits that yes, finally she feels something:

her heart is beating faster. At the end of the session Mariette talks about homework. She asks the members of the group to think about how they deal with tension in their everyday lives. 'What do you do when you are put under pressure, when you are stressed, do you hide feelings away, rationalise them, look for distractions?'

A body can only hope to feel pleasure if it is able to feel in the first place. Thus Mariette creates situations in which feelings are likely to arise, and encourages her treatment group to attend to what occurs. Focusing on their bodies should help people to feel something, anything at all. Seeking words for these feelings and relating to what others say – recognising it, being surprised by it – should help them to explore their sensations further. And all this comes with the hope that in real life participants will get better attuned to their physical and emotional sensations.

Feeling needs

In the control paradigm losing weight depends on abstaining from food even if one feels like eating. One's food intake should not be based on feelings, but on dieting guidelines or a proper calculation of nutritional needs. Self-care, by contrast, includes learning to feel what you need.

> The workshop again. Now two kinds of orange juice are passed around. They look the same. Guido, the workshop leader, asks: 'Note down how they taste and what effects they have on you'. People take sips and make notes. Once we are allowed to talk the agreement is striking again. The first juice has hardly any taste. Someone calls out 'sugar water!' General acclaim. At the same time, most participants report that they felt the urge to keep on drinking. The second juice, by contrast, has a rich taste. There are layers in it: sweet, sour, a tinge of bitter. It is good, but a small glass is enough. Only after this has been collectively established do we learn that juice number one was the light version of an expensive brand and juice number two was freshly squeezed. Guido: 'Isn't it strange that when our bodies ask for juice, we trick them with something light? Why not give them the nourishment they need?'

Guido is convinced that it is not despite its rich, layered taste, but because of this, that freshly squeezed juice does not urge a person to keep on drinking. It is satisfying. Guido contends that light food is a trick, and a bad trick at that, because a body is not so easily deceived. If only people can learn to feel them properly, their desires will appear to be in line with their needs. This confidence in the body's potential to sense its needs is striking in most of the practices that we studied. It may confuse clients who in the past have been given rules (this is what you should eat) or information (this is how to calculate your needs). Things do not necessarily get easier without such handholds.

> As a part of her attempts to lose weight Melanie, who is in her twenties, goes to the gym. But what to eat after the gym? Melanie: 'If I have rules, I'll be fine, I can follow rules'. But Janet, the dietician, tries to take another course: 'That is very good, that you can follow rules. But what about trying to feel what you might best eat? There is a difference between hunger and craving for something sweet, you know. Are you hungry? Then you want proper food, soup, a sandwich, something filling. Do you have a craving? Then you have some of what you crave for. The difference is important.

Would you like be able to feel what you need, instead of thinking: what are the rules?' Melanie hesitates. Janet continues: 'This is hard, we have to take it step by step. Let's start from an example'. Yesterday after her gym, Melanie first had yogurt and then crackers with chocolate spread. Janet asks whether she was still hungry afterwards, but Melanie cannot tell. 'This is the kind of thing you might want to become aware of,' Janet says. 'To get there, it may help to sit down and make notes. Not about what you eat, but about what you experience. How your food becomes you'.

Feeling demands training. Time and again clients are asked to attend to such things as 'how your food becomes you'. What becomes them today may well do so again tomorrow and in this way one's past experiences may come to inform one's future eating patterns. But patterns should not crystallise into fixed rules. Bodily needs may vary from one day to another. While rules seem to offer a stable kind of control, there is no end to the tinkering self-care that involves feeling.

Melanie says that, okay, she will try. But for now she has one last question. She often eats currant buns. Are they allowed? She looks at Janet almost apologetically, realising that she has not quite got it yet. Janet smiles and says: 'That is a good question. You know what? Next time you have a currant bun, try to feel that for yourself. Or you may want to buy a few different kinds, from different bakeries, and try to feel which one satisfies you most. What I encourage you to do, is not to ask 'am I being good?', but rather 'is it good for me?'

While rules may be stabilised and carried along between moments, sensing has to be done in the here and now. While rules that stipulate healthy behaviour are based on measurements done on a population level, sensing has to do with the effects of food or drink on a specific body. Experimenting with different but comparable kinds of food or drink may help in gradually acquiring the ability to feel these effects. In the end, this should allow people to feel and feed their own particular needs.

A mindful eating course. We learn that mindful eating distinguishes between no less than eight kinds of hunger. Joyce, the course instructor, shows a list of them in her PowerPoint presentation. The group has to think up fitting examples. In this way, we come to talk about eye hunger (seeing food makes you want it), nose hunger (walking past the bakery), ear hunger (the cracking of crisps, the sizzling of oil), mouth hunger (sweetness, taste), belly hunger (rumbling stomach, 'real' hunger), body hunger (vague feeling of distress), mind hunger ('I can't eat this, I should eat that, if I don't eat this I can eat that') and heart hunger (warmth, rest, acceptance, cosiness). Then we start an exercise. As we sit in a circle, Joyce invites us to relax and then hands out coffee biscuits with mocha glazing. First we have to rate how much of each kind of hunger this biscuit makes us feel. Then we may choose whether or not to eat it. Only one out of the 12 people present actually does. Then we talk again. 'It looks like plastic, really.' 'The smell is good.' 'Is it? I think it isn't.' 'Once you start thinking about it, you realise: I don't want this cookie!' Most of us say that if the biscuit had been presented during the tea break we would have eaten it without thinking twice.

Even though only belly hunger is granted the adjective real, the point of an exercise like this is not to forbid foods that cater for what, by implication, are unreal hungers. Instead, the idea is that if you realise that, say, you are seeking comfort from a piece of cake, it becomes easier to leave it alone and look for comfort of another kind or, and this is at least as important, to actually find comfort in it. For rather than feeling bad about yourself, you may then enjoy your food. Making the different kinds of hunger explicit helps to open up different perceptions. Food may look appealing, smell lovely, have an interesting texture, a rich taste or provide a gratifying belly feel. Some people even appreciate the sugar rush that follows from their cookie. And as your needs are met and you register your satisfaction, your desires calm down as well. For at least some time all your eight hungers are quietened.

Crafting conditions

The professionals whose work we present here tell people not to forgo bodily pleasures but to cultivate them. As a part of this, people are encouraged to feel their sensations and emotions, rather than to eat them away; and to attune to their various needs and desires so as to better meet them. All this is work on the self. But caring for pleasure does not stop at the boundaries of the self; it also includes care for one's surroundings.

> I tell the adults about the hypothalamus, I explain that this is the satiety centre that regulates how much you eat and makes you stop eating. And then we talk about how this may become dysfunctional. And they get the assignment to give it stimuli again, to start tasting. So we discuss how to do it, this tasting. How to become an aware eater? It starts with sitting at a table, a nicely set table, with flowers, a nice table cloth. Eating with cutlery. Switching off the TV, the radio, putting away the newspaper. Just sitting and tasting. Trying to chew 15 times. Often clients will look at me, like: where's the fun in that? But it does help you to eat more consciously. For if you eat in front of the television, you tune out from your hypothalamus, you do not listen to it anymore. But it tells you exactly when to stop. (Martine, weight consultant)

Care for the self depends on care for the context in which this self is situated. The problem that is tackled here is not an obesogenic environment that induces eating but a distracting environment that shifts attention away from eating. The environment of an eater should not be distracting, but attractive. It should foster pleasures that underline and add to the pleasures provided by food – flowers, a table cloth. It should index care – hence the cutlery.[5] An attractive environment will not alter the flavour of the food but turns the activity of eating into a pleasure in and of itself. And as the body gets pleasure, it registers that it is eating and at some point will signal that it has had enough to eat.[6]

This 'enough' is not a set quantity, like the '2000 calories a day' that results from research done on groups of other people under other circumstances. Instead, it is a locally relevant amount of food that suits your particular body here and now. This body is not caught in a causal chain: the food on offer does not cause your body to eat. Instead this food is, or is not, inviting.[7] You may either respond to this invitation, or not. Such responses are not fixed, they may change over time, they may be tinkered with.

> Amanda, a dietician, encourages Johan, a man in his forties, to try new things. She explains that taste buds only get used to something after at least three weeks. Then they respond with an 'oh, carrots.' It takes another three weeks of tasting before the brain is able to shift to: 'yummy, carrots!' 'So keep trying. Taste a little piece, again and again, and you'll be fine'.

Here, then, pleasure is not enacted as a natural effect, but as a cultivated response. It depends on committed efforts. By attentively tasting new kinds of food one may learn to like them. But while our informants say 'try carrots, they might be good for you', they never say 'you should like carrots'. Luring a body into liking carrots is worth trying, but such self-care techniques do not offer control. In the end pleasure may emerge – or not.

> For children Amanda uses a form that has a long list of vegetables followed by two columns. In the first of these, a child may put a tick every time she tastes the vegetable in question. After 15 ticks she is allowed to rate the vegetable's taste in the second column. The scores are like those of the Dutch school system: 1 for truly bad (or disgusting) and 10 for could-not-be-better-so-very-good (yummy). This form tries to turn appreciating food into a game. Once they have 'done their best' and tried a vegetable 15 times, children are allowed to judge for themselves and score it.

The context in which one eats may be attended to; new flavours may be tried. But caring for pleasure also depends on caring for the food itself. For food is not naturally given, it is grown and transported and sold and bought and cooked. The attention of our informants tends to focus on the last stages of this process. How to prepare food in an enticing way?

Susan works as a dietician with overweight children and their families:

> It strikes me that many of my clients eat very plain food, nothing imaginative. They hardly use herbs or spices. Spicing things up a bit might make meals more appetising. And then it all has to be quick, quick, quick, easy and ready. Of course it then gets boring, especially if it also needs to be healthy, because they all think that's vile. So how to make healthy stuff more appetising? This is difficult, because in practice …
> we can cook with the children, but with the parents it is difficult to organise. Because the parents … you can present them with information, but that doesn't work. They have to experience it. Often they think that they don't like something, but if they make it in a slightly different way, they will experience a different taste. And fun cooking is not necessarily all that difficult or time consuming. (Susan)

Crafting pleasure takes effort. It depends on skills and imagination. While telling people to take control of their food intake presupposes that the food to be taken in is present already, fostering self-care includes paying attention to the work that goes into selecting, buying and preparing good food. This does not easily fit within consultation rooms and current financial regulations, if only because self-care is not a just cognitive task, but involves the entire body. It depends on developing skilled eyes, noses, tongues and hands. It is only by training in practice that a person may become capable of caring.

To conclude

In public health the concern is with what is called health behaviour. In the research that backs up this concern, 'behaviour' is configured as something observed from the outside. It is what one person (the researcher) may see another person (the research subject) do. The researcher-outsider may then seek out the explanatory variables that cause this or that behaviour and hope that interfering with these explanatory variables offers the possibility of changing the behaviour in question. But what if one is the person doing the behaving? Then such knowledge from the outside makes little sense and neither does trying to alter the causes of one's own behaviour (Despret 2008). The professionals whose work we have presented here therefore try to go in other directions. They do not address behaviour observed from the outside but the feelings that, as a person, one may come to sense from within. They do not encourage people to put themselves under their own control but to caringly tinker with themselves, and tinker again, all the while seeking to actively and appreciatively take pleasure from their foods and drinks.

The ideas embedded in these caring practices resonate with phenomenological theory. Phenomenology, likewise, calls for attention to how a body feels from within. However, in a lot of phenomenological studies feeling one's body from within appears to be a naturally given and universally available ability. The practices we studied suggest instead that it is a demanding local achievement. It is not something that 'the' body does, but rather something that some people may learn to do under some circumstances. Hence, rather than a general truth that needs to be theoretically defended, the lived body of phenomenology here emerges as an empirical configuration that may or may not be realised in practice.[8] The professionals who were our informants work to realise it in, with and for their clients, in various ways.

Firstly, they encourage people to feel. The idea is that it is only if people attend to how their food affects them that satisfaction may ensue. One of the complications is that different bodily sensations may intertwine with each other and with a plethora of emotions. As positive and negative feelings are not easy to keep apart, avoiding all forms of feeling may sometimes seem safer. This is a problem: taking pleasure depends on also being able to experience pain. A second set of repertoires addresses the feeling, not of one's responses, but of one's needs. Rather than calling upon nutritional science to stipulate these needs whilst mistrusting one's desires because they know no bounds, in the practices we studied needs and desires are explored together. The ideal is to learn to feel the difference between needing/desiring nourishment, a treat, consolation or something different yet again. A person able to do this will find it easier to meet her needs, fulfil her desires and achieve satisfaction. But satisfaction does not just depend on being able to feel but also on organising one's food world in satisfying ways. Therefore, a third repertoire foregrounds caring for one's eating environment, attuning to different foods, acquiring diversified tastes and, crucially, learning to prepare attractive meals.

Satisfaction, then, is crucial to the practices we studied. The idea is that satisfaction serves weight loss as satisfied bodies send out the signal: 'enough'. But while weight loss is important to both professionals and clients (who, after all, seek help because they hope to lose weight) it is not the ultimate parameter of success. It may be even more important to learn to take pleasure and then being satisfied once in a while; or to be able to feel what you need and which foods and drinks are good for you at which moment.[9] This, then, is how we want to summarise the work of the professionals we studied. While public health messages insist that we should take control over our food intake, here the message is to attend to what we eat. Rather than repeating the admonition, 'mind your plate', these professionals give the encouragement to enjoy their food.

None of this is beyond criticism. 'Enjoy your food' resonates with the advertisement messages of food industries, which makes it easy to be misused. What is more, not all possible food pleasures are being endorsed. Calm enjoyment is being fostered, and wild ecstasy is not. Ignored are the pleasures of transgressing, forgetfulness or, say, of stuffing oneself with fast food while watching a B-movie with friends.[10] There is little about sharing food, feasting, or acting as a generous host or a grateful guest. In addition, the self-care being propagated is demanding. Our informants want their clients to show curiosity by seeking out new food experiences and experimenting with new habits. They risk turning a gourmet model of eating into an ideal for everyone. They hardly attend to money. They work largely through education, like almost everybody else in contemporary public health. And while they give support, once again the people who have the problems have to do most of the care work themselves.[11] All in all, there is a very thin line between liberating the pleasures of the body and imposing yet more obligations on the caring self. Say you find yourself trapped in the station at 5:30 in the evening after a busy day at work. You are hungry, have a long way to travel ahead and little money left. Your food choice then and there is between an expensive luxury salad and cheap, filling chips. Yes, of course, you might have anticipated this moment and brought your own food from home. But you did not. Here yet another sense of failure looms. If only you had taken better care of yourself!

As it happens, our informants know all too well that they are not in the business of creating a paradise. They also know about the socio-material circumstances of their clients. As we talk, they deplore the fact that they cannot change the marketing strategies of the food industry, school canteen policies, supermarket layouts, social inequality, the kinds of skills children are being taught (or not) in schools and so on. Every day again they learn from working with their clients about the structural problems that interfere with eating well. But what can they do from where they stand? Taking their situatedness seriously, we suggest that it is just too easy to write in a social science journal that encouraging people to take pleasure from their food is nothing but another neoliberal disciplining strategy. Once you have heard Annette's clients tell stories of bingeing and feeling miserable; or pushed a balloon with the therapy group of Mariette; or witnessed Maria attending to the details of Helen's responses to foods and feelings; once you have transported yourself to these sites, the conviction imposes itself that paradise may have to wait. It is urgent enough to attend to the question what to do in these sites. What is better rather than worse in a situation where a person wants to (or has to) lose weight (Yates-Doerr 2012)? Is it obligatory to learn to control your eating behaviour while asking yourself the question: am I being good? Or might it also be possible to learn to take more pleasure from your food, while wondering: is it good for me? This is our conclusion: pointing to the difference between these two ways of working is important. It is a difference worth making. Enjoy your food.

Acknowledgements

Our contributions to the present text were not quite the same. AM did a few observations; EV did many more. The analysis and the writing are joint work. The money that made this work possible came from a European Research Council Advanced Grant no. AdG09 no. 249397. We thank the grant givers and taxpayers for this. We would also like to thank our informants for their openness and for the many lessons taught. Thanks as well to the Eating Bodies team: Rebeca Ibanez Martin, Emily Yates-Doerr, Sebastian Abrahamsson, Filippo Bertoni, Michalis Kontopodis, Cristobal Bonelli, Tjitske Holtrop, and on this occasion, especially Anna Mann. For comments on an earlier version we thank the participants of an Amsterdam Bodily Pleasures research seminar in 2012, especially Emilia Sanabria and Bodil Just Christensen and two anonymous reviewers. And, finally, we thank Simon Cohn and John Law for inspiration and support.

Notes

1   The study was undertaken following local ethics committee approval. Consent was verbally obtained and to ensure anonymity the excerpts from transcripts used in this chapter are not identifiable individual interviews or observations.

2   For our work on dieting variants and creative uses of the control/pleasure paradigm, see Mol 2012 and Vogel, 'Clinical specificities: will and drives in obesity care', submitted. Heretic professionals have made themselves heard in self-help or popular science and semi-scientific books with titles like *The Slow Down Diet* (David 2005) *Intuitive Eating* (Tribole and Resch 2003) and *Savor: Mindful Eating* (Nhat Hanh and Cheung 2010).

3   Psychologists who study disordered eating have long since argued that restricted eating and a lack of pleasure have psychologically harmful effects. See Lindeman and Stark (2000) or Westenhoefer and Pudel (1993).

4   For the analysis that affect is not a natural phenomenon but that people may gradually learn to be affected see Hennion (2004) and Despret (2004). For an interesting note on this see Latour (2004).

5   What does and does not index care for one's surroundings is replete with class and cultural markers. In our Dutch materials the norms at work are middle class, though not those of, say, arty or academic elites, who would not care about table cloths. And while in the USA, for instance, eating with only a fork would be acceptable, in The Netherlands this signals a lack of cultivation or of attentiveness. That one might eat as well, and well, with one's fingers, is not considered here. But see Mann *et al.* (2011).

6   In nursing homes, where people risk eating too little, caring for attractive surroundings is celebrated as it incites people to eat more. Hence, there too, pleasure is supposed to help in balancing the amounts people eat. See Mol (2010).

7   For the material aspects of hospitality, see also Candea and da Col (2012).

8   See notably Csordas (1993). In parts of phenomenology the fact that conditions of possibility are precarious, is acknowledged. See Varela's note that being a lived body is not something everyone can easily do, but requires cultivation (2001). For the shift from having/being to doing also, see Mol and Law (2004) and Law and Mol (2008).

9   Healthcare practices have to be justified by proving in clinical trials that they are able to effectively improve a given relevant parameter of success. If a practice has a range of goals, its effectiveness becomes more difficult to prove. For some of the many complications involved, see Mol (2006) and Struhkamp *et al.* (2009) and, for an alternative way of working, Moser (2010).

10   See also the aesthetic regime of comfort, that celebrates the paralysing pleasure of fatty, high-caloric food in Christensen, 'Aesthetic regimes: how good food is crafted through connoisseurship', forthcoming.

11   On possible problems that extending the care-space from the clinic to self-care can bring about, see Miewald (1997). For another discussion on self-care see also Kickbusch (1989).

References

Cadea, M. and da Col, G. (2012) The return to hospitality, *Journal of the Royal Anthropological Institute*, 18, Suppl. 1, S1–19.

Coveney, J. and Bunton, R. (2003) In pursuit of the study of pleasure: implications for health research and practice, *Health*, 7, 2, 161–79.

Csordas, T.J. (1993) Somatic modes of attention, *Cultural Anthropology*, 8, 2, 135–56.

David, M. (2005) *The Slow Down Diet: Eating for Pleasure, Energy, and Weight Loss*. Rochester: Healing Arts Press.

Despret, V. (2004) The body we care for: figures of anthropo-zoo-genesis, *Body and Society*, 10, 2–3, 111–34.

Despret, V. (2008) The becomings of subjectivity in animal worlds, *Subjectivity*, 23, 123–39.

Hennion, A. (2004) Pragmatics of taste. In Jacobs, M. and Hanrahan, N. (eds) *The Blackwell Companion to the Sociology of Culture*. Oxford: Blackwell.

Jallinoja, P., Pajari, P. and Absetz, P. (2010) Negotiated pleasures in health-seeking lifestyles of participants of a health promoting intervention, *Health*, 14, 2, 115–30.

Kickbusch, I. (1989) Self-care in health promotion, *Social Science of Medicine*, 29, 2, 125–30.

Law, J. and Mol, A. (2008) The actor-enacted: Cumbrian sheep in 2001. In Knappett, C. and Malafouris, L. (eds) *Material Agency: Towards a Non-Anthropocentric Approach*. Dusseldorf: Springer.

Latour, B. (2004) How to talk about the body? The normative dimension of science studies, *Body and Society*, 10, 2–3, 205–29.

Lindeman, M. and Stark, K. (2000) Loss of pleasure, ideological food choice reasons and eating pathology, *Appetite*, 35, 3, 263–68.

Mann, A., Mol, A., Satalkar, P., Savirani, A., Seim, N., Sur, M., and Yates-Doerr, E. (2011) Mixing methods, tasting fingers: notes on an ethnographic experiment, *Hau, Journal of Ethnographic Theory*, 1, 1, 221–43.

Miewald, C. (1997) Is awareness enough? The contradictions of self-care in a chronic disease clinic, *Human Organization*, 56, 3, 353–62.

Mol, A. (2006) Proving or improving: on health care research as a form of self-reflection, *Qualitative Health Research*, 16, 3, 405–14.

Mol, A. (2010) Care and its values. Good food in the nursing home. In Mol, A., Moser, I. and Pols, J., (eds) *Care in Practice. On Tinkering in Clinics, Homes and Farms*. Bielefeld: Transcript.

Mol, A. (2012) Mind your plate! The ontonorms of Dutch dieting, *Social Studies of Science*, 43, 3, 379–96.

Mol, A. and Law, J. (2004) Embodied action, enacted bodies. the example of hypoglycaemia, *Body & Society*, 10, (2–3), 43–62.

Moser, I. (2010) Perhaps tears should not be counted but wiped away. On quality and improvement in dementia care. In Mol, A., Moser, I. and Pols, J. (eds) *Care in Practice. On Tinkering in Clinics, Homes and Farms*. Bielefeld: Transcript.

Nhat Hanh, T. and Cheung, L. (2010) *Savor: Mindful Eating, Mindful Life*. New York: HarperCollins.

Rozin, P. (1999) Food is fundamental, fun, frightening and far-reaching, *Social Research*, 66, 1, 9–30.

Smith, C. (2008) Punishment and pleasure: women, food and the imprisoned body, *Sociological Review*, 50, 2, 197–214.

Struhkamp R., Mol A. and Swierstra T. (2009) Dealing with independence: doctoring in physical rehabilitation practice, *Science, Technology and Human Values*, 34, 1, 55–76.

Tribole, E. and Resch, E. (2003) *Intuitive Eating: a Revolutionary Program That Works*. New York: St Martin's Griffin.

Varela, F.J. (2001) Intimate distances: fragments for a phenomenology of organ transplantation. In Thompson, E. (ed.) *Between Ourselves*. Thorverton: Imprint Academic.

Westenhoefer, J. and Pudel, V. (1993) Pleasure from food: importance for food choice and consequences of deliberate restriction, *Appetite*, 20, 3, 246–9.

Williams, J. (1997) 'We never eat like this at home': food on holiday. In Caplan, P. (ed.) *Food, Health and Identity*. London: Routledge.

Wilson, M. (2005) Indulgence. In Kulick, D. and Meneley, A. (eds) *Fat: the Anthropology of an Obsession*. New York: Penguin.

Yates-Doerr, E. (2012) The weight of the self: care and compassion in Guatemalan dietary choices, *Medical Anthropology Quarterly*, 26, 1, 136–58.

Index

From Health Behaviours to Health Practices: Critical Perspectives, First Edition. Edited
by Simon Cohn. Chapters © 2014 The Authors. Book Compilation © 2014 Foundation
for the Sociology of Health & Illness / Blackwell Publishing Ltd.